Studies in Media Management

A. WILLIAM BLUEM, General Editor

Broadcast Management

RADIO · TELEVISION

Studies in Media Management

Broadcast Management

RADIO · TELEVISION

By

WARD L. QUAAL

President
WGN Continental Broadcasting Company
and

LEO A. MARTIN

Chairman
Department of Television and Radio
Michigan State University

COMMUNICATION ARTS BOOKS

Hastings House, Publishers • New York

ACKNOWLEDGMENT

*To our wives, Dorothy Graham Quaal and Jean Martin,
whose helpfulness, patience and understanding enabled
this book to be written.*

*We acknowledge, too, Dan Calibraro and Fran Coughlin,
whose professional assistance and encouragement were
vital to our progress.*

First printing, May 1968
Second printing, February 1969
Third printing, October 1969

Published simultaneously in Canada
by Saunders, of Toronto, Ltd., Don Mills, Ontario.

Text Edition (Paper) SBN: 8038-0708-2
Cloth Edition SBN: 8038-0709-0

Library of Congress Catalog Card Number: 68-17651
Printed in the United States of America

Contents

Studies in Media Management

AN INTRODUCTION

THE SOCIAL, cultural, political, economic and legal circumstances within which any society's communications are transmitted inevitably will shape and control not only what men say to others but what they are allowed to hear others say to them. If the larger socio-political system is democratic, open and possessed of a tradition of freedom of expression, then there will evolve various sub-systems, or media, within the whole which will permit all groups and factions to say and hear what they will. If the system is closed, monolithic and incapable of tolerating dissent, then there will also exist limitations upon what is said and heard by the citizen of that society through all communications media. In either case, technology will be harnessed in service of that system.

But the role of the media manager in the free society is quite distinct from that of his counterpart in nations where the state determines the message. For whatever pressures and influences are brought to bear upon him, the fact remains that all final decisions regarding what is communicated to the society at large must be made by him alone. It is important, therefore, that greater attention be devoted to the study of these communicative sub-systems, not only as they relate to and interact with the external forces in our civilization but in terms of their internal organization and operative procedures. The role of the media manager in American society has simply not been given sufficient analysis in any textual form. To be sure, the interests of the aesthetician, philosopher, historian, educator, and the social and behavioral scientist have been directed toward analysis of our systems of communication, and their work has often proved useful to those who manage the media. The time has come, however, for a complementary analysis of these systems by those who must bear the responsibility for their operation, and whose orientation springs primarily from within.

Studies in Media Management is designed to provide this orientation. It is our hope that the series will create for students and teachers alike a basic analysis of American communications which has been conducted solely from the media point of view. Within this framework, the series is planned to encompass three aspects of media operation: (a) the socio-cultural controls and sanctions within which they operate, (b) the political and economic imperatives underlying their existence (whether sponsored and financed within the public or private sectors) and (c) the specific principles and practices of their sound management.

By intention, the first volume to be developed within this series deals with broadcasting. The impact of the electronic revolution upon the 20th century requires little further delineation, but the unique managerial capacities which are required for our radio and television system have not been sufficiently detailed and codified into a series of principles, approaches and methods.

The combination of professional and scholarly interests which are brought to bear in authorship of this first volume is also intentional. Mr. Ward Quaal is a distinguished broadcaster with a long and productive record in American radio and television decision-making, and Professor Leo Martin ranks among the most respected broadcast educators in this nation. The blend of their interests and insights has produced not only a comprehensive analysis of the unique problems which confront broadcasting management, but a useful pattern of authorship for subsequent volumes in this series.

A. WILLIAM BLUEM, Ph.D.

General Editor, *Studies in Media Management*
Newhouse Communications Center
Syracuse University

Preface

IN AN ERA of social change, often unprecedented in nature, an institution as dynamic as broadcasting cannot afford complacency. It must face a future which will require many changes and it must come to accept greater commitments to social leadership. The time has passed when broadcasters can boast that commercials have effects on people and then claim that most programs do not have effects. So is the time gone when broadcasting was almost exclusively an entertainment medium; although its show-business aspects still predominate, it can no longer disregard the fact that greater proportions of its time in the future will be devoted to news, public affairs and other informational services. New methods of sales and advertising must be designed if broadcasting is to remain competitive in a changing communications climate. The industry needs to overhaul employment practices and its system of personnel relations if it intends to attract competent and creative people. Pressures on broadcasters from outside sources need to be eased by positive approaches instead of the usual defensive maneuvers. Above all, broadcasters need to realize that, whether they like it or not, the public expects them to behave responsibly as members of a profession.

This book is directed primarily to managers of commercial stations and to students taking courses in station management. The commercial station exists to make a profit while offering community services.

It is, however, an overemphasis on profit return that causes some commercial managers to lose sight of the many other rewards to be achieved through broadcasting and telecasting operations. When everything is subordinated to dollar values, standards of good broadcasting are sacrificed. The management of a radio or a television station then holds no more meaning or challenge than the management of a lemonade stand. To be penny-wise is in many instances to be socially foolish. Neither men nor institutions grow in stature through huckster interests in a narrow field.

Intelligent and responsible management cannot be realized by uncreative and imitative methods. There must be a considerable evaluation of the potential that has not been put to use in broadcasting generally. Few station managers have achieved the genuine stature their calling makes possible.

Such accomplishment depends upon the manner in which the true executive approaches his task and the results that he produces. Collectively, the various instances of achievement can change the image of broadcasting.

Throughout this book, we will regularly point to the need for more and greater freedoms for broadcasters in general and station managers in particular. We believe that the broadcast industry has been unnecessarily hampered in the accomplishment of some of its greatest achievements by too much governmental regulation or the threat of regulation; by discriminatory practices which are not experienced by other mass media; and by superficial expectations on the part of superficial observers and groups with little knowledge of the realities of broadcast operations. Yet, with every new freedom gained an equivalent responsibility must also be expected. Freedom and responsibility are parallel expectations of any mature individual or social institution. The mature station manager will know what those responsibilities are because he will have planned for them within the framework of the freedoms which he desires.

We may seem at times to be overly critical of present managerial practices. We believe there are better ways to get better results. We criticize out of a background of devotion to the broadcasting industry. Our professional lives have thus far been bound up in it. We have seen considerable progress since those early days when the mere sound of a human voice coming into the home by wireless was a thrilling and almost unbelievable phenomenon. We are not, however, satisfied with broadcasting's accomplishments, as varied and as marvelous as they have been. We believe that improvement is always possible and generally we have been gratified to find that this is true. To paraphrase Winston Churchill, we have seen not the beginning of the end, but the end of our broadcast beginnings.

This book, therefore, does not attempt to set down minutely detailed and standardized procedures for managing radio or television stations. Such a volume would be obsolete before publication and useless to those managers who want their stations to have distinct images or personalities that make them stand out because they are importantly different. Thus, we believe it appropriate to suggest *areas* for improved managerial leadership, to point out the values of change in those areas and to inspire individual managers to action on the basis of their particular present and future local resources.

WARD L. QUAAL
LEO A. MARTIN
April, 1968

1

The Status of Broadcast Management

Perfection of means and confusion of goals seem in my opinion to characterize our age

—ALBERT EINSTEIN

THE FLAT STATEMENT is all but incredible: Electronic communication has progressed from Marconi to Telstar well within the biblical life span of three score years and ten. Only some forty years lie between the beginnings of mass radio broadcasting and the first international television by satellite. In that short span of time all the technological developments of radio and television were introduced, refined and expanded. From the crystal set grew the marvels of high fidelity, stereo, videotape, transistor receiving sets, color television and satellite transmission.

Superimposed on these achievements were the arts and skills of production and programming as well as the techniques of sales and advertising. Although usurpers of the products of the genius of scientists and engineers, producers, programmers, salesmen and advertisers came to be more closely associated with broadcasting in the public mind than were the people who made it all possible.

Engineering, of course, remains a vital part of the broadcasting service. Without the contributions of station engineers, few producers and salesmen could keep radio and television stations on the air. But the relative importance of the technical contributions to broadcasting made by the engineering fraternity is often overlooked in favor of the social, cultural and commercial applications made of their creations. It was no idle remark when Lee DeForest once exclaimed, "What have you done to my baby?"

Broadcasting would hardly appear to be unique in its reliance upon the products of the scientific mind. Modern society seems to have given top

13

priority to technological achievement—for profit—and often, as in the case of broadcasting, at the expense of equally significant progress in other areas of human endeavor. Walter P. Reuther, whose union assignment keeps him on the opposite side of the bargaining table in conferences with management, has earned the respect of leaders in industry for his pungent observations on the American societal need. In 1964, he opened a speech at the Center for the Study of Democratic Institutions with the following statement:

> "The dilemma of American society is the lag between our tremendous progress in the physical sciences and the art of working with machines and our failure to make comparable progress in the human and social sciences, in the much more difficult art of working and living with man. Having mastered the science of technology and production know-how, we must now develop a comparable human, moral and social *know-why*. The main purpose of society is not to achieve higher and higher levels of economic production or to extend the frontiers of technological progress; it is to find a way to relate and equate material wealth with human values and opportunities for human fulfillment." [1]

If this sounds radical, it is. But it is a radicalism of fact and not of an imagined blueprint for a millennium.

More radical than Reuther is our conviction that broadcast management, given the incentive, freedom of enterprise, inspiration and some sense of direction, can achieve results in programming and in sales that will parallel, if not exceed, the technical accomplishments of the industry.

GROWTH OF MANAGEMENT OPPORTUNITIES

Opportunities for new managers of radio stations opened to their greatest extent following the end of World War II. At that time, there were almost a thousand radio stations on the air. These were managed for the most part by men who had been in radio throughout its existence. Many men who were released from military service were interested in small businesses which they could manage. The possibility of local radio stations as investments was a relatively new development. Those stations which were in operation were, for the most part, high-power operations with network affiliations. The growth of local radio began at this time. Within the five-year period following the end of World War II, some 1800 new radio stations came into existence. In the year 1948 alone, 533 stations began operations. This was the largest number of new station authorizations in any single year since broadcasting had its birth. By the mid-1960s, the number of radio stations had more than quadrupled. The rush to obtain station licenses was so great that the FCC in 1962 established a temporary "freeze" on new authorizations. Yet, in 1963, before the freeze was lifted, some 14,000 American citizens filed applications for licenses.

The sales of receiving sets, amounts of audience listening and station profits have kept pace with the increase in the number of stations. These developments will be treated in succeeding chapters of this book.

One factor which has influenced radio's growth has been the invention and use of the transistor. An advantage which radio has always enjoyed has been its high degree of mobility. The transistor made this advantage even greater. Once people started carrying radios in their pockets, the out-of-home audience, which already was using automobile and "portable" sets, began to expand significantly. In a massive power failure throughout the northeastern section of the United States in the fall of 1965, millions of people were kept informed about conditions through radio broadcasts which could only be received by transistor sets. Shortly thereafter, the broadcasting industry began a campaign to convince the public throughout the United States that at least one transistor receiver should be in every home for use in cases of any possible future emergencies.

The number of FM channels that are available far exceeds the number of AM frequencies. Investors for many years found little success with FM due to various factors, including a general public disinterest in the system. The technological development of stereo-casting added a new public appeal to the system of FM and the channels became more appealing to applicants. The sharpest increase in numbers of applications for radio stations since 1964 has been for FM licenses.

For those aspirants to the more than 1000 available FM assignments, the following advice from Byron G. Wells may be useful:

". . . You're going to need many things before you even get close to going on the air—things like aspirin, money, aspirin, patience, aspirin, money . . ."

"After a while, if your programming is good, if the advertising comes in, and if you get a few lucky breaks, the station may start to pay . . . In fact, you might even start drawing a bit of salary for yourself . . ."[2]

Due to the larger investments necessary for the installation and operation of television stations, their locations have been generally restricted to metropolitan areas. As compared with the 4097 commercial AM and the 1565 commercial FM stations which had been authorized by the end of the 1965 fiscal year, there were only 689 commercial television stations.

Nonetheless, the television penetration of U. S. homes reached 94 per cent by the end of 1965. Most homes had three or more choices of stations, including the offerings of the three national television networks.

Three factors were influential in decisions affecting additional television-station applications. These were whether to apply for ultra-high frequency (UHF) licenses or Community Antenna Television (CATV) franchises and what effect *color* would have on future station operations.

The portion of the spectrum allocated to ultra-high frequency (UHF) can accommodate greater numbers of television stations than that part which is set aside for very high frequency (VHF). The UHF channels run from 14 through 83 positions on the dial, whereas VHF spectrum space, which once was used exclusively for television broadcasting, accommodates only channels 2 through 13. UHF stations were slow to develop due to the small number of sets capable of receiving UHF transmission.

It was common practice for operators of UHF stations, after attempts to provide competitive broadcasting service, to suspend operations and return their licenses to the FCC.

Federal legislation requiring all television receiving sets manufactured after May 1, 1964 to include both VHF and UHF channels led to a steady increase in applications for UHF station licenses. An FCC authorization for low-power UHF stations has opened the way for the construction and operation of television stations in rural areas.

Such growth could somewhat parallel the expansion of radio following World War II if it were not for the questions raised by the developments in Community Antenna Television (CATV). This system was originally designed to bring the services of remote television stations to areas where TV reception was limited or non-existent. Entrepreneurs, including many broadcast-station owners and managers, began to dream of vast profits from investments in such systems whereby monthly subscription fees are collected from users. Consequently, areas which were considered likely prospects for new UHF stations suddenly became high risks due to either the installation, or the threat of installation, of CATV systems. In April, 1965, the FCC asserted jurisdiction over some 400 CATV systems that used microwaves for their transmission, and in March, 1966 some 1200 systems that delivered their service by means of telephone lines were brought under its control. The FCC actions for the first time brought all CATV under government regulation and imposed certain conditions for their operation. The systems were required to give nonduplication protection in the carrying of programs which are broadcast by any local commercial or educational station. Any CATV system which proposes to bring programs from distant stations into the grade-A area of any station in the top 100 markets of the country must first secure FCC approval. Information concerning all officers and subscribers to each CATV system must be submitted to the FCC.

However the CATV controversy is ultimately compromised, the ability of U. S. homes to receive UHF signals is steadily increasing. A U. S. Census Bureau study in August of 1965 showed that almost 23 per cent of the households of the country had sets which were equipped to receive UHF broadcasts; at the end of 1966, the figure had risen to about a third of all

U. S. homes. By 1970, the UHF saturation should make most markets suitable targets for UHF programs.

The color TV issue hinges on a factor of added expense for colorcasting equipment. Suddenly, in 1965, color TV sets began to be purchased in quantity, brought about partly by a healthy economy and partly by the greater availability of color programming together with other incidental factors. Most, if not all, prime-time programming by each of the three television networks for the 1966–67 season was scheduled in color. The local station could hardly afford to offer only black-and-white programs and commercials in the future.

A Confusion of Problems

With the increase in the sheer number of TV and radio stations, competition became a factor for many managers for the first time. Stations that had enjoyed a virtual monopoly of audience found new and aggressive competitors attracting their listeners and viewers. Innovation, change and hard work had not been particularly necessary in a static situation. Now they were suddenly essential.

As the broadcasting industry grew, problems began to multiply. Some were so universal and complicated that associations of broadcasters were needed to deal with them. Others required regular managerial decision-making. Still others were of an annoying nature, postponable but continually bothersome. Included in the latter category was a regular volume of criticism of broadcasting. The chief sources were the FCC, intellectual critics and other opinion makers.

The term "vast wasteland," which former FCC chairman Newton Minow coined and used to describe broadcasting's programs, has haunted station managers ever since. Critics seized upon the phrase and proceeded to blast away at broadcasting in general, often in one-sided arguments. An older industry, with the benefits of experience gained from similar attacks, might have reacted differently. But here was an enterprise, dependent on popular appeal for its success, being buffeted on many fronts with charges not always justified. Broadcasters soon became supersensitive to criticism and devoted far too much time to defensive reactions instead of making positive adjustments in more significant problem areas.

An observer of broadcasting throughout its history is Sol Taishoff, editor and publisher of *Broadcasting* and *Television* magazines. In 1966, he received the annual Distinguished Service Award from the National Association of Broadcasters. On that occasion, he challenged the broadcasters of the nation to establish "a proper heritage of imagination and boldness" for those people of the new generation who would some day be in charge of stations. "The current climate of the broadcasting business," said Mr. Taishoff, "is not especially conducive to imaginative ventures and risky progress." Rather, he said, the prevailing attitude is "conservative," with rallying responses to suggestions not to "rock the boat." Later, and with justification, he lamented: "Everybody has become an expert." [3]

Men in administrative positions usually know more about the problems of their own organizations than the critics know. It is not unusual for them to read ill-tempered and inaccurate critical comments. A common reaction is to suspect all criticism, even that which might have some validity. Broadcasters need to respond more constructively to complaints and comments by non-broadcasters. Over-sensitivity can lead to a tendency to condemn unfavorable comment and to note only the observations which are favorable. Too soon, the general public comes to doubt the objectivity of the broadcaster and to resent his one-sided defenses. It would be more profitable in the long run to show a little less persistence in promoting the medium's virtues and publicly to recognize and work toward the elimination of some communication shortcomings.

Many administrators are reluctant to take positions on social problems. Such stands might limit the amount of future business from possibly dissatisfied clients. Strong stands on problems of vital concern to the public can gain as much business as they lose, and executives can increase their stature as leaders. Broadcasters, especially, have an obligation to assume such leadership since the industry they represent, by its very nature, generates interest in, and in itself is a part of, the social environment. Nothing is so unproductive as to take a strong editorial position on the air and to initiate no follow-up activities of leadership on important issues. Yet, some stations continually exhort the people to "do something" and then leave the implementation of the projects to a disorganized public. Seldom, if ever, does constructive activity follow.

A predominating tendency among managers of radio and television stations is to imitate the successful program formats and business practices of other stations. Evidences of originality or true creativity are rare. Whenever significant issues arise within the industry, a few leaders have to devote great amounts of time toward their solution. The individual station manager's voice is seldom heard.

The ratings services, which we shall treat in a later chapter, are accorded a disproportionate amount of respect by station management at the expense of other measures of success perhaps more significant for the long-range future.

There are danger signs as well. One danger is that people who are given too much of the same kind of programming may grow bored and turn to other forms of recreation for their gratifications. Broadcasting's greatest asset has always been its popularity with the people. If the people acquire a blasé attitude toward radio and television, the industry will indeed be in bad condition. Such a possibility cannot be ruled out as unrealistic by any manager who is concerned about the future and who has the ability to inspire originality in his station staff.

Too often, broadcasters have separated themselves from their listener-viewers by what Gene Accas, Vice President of Leo Burnett Company, has called "an idea-tight, communications-proof wall constructed of ego, misplaced self-importance and misunderstandings." [4] The time is long past when the broadcaster can afford such luxury. Today, an empathy with his audience can reveal much needed information that rating services cannot give him.

Playing it safe is seldom really playing it safe. Imitating other stations' practices and clinging to conservative trends by competing applicants for licenses are hardly challenges at renewal time. With a growing availability of personnel both trained and experienced in broadcasting as well as a significant body of professional consultants, it may well be that alternative proposals submitted by the competition may find a considerable amount of favor in the offices of the FCC. In the two-year period, 1963–65, there were twenty-three competing applications for eighteen AM license renewals Even if the operating station were to assume that it could hold its license, it still would have to face the possibility of a costly and time-consuming comparative hearing process. It would be more efficient operational procedure to make sure of prevention than to have to prescribe and effect a cure.

A constant involvement in defensive strategy has plagued broadcasters throughout the history of radio and television. The time is long overdue for a positive approach. The station manager must be the field commander.

Each manager needs to supplement the work of state, regional and national groups with a considerable amount of thinking in terms of his own station, his own market and his own audience. He should determine where he wants the station to be at the end of another decade and then concentrate a share of his physical and mental powers on achieving that goal. The goal might include greater professional practice, a wide public acceptance, expanded services by the station and consequent profit increases. It cannot —successfully—be a holding operation, sandbagged and dug in.

THE MANAGEMENT POTENTIAL

In the absence of men formally trained in broadcast management, early stations were necessarily administered by people who had been successful in other enterprises. These were as remote from broadcasting as used-car sales, accounting or the raising of livestock. Few were acquainted with business administration although their records as profit producers in many fields had been impressive. None had any previous experience in the curious amalgam of engineering, sales and programming that was to become broadcasting.

Much effective management has been accomplished in broadcasting. Most of it was learned by trial and error and often at a high degree of expense and frustration.

Errors made in the management of stations usually have been errors of omission rather than of commission. As a general rule, those people who have accepted management responsibilities in broadcasting have worked hard for their success. In some cases, it is true, there has been a lack of realization of the true power of the station's programs to inform, to entertain and to influence. In some other cases, there has been an inadequate understanding of the methods whereby the station might be made a true element of community life. There have been instances of shoddy business practices and the broadcasting of questionable materials on the air. But these cases have been in the minority. Examples of downright incompetence have been rare.

Most managers in broadcasting are socially responsible people. The screening of license applications and station transfers by the FCC acts as a safeguard for the public against the possibility that stations might be operated by people of questionable character. Consequently, the man or woman who is in charge of a radio or television station is likely to be a good citizen of the larger community.

Today, owners of stations are in a position to select managers with considerable amounts of experience in broadcasting. In some cases, personnel are available who have successfully managed radio and television stations. Graduate students in a few colleges and universities, often people with years of experience in broadcasting, are now able to study to become station managers of the future. Continuing seminars in station management are arranged for those who are actively engaged in the administration of radio and television stations. Here, management transcends narrow concepts and routine tasks.

The preparation of tomorrow's managers in broadcasting and the services provided for those who are in management today seem to presuppose that there is a common set of principles and methods which can be used to advantage in any station. Is this true? Can the manager of a 250-watt, daytime-only radio station serving a local rural community use the same procedures which are in effect in the 50,000-watt, clear-channel radio station? Are the decisions which need to be made in the independent television station similar to those in the station with network affiliations? And are there significant differences in the management of any broadcast property which makes demands that are not present in the management of other enterprises? Obviously there are differences in all managerial situations but successful methods should apply universally if ingenuity is used in their adaptations.

After some forty years of radio and some twenty years of television, the time has arrived when broadcasters generally have come to realize that two broad areas of need exist. First, the special nature of radio and television as commercial enterprises seems to make an organization of the principles of station management not only advisable but actually imperative. The increasing complexity of the managerial assignment and the probability of significant developments in the future call for a definition of the basic involvements as well as the challenges which confront the manager in broadcasting. First principles can have immeasurable value when used as a yardstick by which the manager can measure his own accomplishments (or lack of them) against others who are engaged in a similar activity.

A second area of need is for a genuine philosophy concerning broadcasting. The public nature of the electronic media and their overall supervision by a government commission have brought an almost constant set of crises to an industry operating under the spur of risks and rewards of private and free enterprise. The station manager in broadcasting has been anything but "free" to conduct his affairs as other businessmen have been able to do. As an individual, he is powerless to effect any changes in the overall system. As a group, broadcasters have seldom been able to mobilize anything approaching unanimity of opinion on any issues except those which would penalize them individually as well as collectively. As a result, they have become sitting ducks for negative criticism, some of it needed, some of it vicious. A positive philosophy is that which defines the purposes of broadcasting, its place in the modern society and the ethics to which broadcasters subscribe. The preoccupation of station managers with governmental pressures and with a constant assault by critics and opinion leaders requires far too much of their time and energies. From the viewpoint of efficient management, surprising advances might be accomplished were these defensive maneuvers supplanted by more constructive attention to station and community needs. A few leaders in the industry are kept busy defending the actions of a majority of their fellow broadcasters and arguing for privileges under which all broadcasters might benefit. All too often, a hard-won right is not used by enough broadcasters after it has been granted. Such was the case in regard to the right to editorialize and the right of access to certain state legislatures. The television executive should not be a faceless proprietor of a peep-show, but a man responsible and responsive to the urgencies of his time.

In the final analysis, the broadcaster will not be given a place in the community unless he earns it. That place is not one of an obsequious servant of survey and profit statements, but of a powerful participant in the free society of the future.

2

The

Station Manager

There is no business that so thoroughly punishes the amateur. In a business such as ours, where boys and girls become men and women rapidly, you have to have a lot more than heart. You have to have that—plus responsibility, sensitivity, judgment and understanding.

—CHARLES BROWER, Chairman of the Board, Batten, Barton, Durstine and Osborne, Inc.

FEW WHO LISTEN to radio and view television programs know the station managers. It is natural for people to identify stations by call letters, positions on the dial or channel numbers, air personalities and programs. Few people not engaged in broadcasting are aware that a station image is developed on the basis of carefully planned policies that are determined and implemented by management. The degree of public response to a station's services is largely determined by the ability, beliefs, attitudes, character, personality and philosophy of the station manager.

A position which carries such power and responsibility should require certain qualifications. Its range of duties should be well defined. The motivations and gratifications of the assignment should be known. We should be able to understand the position better by an analysis of the people who are managers of stations.

Until recently, data which could provide a composite view of station managers was not available. Now, two comprehensive studies have been made which disclose important information. The findings of this research clearly indicate that the management of a radio or a television station requires certain characteristics differing from those usually considered typical of managers of other business enterprises.

One of these studies was a joint research project of the Association for Professional Broadcasting Education and the National Association of Broadcasters.[1] It collected information from 201 radio station managers and 167 television station managers. The other study, made by Dr. Charles E. Winick, involved 287 managers of television stations.[2]

Both studies found that broadcast managers, with an average age in the early forties, are generally younger than other American business managers. The APBE-NAB study shows the television manager to be slightly older on the average than the radio manager (forty four as compared to forty one). The radio industry seems to show a greater diversity of age with more men in their fifties and sixties who entered broadcasting in its beginning and more who are in their thirties. There are many cases of young men in their early thirties who have assumed the responsibilities of radio management in small market stations but few examples of this nature in television where larger markets and greater financial investments are involved. Many present television managers were previously managers of radio stations.

The two management studies disclose that few managers of broadcast properties came to the positions from fields other than broadcasting. The greatest number were employed previously in radio or television sales, far in excess of the number who follow that route to executive status in general business. Many broadcast managers came from backgrounds in programming and a few from station engineering.

Winick found that most television station managers came from small-town backgrounds (under 100,000 population) as contrasted with the city backgrounds of most business leaders. He also identified military service, usually combat duty in World War II or the Korean War in the experience of most of the managers of television stations. His study revealed that most of the television managers made their decisions to enter the field of broadcasting while they were enrolled in a college or university.

The study by Winick found the income of television managers "competitive with that of executives at a similar level of responsibility in other industries." The APBE-NAB study tabbed the average earnings of the radio station managers at $12,500 per year and the average annual earnings of television station managers at $20,000.

Both studies show the importance of higher education for a managerial position in broadcasting. Winick discovered that three fourths of all television managers had been to college and one sixth had taken postgraduate study. The APBE-NAB study found that about half of the managers of radio and television stations were college graduates.

The kind of experience which both the television and radio managers who responded to the APBE-NAB study recommended most often for people who are interested in broadcasting careers in management was sales and/or promotion work. The kind of education which the managers recommended as most valuable for executive careers in broadcasting was training in business, including the study of sales, marketing and accounting.

It is interesting to note that, in another section of the same APBE-NAB study which dealt with responses from employees other than managers in broadcasting, the most highly recommended type of education was a professional curriculum in broadcasting. Significant in this response is the fact that the average age of the employees is somewhat younger and more of them were able to study broadcasting in the colleges and universities. The present managerial group, for the most part, did not find such courses available at the time they attended college; hence, the probable tendency not to equate the value of such training for careers in broadcasting.

QUALIFICATIONS OF STATION MANAGERS

Before we isolate some of the important qualifications for successful station management, attention should be called to the semantic problem of attempting to differentiate between the meanings of the terms "executive" and "manager." While some authorities have drawn a distinction between the two terms, we intend to use the two interchangeably in this discussion. All managers are, by the nature of their work, executives, although not all executives are managers.

We have already noted that extensive experience in broadcasting seems to be accepted as one prerequisite to executive status in the industry. On that point we can agree. Other factors, though, are not so crystal clear. Once, we might have said that station administration is for men. That statement cannot be made today for there are many examples of highly successful women managers of stations.

We would be on safe—and sterile—ground to list such generally accepted traits as honesty, thrift, virtue and love of children. One might as well cite the Scout Law for its pertinence and value judgments.

From a list of many possible criteria, we have isolated seven specific personal characteristics and attitudes we feel vital to success in station management. Even though these are subjective evaluations, we have checked our colleagues who are managers in radio and television and find that they possess these seven characteristics.

The seven qualities which we have chosen to comment upon are leadership, intelligence and knowledge, judgment, personal integrity, sense of responsibility, showmanship, and attitude toward work.

Leadership

There should be little argument over the premise that an effective manager should be a leader. There might, however, be wide differences of opinion as to what human factors tend to produce station managers who truly provide leadership.

The leadership role demands a high degree of confidence on the part of the manager. Normally, his training and experience qualify him to meet many unexpected problems. Essentially a realist and aware that some problems have to be settled without benefit of precedent, he is willing to stake his future on his ability to face issues squarely. He develops the ability to thrive under pressure.

The station manager should be sincerely interested in the welfare of the people who work at his station and people who live in his community. If he has a genuine regard for people plus an understanding of human motivations and aspirations, he can be influential in leading them toward positive growth. The extent of personal development under his influence, as much as any other factor, will characterize his success or failure as a leader. The counterfeiter of human coinage simply invites exposure and disaster.

The successful manager develops skill in correcting the mistakes of others. He is equally adept at showing his appreciation for good work. Employees appreciate his interest in their personal growth and development.

He is an expert at building and maintaining excellent staff morale. Somehow, he causes each person on his staff to feel that his work is vitally important to the success of the station. He is pleased when this feeling exists even among custodial employees.

An important element of leadership is the ability to communicate effectively. The manager needs to be highly articulate in both written and spoken communication, have the ability to say "yes" or "no" with firmness, and know how to ask the right questions at the right times.

The manager needs to have either a high degree of creativity or a fine sensitivity to creative efforts. Otherwise, it would be difficult for him to furnish the interest and inspiration which are needed by the many creative people who work in radio and television. Regular challenges should be made to these people if they are to do their best work.

As a leader, the manager does not confine his activities to his station. He seeks out further responsibilities in his community and in various professional associations. Not content to assume a passive role, he volunteers for active service on committees, runs for office and makes speeches at local, regional and national meetings. His fellow broadcasters recognize him as a leader in his industry and he has a similar image as a leader in his community. Winick discovered a much higher participation in community activities by television managers than by other business leaders. The evidence suggests that their high degree of activity in civic and charitable organizations is motivated, at least in part, by strong inclinations for contacts with a wide variety of people.

Intelligence and Knowledge

It should be obvious that the intelligence of the manager should be well above average. Whether a superior I.Q. would be of any particular advantage to the manager is another question. Apparently, on the basis of the opinions of various authorities in the field of management, success may be achieved in the managerial position with an intelligence which is less than superior but considerably above the norm.

The manager of a radio or a television station is expected to have a considerable amount of knowledge concerning the specialized nature of the broadcasting industry, of his own station, its market and its people. To the degree that his intelligence enables him to acquire knowledge faster, retain it longer and apply it effectively to the various new and continuing problems of broadcasting, we may safely conclude that his intellectual endowments are vital to his success as a manager in broadcasting.

In order to keep abreast of all the changes which occur regularly in the broadcasting industry, the manager is wise to read extensively. He needs to read the important trade publications as well as many periodicals and books in the field of business and other more general magazines and news-papers. Time could be saved if digests of important publications were prepared for him by some suitable member of his staff. In large stations, this is done. But even in those cases, digests of information have been poor substitutes for the reading of original sources by the executive himself. Analyses of the materials are as important as the reading. Again, this is a time-consuming activity but it is essential.

As if the constant study of changes within the broadcasting industry were not in itself a giant assignment, the manager is also compelled to increase his knowledge of his own station. Most station managers are well acquainted with either sales or programming or engineering. Few, if any, are experienced in more than one of those operations. Yet, the manager must be prepared to discuss each department intelligently, analyze the operations and practices of each and provide them with continuing challenges. It is he who must establish effective working relationships between the three de-partments.

Aspirants to management positions would be well advised to acquire considerable amounts of knowledge about all aspects of station operations early in their careers when they are basically involved with only one station activity.

The manager is further obligated to acquire a wealth of knowledge about his market and to use his intellectual capacities to make shrewd anal-yses of the business potential of the market and of the interests and the needs of the people in the station's coverage area. It is all but taken for granted that a complete knowledge of retailing strategies and problems is necessary, as is a specialized understanding of the role of advertising in the business economy.

When a man becomes manager of a station, he enters a new working world with a new set of requirements and demands. He finds much to learn about the whole field of broadcasting which he did not find necessary in his previous communications positions. He develops new curiosities about the audience that his station serves and he becomes aware of research methods and research organizations. Laws and federal regulations become highly important in his new environment. The many allied fields of the advertising agencies, station representatives, trade associations, unions, film and transcription companies, music-licensing companies and wire services take on new meanings. He reads the trade publications with greater purpose. He comes to realize the need for more complete knowledge concerning new broadcasting equipment and he develops a greater understanding of and respect for the show business atmosphere of programming and of talent.

The alert manager notices the pronouncements of the critics of broadcasting more than he did formerly. He finds himself examining the Codes and the merits of Code membership for his station. He becomes public-relations conscious and he reassesses his own station's facilities for publicity, promotion and merchandising. He becomes well versed on the problems and the achievements of all mass media and of all forms of show business. He becomes active in efforts to improve his community. He studies ways to achieve greater efficiencies in budgeting and he learns to be fascinated by the financial affairs of the station. His mind, stretched by all of this new knowledge and experience, can never return to what it once was.

Judgment

Every executive is required to make decisions regularly. In broadcasting, countless problems arise which have few if any precedents. Often, they must be solved in a matter of minutes. In this industry, much is regulated by the clock and the chief commodity for sale is time itself.

Mature judgment is needed to make decisions in broadcasting. Such maturity usually is a product of wide experience and comprehensive knowledge. Some people are capable of intuitive reasoning but the decision must be right most of the time. In this game, a .500 batting average is not good enough.

It would be easy to manage a radio or a television station by imitating the policies and practices of successful managers of other stations. This sort of management hardly appeals, however, to the man who places a high premium on his ability to think for himself. Take away the need for the use of wisdom and the management position loses all of its attractiveness for the man who regards decision-making as a personal challenge.

When decisions need to be made on long-range problems, the most effective managers know how to define those problems, how to gather all of the important facts, how to determine all possible solutions, how to arrive at decisions and how to implement those decisions in a manner which gets employee support. Good managers will not settle for insufficient evidence nor will they be influenced by unimportant or trivial data.

The effectiveness of long-range thinking may depend upon how much time the executive has available for uninterrupted reflection. Any manager would be wise if he were to block out periods of time when he could think about major issues.

Personal Integrity

The station manager must be a man of strong character. His position is in the "spotlight" and he can influence his station personnel and the people who live in the community. He is obligated, by the nature of his position, to command respect.

The manager should be a religious person who has humility and (in the broad sense) depth of character. People should be able to look to him for strength and they should realize that the longer he is known, the stronger he becomes.

An even temper and the ability to control extremes of emotion are distinct assets for the manager. When successes come his way or when he suffers reverses, he needs to be able to react with an outward appearance of stability.

A sense of humor can provide a necessary balance for many problems encountered. Often, tensions can be relieved in other people if humor is used advantageously. Successful executives seem to be able to develop a remarkable facility for laughing at themselves and for being amused at their own mistakes. Amused, but not too self-forgiving, either.

The manager who has a liberal education or background and who maintains a true intellectual curiosity should be able to converse intelligently on almost any subject. His wide range of interests should make him a popular and a stimulating guest at those social events which are important to his professional career.

Sense of Responsibility

Closely allied with the personal integrity of the manager is his attitude toward his various responsibilities. He cannot avoid an awareness of his many obligations to the owners of the station, to the station employees and to the public. There are almost constant reminders that he, and he alone, is accountable for the many decisions which have to be made in their interests.

The most effective managers do not permit material considerations to dominate their existence. While they are fully aware of the importance of profits, they also recognize values which are as important to their success as the accumulation of dollars. This is one reason why they become active in groups which work for the improvement of conditions in their communities. They are aware that such activity usually results in material benefits for the station but only if they are sincere and effective in their interest and participation.

Showmanship

The element of showmanship is perhaps more important to a manager of a radio or a television station than it is to managers of most other kinds of businesses. It is not, however, demonstrated by a flamboyance in actions, speech or dress but it can be recognized in an innate sense of timing and in an intuitive sense of dramatic values, which seem to be basic qualifications of all good showmen.

A large measure of the attractiveness of the station-management assignment is undoubtedly based on the opportunity to work with show people. Their talents add much excitement to a business which might be fairly routine without them. They constitute the station's most valuable contacts with the public. The task of finding the most effective methods to reach that public using the best show techniques that are known to man is a truly challenging kind of work. In broadcasting, the show is the product. Any good manager must fully understand and appreciate his company's product.

Attitude Toward Work

Some people—including, unfortunately, some station employees—visualize the manager's assignment as an easy one. They seldom see him when he is at the station and he arrives and leaves at irregular hours. Usually, his office is carpeted, draped and well furnished. He enjoys personal and social amenities. His secretary(ties) often seems to be in command of the station while he plays golf or goes out of town. Daily on-the-air operations do not require his direct involvement. On the surface, it would appear that he devotes a minimal amount of time to his work and a maximal amount of time to something like leisure.

Most station managers *do* have fun but a large share of their enjoyment comes from problem-solving and decision-making. They work longer hours than their employees and they carry work with them when they go home at night or leave on business trips. The high degree of informality which exists in radio and television stations can be deceiving. A television monitor or a radio receiving set in the manager's office means work rather than recreation. Pressures from stockholders, owners, station personnel, the audience, government and the critics are so constant and the changes in the industry are so regular that the manager becomes preoccupied with thoughts of his station and its problems during most of his waking hours.

To manage a broadcasting station is a privilege which is afforded few men and, as we have noted, there are many responsibilities which go with that privilege. The strong manager not only accepts these duties but he expects them and goes out of his way to create them when they are not present. He knows that his success is dependent upon constant progress. He knows, too, that the *easy* assignment can be assumed by any number of people.

A general public impression of broadcasting is that it is a glamour business. Yet, any description of the manager's position could hardly include the term "glamorous." His job is basically hard work. It is, in effect, a way of life that has to be lived most of the time. That is the way he wants it!

THE ADMINISTRATIVE STRUCTURE

In some small radio stations, the manager doubles as sales manager or as program manager or both; in a few cases he is the station's chief engineer. He may also take a regular shift as an announcer and he may write some of the commercial copy. The total staff of some small radio stations may be no more than five or six people. Such stations are ideal training grounds for the young person who is starting a career in management for he is forced by the circumstances to become engaged directly in all aspects of station operation.

The simplest administrative arrangement in broadcasting consists of three executives who are in charge of engineering, programming and sales and who report directly to the station manager.

The opposite extreme of size is represented by a radio and a television station which are under joint ownership and are located in a metropolitan market. In such operations, it is not unusual to find a *general* manager of both stations in addition to a station manager for radio and a station manager for television. In stations with large numbers of personnel, assistant managers may be added for radio and for television. An illustration of the numbers of people who are involved in executive positions may be seen in the personal structure of WGN Continental Broadcasting Company which is shown on pages 32 and 33. The charts show the administrative alignments for the broadcasting corporation as well as the separate executive organizations for radio and television.

Many group owned stations, in addition to their local administrative structures, have central headquarters offices. Common operating policies for all of the stations owned by the company may be framed in the central office or the company may prefer a more flexible arrangement whereby each station may decide its own procedures. Usually, the central office coordinates financial data from the various stations and often adopts personnel standards and practices that the stations follow. Often, it represents all owned stations which may be involved in union negotiations. In a few cases, the central office maintains a program and production unit which plans and even produces programming for all of the stations.

Duties of the Manager

The varied duties and activities of the radio and television manager will be discussed throughout the succeeding chapters of this book. Yet the essential managerial task is the planning of goals, objectives and operational procedures of the station. This precedes and accompanies all other duties.

Policy Planning

Well defined plans of both a short-term and a long-range nature are needed by all broadcasting stations. Because these immediate and ultimate targets affect and apply to every phase of the station's operation, the manager is the one person who is in a position to evaluate them in true perspective. Key station staff people can supply him with some important data. Certainly, their opinions should be important in his considerations. But all final decisions regarding policy have to be made by management.

Effective planning involves forecasting. Most of the employees of a station work in a "here and now" atmosphere. Their assignments for the most part involve today's deadlines or those of tomorrow or of next week. It is imperative that someone take the long view and make accurate predictions about the station's future. As the person who is most directly responsible to the station owners, the manager is expected to provide answers concerning long-range business prospects and their probable effect on the station's future. He must be aware of trends and signs in program popularity, in advertiser expectations, in new developments in technical equipment. He is expected to analyze and project this knowledge into future plans so that the station can lead, rather than follow, its competition.

Wise planning takes all possible future eventualities into account. Without such planning, unexpected or unforeseen events may occur which could cause temporary chaos. Valuable time can be saved through prior consideration of the measures which could be followed in any possible major emergencies in the future. Such crises might stem from anything from the loss of a tower in a tornado to the possible loss of a valued employee in an accident. Pre-planned actions, while never entirely adequate in emergencies, are preferable to spontaneous decisions which have to be made while in a state of shock or when under heavy emotional stress. The best ad-libs are almost always well rehearsed.

Managerial plans should be clear to the employees of the station. The team nature of the broadcasting activity makes such understanding particularly necessary. A station should be composed of people who believe in the objectives of the manager and who are keenly interested in working toward their achievement. Well conceived planning can reduce tendencies toward employee ideas of indispensability, chances of personality conflicts, displays of temperament and the evils of internal politics in the organization.

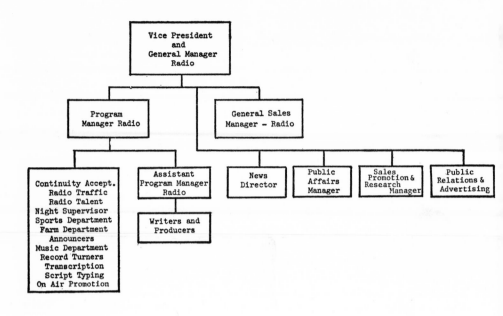

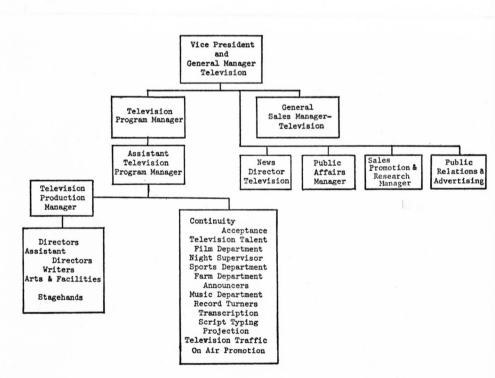

Reporting Relationships
WGN Continental Broadcasting Company

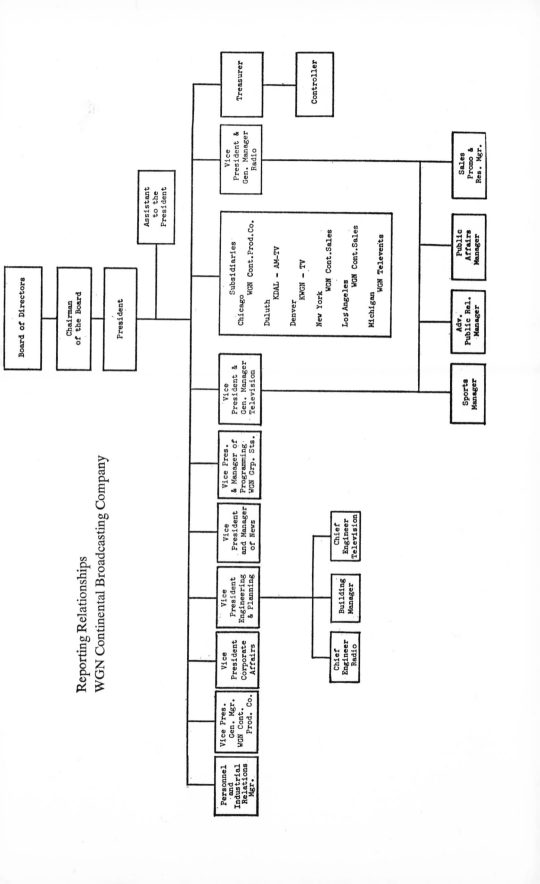

The principal objective of the planning function is to achieve greater efficiency and thus produce maximal returns on the investment in the station. Achievement of this goal is dependent upon a clear policy, a well organized plan of attack and a dedicated staff.

It is as essential to have adequate planning in small radio and television stations as in large stations or networks. All stations of comparable size have basically the same type of facilities and equipment. The important differences between those stations are due to the *people* who work in the stations and the manner in which their activities are coordinated, guided and challenged.

Improvements in or replacements of facilities or equipment, the responses to and actions upon new regulations from the FCC, variations in either individual or overall programming formats, changes in rate structure or in selling methods, revised office procedures—these are examples of variables that require new decisions and consequent alterations in policy. Most of them are made under the pressures of time.

Owners of stations need to give managers the authority to make whatever changes are necessary whenever they are needed. In a business that changes as fast as broadcasting, the manager should not be throttled by a need to obtain the approval of his superiors in all matters requiring decision. He should be regarded as the person fully in charge and he should be authorized to act in the owners' behalf without more than courtesy consultations or advisements.

When a change of managers is made, the new executive should expect to draw his own plans for the future of the station. This same privilege is accorded every new President of the United States, every new Governor of a State or every new manager of a baseball team.

It should be clear that the planning function calls for the most realistic thinking and projection that is possible. In consideration of the responsibility for service and profit which the manager assumes with his appointment, anything short of realistic planning is inexcusable. Some radio and television stations, unfortunately, operate under fantastically unreal goals and there are a few which can produce no clearly defined objectives. These stations properly deserve the various kinds of negative results that they get.

The first important obligation of the manager, then, is to determine the goals and objectives, the policies and the procedures of his particular radio or television station in his market. Some operational practices which have become standard throughout the broadcasting industry may be borrowed from other stations. But the heart of the entity, the *raison d'etre,* for all of the important station decisions, the goals, objectives, policies and procedures should be tailor-made for each particular station. A good manager will want them to be and he will see that they are.

The Station Policy Book

Once station policy has been formulated, it needs to be put in writing and copies need to be given to each employee and to the owners of the station. Some stations have found it advisable to circulate some sections of their policy statements to various community groups which might be interested and affected.

Some of the advantages of having station policies in writing are: (1) the achievement of greater efficiency; (2) a reduction of the chances for misunderstandings; (3) less need for continual routine decisions of a repetitive nature; (4) a provision for additional managerial time for concentration on other station problems; (5) a standard and equitable treatment for all employees; and (6) a guide that sometimes may be incidental to the total station operation but that may be of prime importance to the employees as individuals.

Without a clear station policy in writing, a manager can find himself devoting a disproportionate amount of his time to decision making on relatively minor issues. With a clearly defined policy, many of these cases need never arise. If they do occur, they can be settled quickly by a referral to the station policy.

In the absence of a policy on "moonlighting," plans for rotating announcer's shifts may be upset due to a second job that an announcer is holding away from the station. An employee may be reprimanded for taking excessive sick leave if it has never been made clear just how much sick leave is "excessive." There can be a problem of staffing the station on holidays unless employees know which people are expected to work and why. Station clients may complain about improper treatment on the telephone by station employees if no rules of telephone etiquette have been formulated. Cleanliness can be a continual problem in the various station offices or washrooms or in the reception room if no rules exist. The manager may note that the coffee breaks for office personnel tend to get longer, that the conversations around the water cooler tend to increase, that smoking continues in restricted areas, that more and more attention has to be given to requests for the use of station properties by employees, that official stationery of the company is used for personal correspondence, that the only satisfactory way to deal with letters of reply to people in the audience is to read them before they are mailed, that some people on the staff engage in long telephone conversations of a personal nature during working hours. In such cases, a manager can discover that he spends far too much time issuing memoranda which have been circulated before; the same problems may seem to re-occur involving different people. Most employees, aware of operating policies, accept and follow established rules and practices.

Policy statements can cover a wide range of employee interests, including wages and salaries and the bases for salary increases and advancements, rules concerning vacations and other fringe benefits, and job descriptions.

Complete job descriptions are particularly important in defining the limitations and responsibilities of each staff member and in giving him an understanding of the relationship of his work to that of other people on the staff as well as to the other station functions. Job specifications need to be clearly framed. It is more efficient to define functions and then find people who match them and who will be good members of a team than it is to find people and then attempt to adapt the jobs to them. Station positions should be so well defined that each replacement of an individual will find the basic assignment unchanged.

Written policy is particularly valuable for *new* personnel. In far too many cases, new employees at radio and television stations learn their job routines and absorb the station's philosophy in a most inefficient manner—by talking with other employees, by making mistakes and having to be corrected or by asking questions. Broadcasters have been notoriously negligent of indoctrination procedures for new people. Minimally, a statement of station policy, including the various job descriptions as well as the station rules, should be given to each candidate for a position before he is hired. This policy statement can be regarded as a part of the employee's contract. Any prospective addition to the station's staff has every right to know all the conditions of his employment before accepting a position.

It is next to impossible to compose a complete station policy book in the first writing. New situations will constantly arise and conditions will frequently change. Provision should be made for regular revisions. The most carefully defined rules should cover most cases but there will always be exceptions which are sufficiently different to require separate decisions. It is advisable to create policies that permit a limited amount of flexibility. Then, if exceptions have to be made, explanations can be given without fear of embarrassment. Extreme care should, of course, be exercised in exceptional cases in order to insure fair treatment.

The preparation of a satisfactory policy statement is a time consuming process. It should, however, make for greater management efficiency and it should improve station morale.

Policy Implementation

In the implementation of policy, the human qualities of the manager are extremely important. His skill in administration and his clarity in the communication of his ideas will determine the degree of their acceptance by the employees, the public, the advertisers and the owners. Ineffective communication of the true intent and meaning of the plans or a reliance on an authoritarian approach to enforce their acceptance can result in compliance by the employees out of a sense of duty rather than with enthusiasm. There can be negative reactions of defensive or antagonistic natures. To achieve positive results, the communicative and leadership abilities of the manager are truly put to the test. He must be a good salesman and a good listener.

In the communication of new plans to the staff, it is important for explanations to be given as to why the changes are being made. There should also be clear instructions concerning the benefits to be gained by the station from the changes.

Implementation should never be exclusively a downward process whereby all of the impetus for action is instigated by the manager. If such practice were followed, many good ideas would be lost to the station. All of the station's personnel should be encouraged to contribute suggestions for station improvement. Whenever any employee makes a workable suggestion, he should be given full credit for the contribution which he makes.

Sometimes, the station employees may be aware of changes that might be necessary but the manager may not know of them. Some employees may feel reluctant to report irregularities; others may be inclined to give only a partial accounting of the facts. It is important for the manager to have the confidence of his staff. Often, he may need to convey to them his desire to be kept informed of any irregularities which might affect the station adversely.

The conference approach, whereby an administrator gathers together his junior executives for the discussion of problems and issues, has produced many benefits to organizations. Consideration of possible alternatives is usually more effective when several minds concentrate. But while groups can make effective policy, only individuals can implement and administer that policy. The station manager must provide the insight which brings the problems to the conference table, guide an objective appraisal of the problems and then be prepared for the administration of the policy measures which are adopted.

When duties are delegated to others, there needs to be an explicit understanding concerning the limits of authority. The expectations of all administrative and supervisory roles as well as their relationships to the duties and responsibilities of other station executives should be clearly stated in station policy. General and/or station managers need to make special efforts to keep department heads supplied with all information which has any application to the areas of their jurisdiction.

Delegation of authority is a requirement, of course, for executive efficiency. Station managers need to be freed from detail work in order to be able to concentrate on major policy and on the variety of duties which are combined in the managerial position. We are ready now to identify those managerial duties: (1) a regular study of the *audience* which is served by the station; (2) a close working relationship with the *program manager;* (3) an equally close working relationship with the *sales manager;* (4) a similar close working relationship with the *chief engineer;* (5) the regular supervision of the *office staff* of the station; (6) the preparation of the overall budget and the maintenance of controls over income and expenses in order to earn *profits;* (7) a regular attention to the motivation, rewards and working conditions of the station's *personnel;* (8) the regular acquisition of information concerning the proposals, rules and regulations of the Federal Communications Commission and the maintenance of proper relationships with the FCC and other *government* officials at the national, state and local levels; and (9) an active participation in *professional activities* at the national, state and local levels.

3

The Audience

Don't let anyone ever tell you that people don't change from one generation to the next. They change from one week *to the next. People are better educated and more sophisticated, with more varied appetites, more cultivated tastes, longer weekends and wider interests. They are becoming harder to satisfy, harder to fool, easier to bore.*

—WHIT HOBBS, VP and Copy Director, Batten, Barton, Durstine and Osborn, Inc.

PEOPLE WHO regularly tune in the station comprise its circulation. The advertisers who supply the station's operating revenue are interested in that circulation. Thus, the station's popularity, its income and its consequent profit are directly dependent upon audience receptivity to its services.

Actually, there is no one single homogenized station audience. Any station has different groupings of people who may be listening or viewing at different times throughout the broadcast day, week or month. At one time, for example, the audience may be composed mainly of children. At some times, a station may attract a large proportion of highly educated people; at other times, most of the people in the audience may have very little formal schooling. Some audiences are made up mostly of farmers; other audiences are composed mostly of high school students. We could cite any number of demographic differences in the makeup of the various audience groupings. But woven through all the compositions will be *some* people who have widely different backgrounds from those who predominate. What brings these people together to share common program experiences? What do these people, individually and collectively, really think about the radio and television programs which they see and hear? What causes them to prefer one station's programming over another? How can their loyalty to any specific station be assured? The station manager needs to be able to answer these questions. He'd better!

Most of the knowledge broadcasters have about their audiences is of a *quantitative* nature. This is to say that the approximate size of the audience at any particular time can be known. Various commercial research organizations are able to supply the manager with information concerning the numbers of homes where his programs are accepted.

Size of audience, while useful, if taken as the sole criterion for judging a station's value to the advertiser or its popularity with audiences, can lead to deceptive conclusions. The local manager needs additional *qualitative* information to supplement the findings of outside services. This information should reveal the interests, opinions and attitudes of the listeners or viewers. Such data is not found in program ratings. Unfortunately, this kind of information is not as readily available and the manager may conclude that too much money and effort are necessary in order to get it.

Managers in other forms of show business, such as the legitimate theater, the movies, the night clubs or the concert stage, are able to make a double check on the success of their offerings. They have the box office, which measures the quantitative audience for any performance. In addition, they are able to judge the responses of those audiences while the performance is in progress. The ultimate success or failure of a show has often been determined by these audience reactions after the people have assembled and have been counted. It is not unusual for major changes to be made in the show on the basis of the reactions. In radio and television, the argument is sometimes advanced that audience reaction is not so important for any single offering because the program is only broadcast once and then it is dead. The argument is hardly valid due to the heavy dependence on programs in series, on repeats and on syndication of programs.

In any communication system, feed-back from the receiver to the communicator is a necessary ingredient for maximum efficiency. It is the only true indicator of the effectiveness of the effort to reach people and it provides the only safe basis for alteration of any format.

In the mass media communication is usually a one way, almost authoritarian, process whereby a regular supply of messages is sent to the people. Direct feed-back, on the part of most of those people, is practically non-existent. Viewers and listeners merely receive or consume without any communication of their reactions to the originator of the messages.

The broadcaster may hear from a small segment of his audience when something is disliked. Seldom does he receive praise from the people who appreciate what has been transmitted. Most of his audience appears to be apathetic or lethargic. The station manager cannot meet with members of his unseen audience to learn their opinions and attitudes about his station. He cannot check his sales effectiveness with them directly as does the merchant with a customer in a store.

Most managers have resorted to either a reliance upon comparative numerical sizes of audiences or to reports of store traffic after commercials have been broadcast. Neither has been a very accurate barometer of public opinion. Both, in the absence of more revealing information, have given some indication of a station's relative popularity in comparison with other stations.

Until recently, broadcasters were content to settle for quantitative information, which comes down to a kind of nose counting. The costs of securing qualitative data and the absence of pressures from advertisers or agencies for such information contributed to the almost total concentration on the quantitative figures. The time has come when the counting of noses will not provide the information that the broadcaster needs.

So long as most markets with broadcasting service had only one station, evidence of station popularity was easy to assess. Indications were the numbers of receiving sets purchased in the area, enthusiastic telephone calls and letters from those early audiences, and the regular references to broadcasting in most people's conversations. And, since local broadcasting meant only one station, there was little doubt concerning the existence of an audience for that station's programs.

As two or three or four or more stations came into those markets, the competitive nature of the broadcast service forced a burden of proof of audience on each station manager. He had to find out how many people preferred his station over his competitors in order to be able to sell his advertising at a respectable rate. Information relative to his audience could be purchased. Thus began the "battle of the ratings" from which the industry has never recovered. Decisions on the nature of programming began to be based not necessarily on whether a program was good but on whether it would be popular. Stations claimed dominance at various periods of the broadcast day often on the basis of a decimal point or two. With the widespread public that is attracted to radio and television, even a decimal point in the ratings can represent thousands of people.

DIMENSIONS OF THE BROADCASTING AUDIENCE

Both radio and television achieved almost universal public popularity within the relatively short period of a decade after their inception, then continued to expand with each subsequent year of their existence. The initial enthusiastic public reaction was shown by the purchase of receiving sets almost as fast as they could be produced and marketed. Brigadier General David Sarnoff predicted in 1920 that his "radio music box," which could be placed "on a table in the parlor or living room," would bring $75,000,000 in sales within three years. He was $8,500,000 short of his estimate.

Two years after the licensing of the first radio station in 1920, there were some 500,000 radio receiving sets in homes. At the end of the first decade of radio's history, there were 13,000,000 radio sets in use. The profile of growth has gone steadily upward each year. Now, the number of sets which are produced annually exceeds the total number that were in use at the end of radio's first decade. Radio sets are now in some ninety-eight per cent of the homes of America and it is estimated that more than half of those homes have two or more sets. The total number of radio sets in working condition in the United States approaches 200,000,000.

We are told that four out of five radios sold at present are either self-powered portables or car radios. Eight out of ten new automobiles which are sold are equipped with radios; surveys have shown that the number-one accessory choice of most buyers of new cars is a radio. Transistor sets are in use today wherever people can go. Programs may be heard at the beach, in parks or picnic grounds, on hunting or fishing trips, in the cornfield, on excursions, in the retail store.

FM radio has begun to show some indication of becoming a profitable broadcasting service with sizeable and loyal special interest audiences. It has proven its ability to reach the quality audience on the local and the regional network levels.

Some 20,000,000 American homes are equipped with FM receiving sets and the rate of increase has averaged about two million additional homes each year. Studies have shown a higher proportion of people with high incomes, college education and professional status in FM homes than in non-FM homes.

It appears that the economics of the FM audience will continue to support specialized program services, especially when the census figures reveal that professionals, executives, proprietors, and technical workers make up approximately twenty-five per cent of the civilian-male working population.

The manager of an AM radio station or a television station would do well to bear in mind that most of the FM homes are duplicated *homes* but not audiences. This is to say that most of those same homes could be reached through television or by AM radio if these stations were disposed to try to reach them.

The initial acceptance and expansion of television has been equally phenomenal. At the close of World War II in 1946, when television began its growth, only 8000 homes had television sets. Twenty years later, television could be seen in close to 60,000,000 homes and almost twenty per cent of those homes had two or more sets. Television's national coverage extends to some ninety-two per cent of American homes. While this is short of the ninety-eight per cent of the homes that have radio sets, it exceeds the eighty per cent of American homes with telephones or the seventy-three per cent with bathtubs. The television antenna has become a familiar characteristic of the American landscape. People have invested millions of dollars in television sets and antennas and in their service and maintenance.

It should be borne in mind that all the dollars people spend on radio and television receiving sets and on their repair and maintenance are purely voluntary expenditures. Here is true evidence of a high degree of public acceptance of broadcasting. It has become a cliché to say that the average American spends more time in listening to the radio and in viewing television than he spends on any other activity, with the exception of working and sleeping. It has been noted that some people often combine the latter two activities.

Managers of stations can hardly afford to become complacent over the relatively high availability of audiences in comparison with other media. Broadcasters know that a figure of fifty per cent *actual* audience, representing one-half of the available audience, is considered high most of the time. The term "actual audience" is the same as another term used to describe the percentage of tune-in, namely, sets-in-use. It is in the matter of expansion of actual audience or sets-in-use that many broadcasters have been lax in their cooperative efforts with other broadcasters to increase the percentages. Concentrated efforts by all broadcasters in an area to provide motivations for the listener-viewer to make greater use of the receiving set might result in a consistently larger actual audience in the area.

Competition between stations for the attention of the actual audience results in a "share" of that audience for each of the stations. That station which, at any particular moment, provides the programming which appeals to the largest segment of those people who have their sets in operation gets the largest share of the audience at that time. If it is consistent in achieving this result, it becomes the most popular station in the area on an overall basis but not necessarily during all of its hours of operation.

Broadcasters have had a tendency to devote most of their attention to increases or decreases in their share of audience. While this may be the logical focus of any individual station, it would be wise for all broadcasters in an area to give some of their attention to the increase of both *actual* and *available* audiences.

GROWTH OF BROADCASTING STATIONS

In order to complete our look at the dimensions of broadcasting in the United States, we should note the growth of the radio and television stations serving the public.

The number of AM radio stations grew from a total of 30 at the end of 1921 to 955 by the middle of 1945. Fewer than a thousand radio stations provided service to the public through the period of the World War II years. In the five-year period from 1945 to 1950, more stations *began* broadcasting than had been on the air in all of the twenty-five year history of radio up to 1945. By the middle of 1950, there were 2303 AM radio stations in the United States. Since that time, there has been a steady growth in the number of stations. Toward the end of 1967, there were more than 4,250 commercial AM stations.

The growth pattern of FM stations was quite different, although the present signs are indicative of a healthy growth of FM in the future. The first year of recorded totals of FM stations, 1945, showed a total of fifty-three stations in the United States. There were 732 stations in operation by July 1950. Then, for the next seven years, the number diminished year by year until there was a surviving total of but 541 by the middle of 1958. Since then, FM has had a rapid rate of growth in each subsequent year. There were 2,016 FCC-authorized commercial FM stations by the end of 1967, with an additional 356 educational stations.

It is difficult to equate the growth of FM stations with particular audience interests since there are different kinds of FM. In addition to the independently owned and operated FM properties, there are those owned and operated by AM interests. Of the latter types, some duplicate many AM programs; others maintain a completely different program service on the FM outlet.

The growth in the number of television stations was a post-World War II phenomenon. At the beginning of the year 1947, there were only six television stations in operation; there were only seventeen by the end of that year. Enough applications for licenses were processed by the FCC prior to the 1948 "freeze" so that thirty-three stations were able to begin operation in 1948 and forty-seven more were added in 1949. Then the increase of stations slowed down considerably, with but ten taking the air in 1950 and only one new station in 1951, bringing the total of stations on the air to 108 at the end of 1951. As soon as the "freeze" was lifted in the spring of 1952, there was a flood of applications. Twenty-one additional stations opened in that year. Then the industry really began its expansion, with an additional 227 new stations during 1953. Since that time, the total number of television stations on the air has increased each year. As of December 1967, there were 823 FCC-authorized commercial television stations in the United States. In addition, 186 non-commercial educational stations had been authorized by the FCC.

RESEARCH IN BROADCASTING

The beginning of commercial research in broadcasting dates from 1935. In that year, the C. E. Hooper Company began supplying ratings of network radio programs, using the telephone coincidental method. For years, the Hooper rating was a powerful factor in the determination of the success or failure of many network programs. In 1950, the national services of the C. E. Hooper Company were purchased by the A. C. Nielsen Company but Hooper continues to provide audience measurement services for local stations.

Cooperative Research Efforts

There have been two major attempts to establish cooperative research companies in broadcasting. Both were ill-fated.

Pre-dating Hooper as the first broadcasting-industry research organization was the Cooperative Analysis of Broadcasting, which was started in March of 1930 under the sponsorship of the Association of National Advertisers. By 1934 it had become a non-profit cooperative organization. The ANA was joined by the American Association of Advertising Agencies and later by the radio networks as financial contributors and joint managers. CAB, as the research company came to be known, used the telephone-recall method as developed by Archibald Crossley for the measurement of comparative sizes of network audiences. Later, a change was made to the use of the telephone-coincidental method, which was already used by Hooper. In the summer of 1946, CAB announced that two ratings services using the same methods were superfluous and therefore it would terminate its existence.

The idea behind the formation of the Broadcast Measurement Bureau in 1945 was to try to give broadcasters a kind of standard measurement service similar to the Audit Bureau of Circulations in the publishing field. The governing board of BMB was made up equally of representatives from the National Association of Broadcasters, the Association of National Advertisers and the American Association of Advertising Agencies. Only two national studies were undertaken, the first in 1946 and the other, after considerable difficulties in financing and administrative changes, in 1949. A mailed postcard survey, covering a million people, was conducted in each study. The advertising agencies seemed to see great possibilities in the data collected but many radio station managers believed that the information did not provide them with sufficient sales ammunition. BMB was dependent upon station subscriptions for its financing. The indication of weak support from the broadcasters for any further studies caused the failure of another cooperative venture into broadcasting research. BMB came to an end in 1950.

The Big Three of Commercial Research

Three commercial research companies entered the field of broadcasting in the decade of the 1940s. All have remained leaders in broadcast measurement ever since.

The A. C. Nielsen Company, an established marketing research firm, began its work in broadcasting in the early 1940s. The company holds the patent on a mechanical recording device called the Audimeter. This device, when attached to the receiving set, records which stations are tuned in and the amount of time the set is tuned to each station. Since the Audimeter operates continuously, it captures a profile of the complete activity or inactivity of each set to which it is attached.

The Pulse, Incorporated entered broadcasting in the mid-1940s after notable success in the use of the personal-interview method in the field of public affairs. Adapting this method to broadcast measurement, Pulse began to supply some qualitative as well as quantitative information about audiences.

A third company was organized in the late 1940s and opened its national offices in 1952. The American Research Bureau, now commonly referred to as the ARB, selected the diary method, using a different sample for each survey period.

Other Commercial Research in the 1950s and 1960s.

Trendex, Incorporated was the first research organization in broadcasting to develop an instantaneous overnight rating service. The company, which was started in 1950, adopted the coincidental-telephone method of measurement. Through the middle of 1961, Trendex offered its clients the fastest national service in broadcasting by making 1000 telephone calls every half-hour in twenty-five cities throughout the country. Only the evening programs of the networks were rated. Trendex national reports have not been prepared since June of 1961 but the company continues to make reports on special order from the networks and agencies.

Sindlinger and Company, using the telephone interview method, measures all of the mass media. Prior to its involvement in broadcasting, the company achieved success in its research on box-office reports from the motion picture industry. In the early 1960s, the company started a national radio and television measurement service which matches information about audience makeup with probable buying plans for specific products.

A research organization called Trace operates mainly on the West Coast, using an automobile coincidental system whereby motorists are interviewed during their stops at traffic lights.

A research organization that stresses the qualitative approach is TV-Q, a division of Home Testing Institute, Incorporated. This national service uses the mailed questionnaire method and contacts different families for each monthly survey. Attitudes and opinions about specific television programs are tabulated.

A complete description of the various services of these and other major research companies in broadcasting has been reported by Dr. Harrison B. Summers, formerly in charge of instruction in broadcasting at Ohio State University. This excellent report appeared in the Spring 1961 issue of the *Journal of Broadcasting*. It is recommended as a source for further information on this subject.

Changes in the Nature of Research Information

In the early days of program research, information supplied to the subscribers consisted of quantitative data including how many homes had receiving sets, the numbers of respondents who were listening to the sets, the stations and programs to which they were tuned and the percentage who could identify the sponsors of the programs to which they were listening.

By the early 1960s, audience information was more detailed and included some demographic characteristics. Demography as here used expands the academic concept from a statistical study of populations with regard to birth, death, health, growth rates and so on to include cultural, socio-economic and compositional data. In television terms, demography embraces a study of the audience as a potential viewing and buying group. Demographic techniques are available. The mystery is why so many station managers continue to rely upon guess, hunch and luncheon-table oracles. In general, top communications executives are alert to the advances of engineering and technology while remaining aloof from the resources of the social sciences.

Demographic disclosures have increasingly proved to be advantageous to the advertiser who wanted more understanding of the audiences for his commercials. Trendex, Nielsen, ARB and Pulse all began to publish additional data for their respective subscribers, including such information as the number of viewers per home for each program, the proportions of men, women and children in the audience, and income, occupation and education stratifications.

PROBLEMS FOR COMMERCIAL RESEARCH

In spite of the present availability of additional audience data, various commercial research companies became the targets for a steadily increasing wave of negative criticism. It was the broadcasters who first raised doubts about the values of quantitative research findings.

The wide disparity of results from the various research companies bothered some broadcasters. The top-rated program or station in one research study might be considerably lower in the ratings of another organization. Performers, writers, directors, producers and others in programming became particularly sensitive to the variance in ratings. Often, their future careers were dependent upon where they stood in comparative rankings. When different audiences were measured by different methods, it was not too surprising that the results did not always agree. Nevertheless, the slavery to the decimal point decided the fate of many a program and it caused the renewal or termination of the advertising contracts of many sponsors. Casualties were common every season in the network schedules.

The trend in radio research on the national level seems to be toward cumulative studies. Rather than reports on the shares of audience during segmented parts of the broadcast day, the "cumes" show how many people listen to radio, or to a specified station, over a longer period, usually a week's time. This information is comparable to the determination of circulation of a newspaper or magazine, where total numbers of sold copies of a particular issue are determined but not the readership of specific features.

From a competitive standpoint with other media, the cumes may be sufficient. A certain amount of education in their use will be needed by broadcasters. Hindsight now reveals that the early projects of BMB had considerable merit.

While national radio research is in transition, two major research companies continue to provide *local* area radio measurement. C. E. Hooper, Inc. issues telephone coincidental reports in some 160 markets. The Pulse, Inc. issues from one to eight roster-recall reports per year in some 150 markets.

Writings on the nature, reliability and influence of the rating system are voluminous. Probably, the fairest evaluation issued in 1966 by the Committee on Nationwide Broadcast TV Measurement (CONTAM), formed by the networks themselves, was simply that "Ratings are an aid to decision-making, not goals in themselves." Unless and until the computer takes over human affairs completely, management will be well advised to rely upon courage and creativity. Broadcasting will otherwise abdicate the management of its own house.

A Look Ahead

Out of the welter of confusion over the ratings issue, several hard facts should have emerged.

First, ratings are basically accurate in measuring what they claim to measure—audience size. In the absence of means whereby audience response can be surveyed as rapidly and as comprehensively, ratings are essential to broadcasting. Stations and networks need to know how their programming is received. The quandary of ratings seems to stem not so much from their existence as from their frequency and their interpretations.

It is highly questionable whether surveys of audiences are needed every hour of every day. Some variation of the cumulative circulation tabulation would seem to be sufficient for competition with other media which are already established on that kind of long-term average basis.

The necessity for realistic interpretations of ratings should be obvious. Gross numbers of people, even when stratified by demographic characteristics, reveal comparative sizes and nothing more. Any inclination to read other meanings into the ratings can produce false conclusions which may be dangerous.

Second, it is now a certainty that the industry will control the research which is conducted among its audiences. This must be a control based on complete objectivity and not, to any extent, on the profit motive. Pure or basic research must take precedence over the numbers game and methodologies must be validated for their accuracy.

Third, the industry cannot bargain for cheap research; research that is meaningful is expensive and is worth supporting. We should have learned that much experimentation is necessary in order to discover the true scientific facts and we must be patient while such experimental projects are undertaken.

Fourth, it has become evident that too many station managers either have not properly understood research or they have not had people on their station staffs who could interpret research realistically for them. Such understanding will become more and more of a necessity for every radio and television station in the future.

Fifth, it should now be obvious to every broadcaster that there are other factors which are as important as, and perhaps even more important than, ratings in the determination of his success in reaching the people in his coverage area. Such factors as station image, creativity in programming, flexibility of station performance, the availability of the station to the community and the costs of the station services to the advertiser in relation to the results the station is able to deliver should be equated in proper relationship with any ratings used.

The *composition* of the audiences should be of far greater import than the total size of those audiences. The race to be more popular than the competition throughout the broadcast day has perhaps caused more distortion of the research effort in broadcasting than any other single factor.

Will audience measurement methods in use today be outmoded in tomorrow's broadcasting service? Unquestionably they will need modification. Already, advertisers and agencies are asking for more definitive information about stations and about the people they serve. Rather than measurement of households, the research of tomorrow will need to concentrate on individuals. The multi-set homes in both radio and television involve varied selections of programs. The increase of UHF stations should mean an expanded competition resulting in greater audience selectivity. In the future, information concerning predefined *groupings* of people will be needed by advertisers. The coming fractionalization of the total mass audience by multi-sets and more stations may itself condemn a system which equated success with the largest audiences. Increasingly, the opinions and attitudes of the listener-viewer will be as important as the simple fact that he chooses a specific program or station at a specified time.

CHANGING AUDIENCE CHARACTERISTICS

It would be easier for the broadcaster to understand his public if people had not changed so radically in such a short time. These changes can be illustrated through an examination of three of the most basic categories of a society: age, education and income levels.

Age Categories

There are now more people under the age of ten in the United States than there were people of all ages in the total population of the country one hundred years ago. We are nearing an unusual phenomenon whereby more than half of the population in the United States will be under the age of twenty-five. Before 1970, some twenty per cent of all the people in this country will be teenagers.

At the other extreme of the age spectrum, another bulge continues to grow. In the decade between 1950 and 1960, the over-sixty-five age group increased twice as fast as the expansion in the population as a whole. In the past fifty years, the over sixty-five populations increased almost three times as fast as the total population. Seventy years ago, 2.9 per cent of the population were over sixty-five; today, that group approaches ten per cent. A century ago, the proportion of people over the age of sixty-five was one in every thirty-five; now, we are close to one in every ten.

As increases have occurred in the "under twenty-five" and the "over-sixty-five" age groups, the percentages of people in the twenty-five to sixty-five age range and more particularly in the twenty-five to fifty range, have decreased proportionately. This, of course, should be an obvious conclusion. What is apt to be overlooked is the ever-increasing audience of youth and senior citizens for the mass media.

Another general projection foresees a heavier burden on the working population to finance the increased needs of the young and the elderly, both of which groups are largely dependent.

Education Categories

In the fifteen-year period 1951–1966 the proportion of people between the ages of eighteen and twenty-one who were enrolled in a college or university changed from twenty-five per cent to forty per cent.

Yet, this is only the beginning. It is generally agreed by educational administrators that, at the current rate of growth, enrollments will increase from a present annual total of over four million to nearly seven million by 1970 and to eight and a half to nine million by 1975.

These figures pertain, of course, to just those students enrolled in colleges and universities at the respective times. It is perhaps even more revealing to add to those millions of people another nine to ten million who are graduates of colleges or universities.

Elementary and secondary schools have shown proportionate bulges as a result of the population explosion following World War II. In 1940, some ten million people in the United States had completed high school. By 1960, that total had increased to some twenty-five million and the projected total for 1970 is some thirty-five million.

Income Categories

Educators have long been aware of a direct correlation between education and income. A 1963 study made by R. H. Bruskin Associates[1] concentrated on people in the twenty-five to sixty-five age range. In this group, those who had completed high school had an average annual income of $6102. The average annual income of the person with some college was $7392 and for the individual with four or more years of college, it was $9350.

The number of American people who have moved into higher income categories has increased significantly in the past twenty years. It has been noted that in 1947 only three per cent of U. S. families and individuals had incomes between $10,000 and $15,000; in 1963, twelve per cent were in that category. In 1947, only two per cent had incomes above $15,000; the percentage had increased to seven by 1963.[2]

The other end of the family-income range is anything but a pleasant picture. In 1963, half of all the families in this country had annual incomes of less than $5000. Almost a third of America's families had annual incomes of less than $4000, twenty-two per cent were under $3000, thirteen per cent earned less than $2000 and five per cent subsisted on annual earnings of less than $1000.[3]

Signs of Changing Interests

So the "average man" is somewhat different from his counterpart at the time of the beginning of broadcasting. His environment has changed, too, affecting his outlook, his interests and his tastes. Radio and television, along with the other mass media, have been important factors in determining the directions of that change. Conversely, the new social climate has had its effect on the media and should continue to condition necessary changes in the nature of communication messages in the future.

There are signs, for example, of a growing public interest in the fine arts. Perhaps loosely referred to as a "culture explosion," this increase of interest in the fine arts should not be regarded lightly. Nor dare we disregard the increasing existence of leisure time.

The question as to what people will do with their increased participation in cultural interests and the growth of leisure time should concern every station manager. A search for the answer can hardly overlook some of the signs of a new appetite for cultural pursuit.

Some authorities are highly skeptical of the cultural trend. They believe that there is a lack of depth and meaningfulness in this search for culture. Other authorities maintain that the American society is in a period of change leading toward a time when there will be a general public appreciation for the fine arts. The station manager need not concern himself too greatly here. He must appeal to the young, the elderly, the working population. Culture is not for him to invent, but to understand, to foster and to transmit.

THE CRITICS

It is in this confused area of public taste that broadcasting's critics find their most fertile ground for provocation. Regularly, they denigrate the programming of radio and television, usually through the print media. Their highly vocal attacks have caused some people in the audience to question whether they should be as interested in broadcasting as they once were. Guilt complexes about time wasted in watching television have been detected in recent studies. Any personal indulgence—be it the afternoon cocktail, motorcycle riding or reading comic books may be assailed by charges of unrespectability or called a waste of time by "authoritative" people and thus made suspect.

What troubles broadcasters is the amount of influence critics seem to possess, particularly when so many of them are poorly qualified commentators on broadcasting itself. Too often, broadcasting is indicted by the critics for not having enough of the kinds of programs the critics themselves would prefer. Any wide appeal of such programs to the majority of the public would be purely coincidental.

The fact is that many ambitious broadcasters receive very little critical support. Brilliant and dedicated men have fought against odds to produce programs of dramatic value, information and art appreciation. And, when, at last, some of their efforts are successful, who praises, acknowledges and argues for them? The lofty esthete? Hardly ever!

How many leading citizens of any given community who complain that broadcasting has nothing to offer watch the splendid documentaries and cultural programs on television, or listen to the news roundups, or fine musical programs on radio? True, this calls for selective tuning but there are enough programs of this nature to occupy hours of a person's time each week. And that's precisely the point! Fine programs are available!

The critical minority exercises great care in the selection of the fine arts that they attend and they buy tickets for the events weeks in advance. Yet its members are perturbed because they have to make some effort to seek out what they want in broadcasting.

Millions of people have had the opportunity to hear the works of Shakespeare, Ibsen, Shaw, Conrad, Henry James, Stephen Vincent Benêt, Dickens, Cervantes, Maugham, Hemingway, Maxwell Anderson, Wilder and many others performed. They have been given performances by Leonard Bernstein and the New York Philharmonic, the Moishiev Dancers, the NBC Opera Company, the Firestone Hour, the Bell Telephone Hour, the Boston Symphony, the Chicago Symphony with its Great Music Series and the best of the concert stage. They have had the chance to hear and see every important leader of the world. It is true that the majority of programs are not of this nature but neither are the majority of books written (consult any list of best sellers), plays produced and musicals presented. We suspect that there is a tendency on the part of certain critics to judge the traditional fine arts by the best produced and then to condemn the mass media by the bulk of popular offerings.

Much of that which concerns the critic today will be taken care of in time. Once, there were those of the elite who looked with disfavor on the silent film; now it is exhibited as an art form. The same reaction has been in process with jazz. Who is to say that some time in the future a Red Skelton or a Bob Hope or a Jack Benny may not be regarded as classical artists? It is even possible that some of the Westerns that the critics deplore may one day be exhibited as American classics.

The commercial message is a particular target for abuse. Yet, the printed media carry the same kinds of commercial messages as are carried on radio and television and in as great, if not greater, volume.

It should be a source of pride to broadcasters that they have been instrumental in the widening of public understanding. The majority of the achievements of broadcasting have been positive but broadcasters have permitted a few deviant stations and biased critics to distort their image. They need to take action while they are still popular.

Of all social institutions, broadcasting should—indeed must—be as modern as the people it serves. If it is true that people are becoming harder to satisfy and easier to bore, then there is a profound risk in operating a station by yesterday's standards. No one will detect out-of-date methods faster than the people, who can always tune to those other stations and make comparisons.

People with significant shifts in age, income, interests and with greater amounts of formal education, with developing interests in culture, can hardly be expected to settle for the same values which they had formerly. It is vital to the future success of any radio or television station to find out in advance in what direction the people are moving.

We, all of us, have a long way to go before utopia arrives. Given the opportunity to provide either popular entertainment or self-conscious cultural offerings, most station managers would not hesitate to give the audience what the majority prefers. The manager, charged with the responsibility for the making of profit for his owners, has small choice but to satisfy the majority. On occasion, popular programs are canceled in order to carry special programs of an informational or a cultural nature. When this is done, the reactions from the audience are anything but conducive to re-peated efforts. Networks and stations have been flooded with complaints, for example, when they have pre-empted regular offerings in order to carry the Republican and Democratic national conventions. Sizeable numbers of people have reacted negatively to stations when programs have been inter-rupted to carry news bulletins. And who can forget the time when the edu-cational television station, WNDT, in New York received a reported 350 complaints when it carried an important session of the United Nations in-stead of the scheduled ancient Charlie Chaplin film?—and from a cultivated audience, too.

In March, 1966, the three television networks pre-empted their regular programming one evening in order to provide coverage of the emergency splashdown of the Gemini 8 spacecraft. The cost to the networks was re-ported as approximately $3,000,000. Even the cost was incidental to the service performed in providing instantaneous coverage of an important event. Nevertheless, there were thousands of angry telephone calls to the networks and their affiliated stations. Plenty of viewers resented the cancel-lation of *Batman, The Virginian* and, ironically, *Lost in Space*.[4] There's little to be gained by laboring the point. It should be clear to most people that whatever the signs may be for the long-range future, the present status of mass audience taste favors the popular arts.

Whether commercial broadcasters have an obligation to try to upgrade audience tastes continues to be a debatable issue. There is much to be said for knowing the audience well enough to be able to aim consistently a little higher than existing tastes and thus raise standards by degrees. But it would be financial suicide for most stations to move too fast too soon in that direction. There would seem to be an equal danger in playing down to an audience; condescension has a way of alienating people.

It should be a sensible approach for any manager to make a sincere effort to learn the true interests of any specific audience. It would appear to be folly to make decisions on the basis of critical diatribes, personal prefer-ences and aesthetic guesswork.

STUDIES OF AUDIENCE BEHAVIOR

There have been several comprehensive studies of the motivations and attitudes of viewers and listeners. Glick and Levy[5] discovered a certain degree of dissatisfaction among television viewers. The excitement and en-thusiasm which existed in the first years of set ownership had somewhat subsided and had been replaced by a greater discrimination in program selection.

The late Gary A. Steiner[6] found that the factor of college attendance made the most significant difference in the amount of time devoted to tele-vision viewing. Those who had no more than a high school education were the most devoted fans. Steiner noted that people who had attended college were more selective viewers. They had a wider range of interests outside television and more sources of entertainment. Yet, they viewed few informational programs on either commercial or educational channels, even though they said they would like to have more of this type available.

If those people who are the better educated and are in the highest income groups view television less than other people do, then an NBC study,[7] conducted by the American Association for Public Opinion Research in 1963, is particularly interesting. This study found that the "heavy" viewer watched the most informational programming; the "light" viewer usually chose entertainment programs.

Elmo Roper and Associates have conducted opinion studies at two-year intervals since 1959 for the Television Information Office.[8] In all of these studies, favorable attitudes toward television have heavily outweighed unfavorable ones. Since 1963, most people have reported that they receive more of their news from television than they do from any other medium. Television also leads all other media in public believability of news reports, according to the Roper studies.

Media Statistics, Incorporated of New York City, in a study of New York City residents in March, 1965, found that the heaviest viewers of television were men and women over the age of sixty-five and the heaviest users of radio were people between fifty and sixty-four. Heavy users of both radio and television included men over sixty-five and women in the fifty to sixty-four age group.

The Mediastat study revealed a surprising finding about the teenage audience. Contrary to popular opinion, the teenage group in the New York Study was the lowest of all age groups in heavy radio listening. It was also surpassed by women in all age groups and by men sixty-five and older in amounts of television viewing.

New York City has a multiplicity of radio stations offering a wide range of choice for the person who is disposed to listen. Yet, the Mediastat study found that the average radio listener seldom tuned to more than two stations.

PROFILE OF THE AUDIENCES

In general, what do broadcasters really know about the public? First of all, and of prime importance to broadcasters, they know that it is composed of many diversified publics. Each of these smaller units has its own particular interests and its members are apt to believe that their views are the correct ones.

Broadcasters know that most audiences for radio and television are far more interested in entertainment than they are in education or information. Whether a particular audience preference is for homemaking programs or baseball or music or dramatic fare, they *do* want to be entertained. Even those groups which prefer the fine arts find their own form of entertainment in that programming. A sure way to fail in any format is to neglect the element of showmanship.

It may be granted that the American public responds to the sensational. So does every other public from Peshawar to Patagonia. It is regrettable that vast numbers of Americans would rather see an attractive woman in a skimpy bath towel than hear good, sound scientific reasons for the superiority of a particular deodorant. But these are the conditions that prevail among human viewers. Any leadership by any broadcaster must take into account a realistic understanding, not a concept arising out of an idealistic notion. And it is true that more people can parrot a cigarette jingle than can quote the First Amendment. Why not? The Amendment is in the Constitution and it can be looked up if needed.

Most people tend to give perhaps too much credibility to radio and television sources. They tend to believe whatever Cronkite or Brinkley or the local newscaster or announcer tells them. In most cases, this faith is well placed but it is almost too much responsibility for the broadcaster to bear. Since the tendency does exist among a people not accustomed to look very far beyond the headlines of a single newspaper, the trust of those people must never be taken for granted. Certainly, any exploitation of that trust must rank as one of the lowest forms of misbehavior.

Granted, it would be naive to expect the audience to appreciate all the efforts of the broadcaster. The moods of an audience are often fickle and difficult to estimate. This unpredictability factor, as much as anything else, is sufficient reason for broadcasters to extend themselves to acquire a sounder understanding of the people they serve.

The audience has been conditioned to expect regular *changes* in station offerings. The wide variety of programs which they have come to expect from broadcasting may have spoiled them somewhat but variety must be continued as the spice of quite ordinary lives. Broadcasters may be grateful for the general *optimism* which the public has concerning changes. Next year's programs will be better, they believe. The resultant excitement over new offerings is in the station's favor.

Certainly these are *impatient* people. They have been given so much by the media. They have seen most of the forms of show business and all of the established story plots and they have been eyewitness to the great news stories. Their expectation level for new and for novel programs is insatiable. At any particular time, given too much repetition, they could turn to alternative forms of entertainment and recreation as they once turned to broadcasting over their former interests.

STATION RESPONSIBILITY

✝ If it can be established that broadcasters are both leaders and servants of the public, then a question of proportion must be raised. When, how often and under what conditions should the leadership function be exercised? How much of the broadcast schedule should be what the public wants and how much should be devoted to what the public needs? It must, of course, be assumed that the broadcaster is aware of the specific needs and wants of his audience. It must also be assumed that he knows some of the needs and wants of the people which they themselves may not realize. The problem is further complicated by the changing nature of the public's desires.

Two problems arise from attempts to give the audience what it wants. First, it is doubtful whether most people *know* what they want at any particular time. Tuning usually involves two choices: whether to turn the set on or leave it off, and which station to choose from the several that are available. The latter selection may not supply what the consumer wants at that moment. Rather, he makes his choice from whatever is being broadcast. In this sense, the listener adjusts to the media rather than vice versa.

A second problem is posed when ratings are used by the broadcaster as a basis for giving the audience what it seems to want. The fallacy of this reasoning is that the ratings show what may have been wanted *yesterday* or last week or last month. Ratings represent measurement of *past* choices. There is no assurance that the listener wants more of the same *today*.

It is no easy task to determine the best methods for satisfying most of the people most of the time. Certainly, the ideal combinations have not as yet been discovered. The FCC asserts that broadcasters must serve the public interest, convenience and necessity. No one disagrees. This is something like discussing the weather. We'd like it improved but how to improve it escapes us.

The balance has to be somewhere between the extremes of a complete responsibility toward the public welfare and a complete irresponsibility toward commercial obligations. Perhaps the problem should not be expressed in terms of *giving* but rather *selling* the station's programs to the public since commercial broadcasting operates in a sales atmosphere. If so, then the test of effectiveness, as in sales endeavors, should be the mutual satisfaction of both parties.

A strange dichotomy exists in the area of alleged effects of programs on people. It is claimed by some critics that some broadcast materials make radio or television addicts of some people, or that they may delay or prevent normal maturation or make some people select unrealistic goals or become generally apathetic. The very same materials are said to provide healthy relaxation for other people, to aid them in their normal maturation and to serve as an escape valve for channeling off certain aggressive impulses.

We would do well to remember that one man's meat is another man's poison. After all, almost any wife might agree that television has some adverse effects if she were to be questioned at a time when her husband wants to watch double-header baseball games and she wants him to cut the grass.

Joking aside, broadcasters must admit that these powerful media do have effects on people. Such an admission is pure realism.

Zsa Zsa Gabor's opinions can be more important than the opinions of a college professor to many people because she is more physically attractive, she is seen more often and she more closely represents the social aspirations of many admirers. Whether those desires are in the people's best interests is moot. They do exist and the public reacts accordingly. Broadcasters may not determine social standards but celebrities and the roles they play do influence the public through the status which broadcasting confers upon them.

People with unstable characteristics who watch considerable television very possibly could get destructive ideas and miss the constructive elements completely. True, they may get the same ideas in other places but perhaps not as graphically or as attractively demonstrated. Programming which might seem quite innocent to a normal person can be interpreted in an altogether different manner by an abnormal person.

When a President of the United States is slain by an assassin's bullet, when eight student nurses are murdered, when forty-five people are hit by the bullets of an unbalanced person on a major university campus, it is time to ask, "What and who will be next?" It is also time to ask whether the pleasurable rewards of violence in broadcast programs for some people are worth the consequences. There still remains the question as to the amount of influence which broadcasting has, if any, on these and other acts of crime. If there is any chance at all that the media may be contributory factors, then broadcasters have their work cut out for them.

Certainly, the opposite extreme of naive, pollyanna types of programming would be just as questionable in its effect on people. There is evidence that some people would prefer a saccharine-treated program instead of the display of battlefield corpses.

One of the broadcaster's greatest tasks is to discover a balance which neither narcotizes the public nor places individuals in danger.

Possible negative effects on children are concerns unto themselves. When a seven-year-old child is caught sprinkling ground glass in the family's lamb stew, we can hardly charge the child with evil intent. In this actual case, there was a curiosity on the part of the young scientist to learn whether it would work the way it did on a television program.

A young person may be instructed carefully in the principles of good driving on the highway and then lose his life to one who has not learned to respect the rights of others.

So long as broadcasting is so all pervasive and can get into those homes where parental guidance is non-existent, it should take advantage of its opportunities. It should not shift its responsibilities to sources which are not inclined to accept them.

Broadcasters *can* help make and shape the values people live by. People can, through radio and television, come to feel a sense of participation in current history. They can learn life's deeper satisfactions and, as a result, become active in the reduction of the many injustices of modern society. They can come to believe in the values of man's compassion for his fellow man.

What is wrong with the stimulation of *thinking* of the members of the audience? One of the noblest accomplishments of the electronic media could be the raising of significant questions rather than the providing of neat answers. One can be accomplished as easily as the other without any discernible difference in the size of the audience. Either can be achieved within entertainment programs as well as within informational or educational formats.

The job broadcasters can do to protect and explain the true democratic ideal is practically unlimited. Here is a way that the industry can partially pay the public for the use of its airways.

The individual station must take the initiative in establishing rapport with its audience. Involvement in community affairs can be followed by on-the-air reports of those activities. The station's facilities can be used regularly to tell the people in the audience what the various staff personnel are doing for community improvement. The station's interest in the people in the audience and its efforts to serve them better should be told on the air.

If the broadcaster expects public support on important issues, he must begin to encourage a more vocal response from the people in relatively minor matters. He cannot anticipate sympathy when he needs it if he cultivates a one-way communication system. It is time for broadcasters to realize that an absence of audience response is a reflection on the management of stations. Oversensitivity to opinions that do not happen to coincide with those of management is not a healthy trait. It is through the conflict of ideas that any democratic institution is able to achieve greatness.

Apathetic audiences are of little practical value to the broadcaster in the selection of his program schedules. Yet, they can be highly critical of those offerings once they have been aired. The situation is somewhat comparable to the person who does not vote on election day, and then months later stands on the street corner to cuss-damn the administration.

Manufacturers have discovered that their products are successful when they are "people-centered." Studies are made regularly to be sure that the understanding of the "people" is accurate.

The station manager needs to conduct his own personal involvement with the "people" in his area. He won't necessarily find representatives of the majority at country clubs or among his associates. Lest he become isolated from the mass audience he serves, it is essential for him to keep in touch with them. He should ride a bus and talk with the people who are on it. He should converse with garage attendants, laborers on construction projects, taxicab or truck drivers, radio-repair men and the myriad of people who live outside his ordinary world. One of the most enlightening and profitable experiences he could undertake would be participation for a day or two in one of his station's personal interview surveys in the homes of his audience.

LOCAL STATION RESEARCH

We have touched base in this chapter with some revealing studies of the national audience. The studies we have mentioned do not, we repeat, provide information about any particular station audience or audiences. Qualitative information about local audiences must still be discovered through local effort. The station manager may choose to remain unenlightened concerning the real image of his station in the community. If, however, he wants to provide the best possible service to the local public and to local advertisers, he will want to learn the people's true thoughts.

Local audience research needs to be undertaken as a supplement to the other research services which the station buys. Its usefulness lies in the information it can disclose to indicate how well the station is presently communicating and how it may improve its communication in the future. The results of local station research should be considered by management as an important aid toward the achievement of more efficient operations.

Local audience research may reveal some shortcomings in the station service and it may confirm some station achievements. It is this kind of revelation, positive or negative, that the station manager needs to know. The true public attitude toward his station is of far greater value to a good administrator than distorted impressions based on guesswork. Local audience research, then, should be conducted primarily for the values which it will bring to station administration. Dr. Sydney Roslow of The Pulse, Incorporated, has said:

> "There will be a lot less mis-use and abuse of research as more of us discover that research is not the action. It is not the judgment. It is only an aid to judgment . . . It is a tool to complement all the other tools management needs for its cerebral decisions."

Who should be in charge of local research? In order to answer that question adequately, the *purposes* of the research should be kept in mind. Those purposes should be to confirm or deny the effectiveness of past operational patterns and to provide guidelines for the future. Since any use of data for general circulation outside the station would defeat the diagnostic purpose and could also advise the competition of possible future station action, it is advisable that the research be conducted by a member of the station staff. Then, whether favorable or unfavorable reactions are received, the information can be used only by the station administration and in ways that can be determined internally.

In some of the larger stations, a director of research has been designated. In most of those instances, his assignment has been one of coordination of various existing research efforts. Seldom have these men been given the opportunity to initiate and supervise significant independent local station research. Yet, with minimal rearrangement of job functions, the way could be cleared for them to begin to feed important information to management. We cannot overstress the caution that local research studies, when undertaken, should be completely divorced from the activities of the sales and promotion departments.

Many stations are not in a position to add a research director to the staff. In those cases, the manager may find benefits from the employment of someone qualified to perform regular staff duties who is also qualified to conduct qualitative research. Many young persons who graduate from colleges and universities after having majored in radio and television have received research training as a part of that education.

In the event that some stations may find it impossible to organize for any staff conducted research, investigation might be made of the possibilities of studies by either colleges and universities or by state broadcasters' associations. The advantage of the confidential nature of the station conducted studies may be impossible to achieve in these "farmed-out" or cooperative efforts because their results will be known by the sources which do the research. However, the information discovered can be useful and such studies certainly would be better than none at all.

Often, a radio or television station is located in close proximity to a college or university. In too many cases, the research facilities and resources of the academic institutions have not been adequately utilized by the broadcaster. Educational researchers are particularly suited for the kinds of studies which the local station needs to make of its audience. They, as a rule, have little or no interest in the quantitative "ratings" type of research but they can become interested in projects which propose to study audience opinions and attitudes.

How often should local research be conducted? It would seem that a local audience could be over-researched; this condition could be as wasteful for a station as no research at all. A good, thorough, continuing study of the local audience once each year should provide a realistic venture for any station. The returns to management should far outweigh the investment.

The possibility of cooperative studies with leading merchants in the community should not be overlooked. Some stations have had outstanding success with return-postcard mailings in monthly statements of banks, public utilities or savings and loan associations. Information can be gathered relative to station or program popularity. In the ordinary arrangement, the station pays for the mailings and the financial institutions contribute the time for the tabulation of the results. Local businessmen accept the findings because of the position of trust which businesses hold in the community. The element of respect is also an advantage in terms of the reliability of the public response to the mailings.

OTHER STATION-AUDIENCE RELATIONSHIPS

A station manager dare not stop at the acquisition of knowledge about his audience. He needs to use all of the methods at his command to maintain cordial relationships between the station and the people. His attitude toward the audience will be reflected in the attitudes of his employees and in the nature of his service to the people.

Those stations with the best records of successful audience relationships usually are managed by men who are truly concerned about, and who work to maintain, a feeling of mutual understanding and respect between the station and the people served by the station.

The not-so-simple matter of insuring the proper handling of telephone calls and mail from the audience can reflect to the advantage of the station. The cordial telephone voice and manner can win people and influence them favorably. A lack of courtesy and consideration can destroy goodwill that has taken years to establish. Some stations have a practice of using recorded answers to telephone calls during nighttime or week-end operations. Such a practice can provoke people so much that the loss in favorable image can be far more than the station can afford. The personal touch is essential for close relationships.

Unanswered mail is inexcusable. The use of form letters should be avoided except in cases where mass mailings are necessary in connection with contests or promotional efforts. Even letters which might come to the station from "crackpots" deserve the courtesy of a reply, even though they may be difficult to answer.

Stations can achieve tangible benefits from the organization of a working advisory council made up of responsible men and women from the coverage area of the station. Such a council might be composed of active men and women prominent in general civic affairs and in club work throughout the coverage area.

The WGN Continental Broadcast Advisory Council is an example of a going concern. Full membership meetings of two to four hours' duration are conducted at least semi-annually with frequent additional meetings with some segments of the Council membership. The members of the Council have an opportunity to talk with key department heads and other station and corporation executives. Suggestions for changes in programming are made. Many of the ideas have been excellent; some, while well meant, have been thoroughly impractical. The members of the WGN Continental Broadcast Council, representing persons from Illinois, Indiana, Iowa, Wisconsin and Michigan, are fully aware that theirs is an advisory capacity and that the station officials can and must make all final decisions. These dedicated men and women have contributed to the benefit of everyone in the audience under the umbrella of the station's broadcast signal.

In a smaller community, such a council can have an immediate and highly personal impact. It can be extremely beneficial in aiding those broadcasting operations that are limited in their program resources. It can direct people's attention to the station and, through the various organizations represented by the members of the council, advise the general public of what the broadcaster has done and is doing to contribute to the good of the home community.

When the broadcaster, his audience and the critics pool their resources, self-interest can change to mutual cooperation. Then, all of the true benefits of broadcast communications can be realized.

4

Radio Programming

"I don't know where you happen to be.
If you're on this world,
You can listen to me."

—Song lyric by JACK NELSON, Program Director of WDAP on the
Drake Hotel, Chicago, 1923[1]

THE PROGRAM DEPARTMENT is the "showcase" of a radio or television station. It normally employs more people than any other department of the station and produces the only *product* the station has to offer, whether it be entertainment or information. It, more than any other part of the operation, creates the station image or personality.

There are two broad areas of activity of the program department: (1) the planning of the overall program schedule and (2) the development and production of individual programs to fit that schedule. The station manager is involved in both of these activities, principally with the first.

It is the station manager's function to serve as the architect of the station's program framework. He provides the philosophy out of which program policy grows. He knows the expectations of the stockholders and of the public and he accepts the responsibility for the success of the overall program structure of the station.

The manager's programming blueprint needs to be clear and realistic and it should be flexible enough so that it may be adaptable to future change. It is finalized only after considerable appraisal of the resources and the objectives of the station.

Implementation of the blueprint is assigned to the program manager but the station manager must continue to evaluate the station's programming. He spot-checks concepts and performance. He notes places where improvements can be made. He confers with the program manager to suggest changes or corrections.

64

The ability to recognize where change is needed and to offer constructive advice is developed by experience in programming. Station managers, whose earlier experiences in broadcasting were confined to sales or engineering need to make special efforts to approach programming. Leadership is particularly necessary in this department where so much of the station's success is dependent upon the inspiration of sensitive and creative people. Selection of an outstanding program manager is an important consideration.

The program manager's role in radio has undergone radical change since the early days of broadcasting. There are signs that it may be on the verge of further alteration. To understand properly the background of the change as well as the evolution of programming, one needs to know some history of what has been broadcast.

CHANGES IN RADIO PROGRAMMING

On Friday, November 25, 1960, a successful format of radio's "golden age" of programming died. On that day, the seven surviving radio network daytime serials broadcast their concluding installments. All seven were on CBS; NBC had dropped daytime serials on radio some months before. In their heyday, just prior to World War II, there had been twenty-five of them a day on CBS and twenty a day on NBC, filling an uninterrupted six to eight hours a day. They came to be known as "soap operas" because most of them had been sponsored by soap and detergent companies.

These hardy perennials of daytime radio had represented one of the truly original art forms the medium had created up to that time. Noted for their chronicles of human misery and misfortune, these serials had brought comfort to many women by dramatizing problems that were greater than those in the lives of the listeners. Following the daily episodes had become a regular habit and, as a result, the cumulative audience for the broadcasts was enormous. It was estimated that over half of the housewives in the country followed the serials. No other radio format had ever been so successful in captivating so large an audience for so long a period of time.

The serial which, perhaps, will hold the all-time record as the longest-run "soap opera" of them all, *Ma Perkins,* played for twenty-seven years and closed after 7065 consecutive installments. Three others, *The Right to Happiness, Young Dr. Malone* and *The Second Mrs. Burton,* each ran for almost 20 years and more than 500 broadcasts. Three relative newcomers perished with the veterans: *Whispering Streets, Best Seller* and *The Couple Next Door.*

It is characteristic of radio men to remember the period of network dominance in radio programming with nostalgia. There is good reason for them to do so. Once, the great bulk of radio programs featured the best live talent in show business. Those were the times when families came together night after night in their living rooms to share the comedy of such greats as Ed Wynn, Eddie Cantor, Fibber McGee and Molly, Fred Allen, Jack Benny, Bob Hope, Jimmy Durante and Burns and Allen. Those were the years of giant variety programs, *Maxwell House Show Boat,* Rudy Vallee and the Connecticut Yankees, Edgar Bergen and Charlie McCarthy, and Kay Kyser and the *Kollege of Musical Knowledge.* Live drama was popular, too, in such programs as the *Lux Radio Theatre, First Nighter, Mr. District Attorney, The Easy Aces, The Goldbergs, Lights Out* and the productions of Norman Corwin and Arch Oboler. In an era of great dance bands, most of the late-night offerings were live, on-the-spot pick-ups of bands such as the Dorseys, Glen Gray, Benny Goodman, Fletcher Henderson, Jan Garber, Gene Krupa and Artie Shaw. Earlier in the evening, the orchestras of Paul Whiteman, Phil Spitalny, Guy Lombardo, Wayne King, Ben Bernie and others were standard listening. Vocalists drew their share of the audience, too, with popular singers such as Kate Smith, Bing Crosby, Morton Downey, Al Jolson and the Street Singer (Arthur Tracy) featured on daily or weekly programs. People arranged their Saturday-evening schedules so that they could listen regularly to *The Chicago Theatre of the Air.* They followed the speeches of Father Coughlin on Sunday afternoons even though many people disagreed with his remarks. Major Bowes and his original amateur hour encouraged local-talent contests. Nor was information neglected; people listened to the news through the voices of commentators Gabriel Heatter, William Shirer, H. V. Kaltenborn, Edward R. Murrow, Raymond Gram Swing, Elmer Davis and others. And every weekday evening around 7:00 P.M. local time, most other activities ceased while millions of people listened to the daily episode of those favorites of comedy and human affairs, the radio *Amos'n' Andy.*

In the 1950s, the growth of television and the increase in the number of radio stations brought about radical changes in radio programming. Many of the network stars and the lavish productions moved to television. The country over, radio stations began to shift from network affiliation. Within a few years, two-thirds of the radio stations in the U. S. were independents.

Most of the independent radio stations were then faced with more hours than they knew how to fill. Many were not budgeted or staffed for live production and they could not have produced very much original programming even if they had been so inclined.

A kind of bandwagon effect began among the independents. Some successful formats were hastily duplicated. In the process, much of the appeal of the originals was lost. In many cases, the second-hand versions were comparable to a small-town high-school stage production of a Broadway success.

Sometimes the original was not worth imitating. Many programs consisted of hard sell, high pressure materials tasteless in content and skimpy in production.

Into management positions in radio during this period of change came eager young men who had had little or no background in the great traditions of radio and apparently no interest in the future professional status of the industry. They were blessed with considerable energy, egotism and promotional ability and a consuming interest in the "fast buck." In another age, they could have been successful circus-sideshow or carnival operators.

In their search for successful formats, some of these young men began to scan the lists of the best sellers in recordings and then to feature those records on their stations. It was not long before the "top forty" records of the day were played repeatedly. It was not long, either, before record manufacturers recognized a potential gold mine complete with free advertising for their product. Stations were soon using recordings as a vehicle to advertise the merchandise of local businessmen. The merchants paid for the service while the record companies received their advertising free. Station after station began to adopt the formula. It was not long until most radio stations sounded alike.

Much of radio's programming became cheap and blatant. Music was largely rock and roll, disk jockeys were arrogant and verbose, news was surrounded by the noise of teletypes or trains or rockets and commercials were hard-sell. What appeal the format had was largely confined to teenagers and to adults who had the interests of teenagers. The formula seemed to be: do it cheap and without imagination for people whose desires are simple and undemanding.

Most broadcasters by the early 1960s were aware that the radio industry was operating far below its potential. Some managers changed their station formats. Others wanted to change but did not quite know what to do to replace them. A few managers had never accepted formula programming. Most stations continued to broadcast what came to be known as raucous radio.

Payola

The radio industry was hit hard by the "payola" investigations. Much of management's authority and initiative was forfeited to the "play for pay" people. Some managers claimed to have learned for the first time that their stations had been involved in the unethical practices of the disk jockeys. This seemed to amount to an admission that they had neglected the supervision of their programming.

In May of 1963, the FCC issued final rules on payola. Stations are now allowed to accept free records from manufacturers or distributors but not in excess of the amount needed for regular programming. No promises can be made to play any of the free records on the air. Any form of payment or service to a disk jockey or to management in return for a free air plug is prohibited. AM and FM, as well as television, stations that accept "money, services or other valuable consideration" in return for an agreement to broadcast any materials must make an announcement on the air that those program materials were sponsored and must inform the listeners "by whom or on whose behalf such consideration was supplied." Licensees and managers also must "exercise reasonable diligence" in discovering all cases where considerations are made. Both giver and receiver become equally liable for criminal prosecution under a law enacted by Congress following the investigations. All this was necessary enough. It is mortifying to admit it was necessary at all.

Clearly, the evils of payola need to be policed regularly by station managers. Disk jockeys need to be given explicit rules and instructions. There should be no excuse for keeping any employee who is unable to resist this sort of temptation on a station staff. Payola is sellola. The things sold are station quality and integrity.

REAPPRAISAL AND REASSESSMENT

Perhaps this is the time for a reassessment of radio's unique resources. Many broadcasters, caught up in the hectic day-to-day struggle for some kind of dominance, have not fully realized that a whole new generation of people has come along to whom radio is as novel as television. Radio's inherent strengths are still present in the medium even though they may have been discounted and overlooked.

No other medium of mass communication can utilize the factor of *imagination* as radio can. No other medium can isolate sounds, which by their very isolation are conducive to strong emotional impact. Copy can be written which can make a man hungry, or happy or excited. In some instances, pictures may be worth 1000 words. In others, words may be worth 1000 pictures. Speech, persuasion and eloquence are still prime movers of human response.

The intimacy of the illusion of the person-to-person communication is another of the advantages of radio. The listener can select his own particular kind of program and listen to it by himself if he chooses. The ability of radio to reach the listener in his own selective environment should not be discounted.

There are other important factors unique to radio. Its *economy* of transmission and of personal reception is one. The cost-per-thousand for radio is less than for any of the other mass media. The *portability* of radio cannot as yet be matched by television. The radio listener can take his chosen programs with him wherever he goes. Radio is the most portable source of instantaneous news and entertainment. Radio is *flexible*. It can adapt to needed changes of program content faster than any other medium.

It has the freedom to experiment with new program formats and to create new modes not common to other media. On radio a man, a voice and an idea can initiate a promising experiment. It need not be an elaborate or a costly innovation. Radio is everywhere. It has something for everybody.

All these advantages are inherent in the radio scheme of things. Their exploitation, however, requires careful study, original thinking and hard work.

Music and news formats seem to be admirably suited to the radio medium. They are the basic program elements which radio probably communicates best. The task ahead involves a search for new ideas and techniques for their presentation. It comes down to this: if you would presume to address the public ear, then you will do so successfully if you have something to share and something to say. If so, those stations which lead the way in programming should expect a high degree of audience loyalty in return. The route to leadership appears to be open to those who want to take it. Once again, radio must call for strong program managers.

THE PROGRAM MANAGER

In those early days of radio, when the title of the chief of station programming generally was program director, this was a key position. The assignment was challenging because of the numbers of programs that were planned, rehearsed and broadcast live from the station's studios. Even with heavy network schedules, there were many hours to be filled locally and the program director considered it a challenge to match the network quality of production. They created an aura of excitement in the radio stations.

With the advent of formula radio, which was radio's first major solution for the competition of television, there was little need for live production. In a majority of stations, the program director served as a kind of chief office clerk. He arranged announcer's schedules, counted the number of times a particular record was played in a day, tried to maintain a measure of authority over the disk jockeys and waited for direction from the station manager. He became a follower, riding gain on mountains of paper. Today, with radio stations striving for identity, a premium is again placed on station creativity.

The good program manager is one who personifies show business. The world of entertainment in all its forms should be his number-one interest. In addition, he needs to be concerned about the communication of information.

Company product is as strong as the man who supervises its growth and development. Projections into the future in station programming depend upon the vision and the wisdom of the manager of this department.

Given a program manager with these and other qualifications, combined with the desire of station management to give him the right climate for growth in his department, there can be little limit to the constant progress which a station will make in program development and improvement.

THE STATION FORMAT

The determination of the overall station format is the first step in the creation of a station image. The possibilities for unique identification of a radio station in any market seem to be considerably more numerous than for the special identity of a television station. Radio stations are, for the most part, independent of network affiliation and are in a more flexible position to change their formats completely at any time. With some eight times as many radio as television stations and most of them in search of some kind of distinctive image, several standard formats have emerged with more undoubtedly ahead in the future.

The *top-forty* station is fast-paced and loud. It has tight production. The sound of "rock" is the same throughout the broadcast day. News is minimal, consisting mainly of headlines. Many promotional gimmicks are used on the air, including contests of various kinds.

The *good* music station uses a middle-of-the-road popular approach. Its pace is conservative and its music is light. There is a predominance of instrumental popular and Broadway Show music. Older tunes are favored. Newscasts are more complete. On-the-air promotion, when conducted, is presented in a dignified manner. Contests are seldom staged.

The *background* music station, usually FM, has neutral music as its basic commodity. The music has few breaks for commercials. There is as little talk, including news, as possible. Consequently, the role of the disk jockey is diminished. The sound of the station resembles that of commercial-music services for offices and restaurants.

The *classical* music station has a calm, deliberate pace, in direct contrast to the top-forty station. It may depart from lengthy programs of symphonies, operas and other music to present discussions of the fine arts and of contemporary affairs or education. News commentaries are broadcast in addition to news reports.

Specialized appeal stations concentrate on program fare that appeals to specific tastes and interests. Examples are: foreign-language, race, jazz and sports stations. The *country-western* station merits special attention given later in this chapter.

The *all-talk* station offers a variety of non-musical fare with the exception of some commercial jingles. Conversation programs dominate the broadcast day with audience involvement in many of them. News is presented in quarter-hour or longer segments, augmented by specialized news programs dealing with sports, business, women's affairs, etc.

A variant of the all-talk station is the *all-news* station. This station format seems to appeal to the information seeking public even more than the all-talk station does. There are no programs which are primarily entertainment on the all-news station.

The *small-market* station, located in areas of minimal direct competition, is free to offer a variety of program fare. At times during the broadcast day, several of the formats of other kinds of stations may be offered. The image of the station is achieved primarily through its coverage of local events. The smaller the market and the fewer its competitive stations, the greater is the tendency toward a variety of program offerings.

PRODUCTION QUALITY

Are there identifiable characteristics of production that can make the difference between good and poor radio stations? There are! How much can the quality of production affect a station's popularity with its audience?

In the achievement of professional production standards, there are few cut-rate bargains. There is no substitute for quality. The basic excellence of radio reflects station pride and performance. Lacking one, apologetic management has neither.

BALANCED PROGRAMMING

Program balance, balanced programming—no one seems to know just what the terms mean. Perhaps this is as it should be. If there were a standardized definition universally accepted, then programming would tend to be similar on all stations.

Certain allocations of interest are obvious. It makes little sense, for example, for a station with a completely urban audience to devote part of its schedule to farm programs. On the other hand, farm programming is needed on the clear-channel stations, the regionals and the local stations in rural areas.

The alert program manager recognizes that the real key to program balance lies in a variety of offerings. A station format that provides a day-long diet of five minutes of news on the hour and fifty-five minutes of music all of the same type cannot be said to offer much variety.

MUSICAL FORMATS

Some eighty per cent of all the programming of the radio stations in the U. S. consists of music. The introduction of long-playing and 45 RPM records in the late 1940s, with their extended playing times, better sound quality and non-breakable materials helped to insure the use of recordings as a staple of radio broadcasting. It also gave new impetus to the recording industry that earlier had been the target of predictions of collapse due to the availability of radio.

The Teenage Listener

The teenage market is important, but it would be a mistake for many stations to adopt formats especially designed for this age group. There is a place, however, for a few stations with basic appeal to teenagers. The teen-age group in the U. S. is expanding three times faster than the total population. Teenagers have a spendable income of some thirteen billion dollars annually. They own one-fifth of the automobiles and spend a billion and a half dollars a year on entertainment. This group also has a major influence on many of the purchases their parents make. The amount of family purchasing they are said to influence has been estimated at thirty billion dollars a year. By 1970, teenagers will constitute one-fifth of all the people in the country and their annual spending power at that time is predicted at about twenty-one billion dollars.

Those broadcasters who offer "rock" music have no easy task, however. Whether broadcasters enjoy a censorship role dealing with racy lyrics, a decision to program "rock" music automatically carries an obligation to edit it first.

Country Music

Country music is folk music with a beat, given elaborate production and sophisticated renditions. Stations lowest in popularity in their markets have switched to the country format and their ratings and their billings have increased.

The country music listener is not restricted to the rural population or to people with little spending power. A survey of country western homes in twenty-three markets was made by Pulse in 1965. The results showed that the median family income was $5675. Over seventy per cent of the families surveyed had savings accounts and over three-fourths lived in non-rental homes. Ten and a half per cent of the heads of households held executive or managerial positions or were proprietors, 16.3 per cent were skilled craftsmen, 20.5 per cent were semi-skilled craftsmen, 5.9 per cent had professional or technical positions, 3.8 per cent were in clerical work, 3.9 per cent were in sales, 2.6 per cent were students or were in the armed forces, and only 10.5 per cent were unemployed or retired. Again note the application of demographic data.

A country western band can be a powerful promotion arm of the station through bookings at county fairs and community events. Live local country western talent adds a dimension to a large number of local radio stations.

The key to the success of the country music format seems to be exclusivity. So long as one station in a market offers this brand of music, it seems to do very well. When competition occurs, the share of audience left is too thin for any station to prosper.

Middle-of-the-Road Music

While such formats as all-rock or all-country-western or all-jazz or all-classical music may result in a clearly identifiable image, managers of stations with a middle-of-the-road music policy have a more difficult task in impressing both listeners and advertisers with their individual images. Actually, the middle-of-the-road station has built-in variety right on the shelves of its music library. Imagination plus time devoted to planning can produce real rewards.

The big bands of Glenn Miller, Benny Goodman, Ray Anthony, Freddy Martin, Les Brown, Guy Lombardo, Harry James, Count Basie, Duke Ellington and others are still popular today and will be for quite some time. These are good sources of program material, along with present-day vocalists.

Modern jazz that appeals to the "middle" group is provided by such artists as Oscar Peterson, Jonah Jones, George Shearing, Andre Previn, Dave Brubeck, Al Hirt, Pete Fountain and the Ramsay Lewis Trio.

Broadway original-cast albums are always good series possibilities. The "middle" audiences request them often.

Another type of middle-of-the-road program material is available from original motion-picture soundtracks.

The comedy or spoken albums of people like Jonathan Winters, Bob Newhart, Phyllis Diller, the Bickersons and Stan Freberg can be made into a series of popular programs that can provide a balance to the musical offerings.

All major recording companies offer monthly releases of their new albums to radio stations for a nominal annual fee. Their best packages consist of a combination of pop and classical albums. The variety of music is outstanding. When supplemented by current single releases of the popular vocalists and instrumentalists of the day, any station can provide middle-of-the-road programming for all tastes.

THE ALL-TALK FORMAT

The economic necessity for station specialization and the need for a different and an exclusive image probably spawned the all-talk format; otherwise, it might not have come into being. Most stations regularly schedule some talk programs in addition to news during the broadcast day. About two dozen stations have gone all the way and offer nothing but talk programs all day long.

There is no inclination as yet to adopt its format in the small markets.

Thus far, it is confined to the largest metropolitan areas. It is questionable whether the small market would support this kind of format. The needs for a large reserve of talent and a large participating audience are probably beyond the resources of such areas.

Studies have shown that the listener to talk programs, once he is involved, gives closer attention to what comes over his receiver than does the listener to music.

Some stations make considerable use of the telephone to involve the audience. Questions for people to answer (either pre-planned or suggested by members of the audience during the calls) or discussions of a wide variety of topics are often the themes of entire programs. Conversations are often broadcast live. The only insurance against profanities, obscenities and libelous comments is a sharp, intelligent and genuinely witty announcer who can think extremely fast. His only means for cutting what is said is a tape recorder that gives him a few seconds delay. In these few seconds, he must decide what needs cutting and delete it before the tape hits the air.

If not overdone in a market, the advantages of an all-talk station can outweigh the disadvantages. Increased audience, higher ratings and increased billings may be delivered.

A variant of the all-talk format is the all-news station. This is a relatively new attempt to achieve an exclusive image in a market. Consequently, the all-news service must be considered experimental at this time.

Whatever may be the future of all-talk and all-news stations, much credit is due the owners and managers of these properties for their innovation and foresight. They have refused to be imitators, with sounds similar to other stations in their markets. Radio as an institution could be more progressive if more managers sought more ways to be different.

Radio News

In some ways, the radio industry missed a golden opportunity in the news field. Radio could have become the number-one medium for news. Instead, it lost this distinction to, of all media, television! Not content with taking over radio's former dominance in many forms of entertainment, the television industry boldly moved in to establish its leadership in the news area. Its network daily evening news coverage was expanded from fifteen minutes to a half hour, it moved into the field of public affairs documentaries and, in spite of its more cumbersome equipment, it initiated more remote coverage than radio had ever done.

What was radio doing all this time? For the most part, it continued to be dependent upon the wire services for its news and it concentrated on five-minute summaries of news highlights or headlines. The radio industry showed little disposition to seek out local news on its own.

At many radio stations with a program policy of music and news, the five-minute newscasts make the policy a misnomer. Music is given predominant attention and only token recognition is given to news. The news programming on those stations has been described "as something you sandwich in between music and disk jockey commentary, like a piece of processed ham between two stale pieces of bread."

Furthermore, by the time the gimmicks that introduce the news (sounds of teletype, echo-chamber effects, filter mikes, sounds of fire engines, supersonic jets, etc.) and the commercials have been taken care of, there isn't a fair *five* minutes left for the news.

Most independent stations rely upon the radio wire services of Associated Press (AP) and/or United Press International (UPI) for their national and international news. Most small-market stations purchase the services of one or the other. The large-market stations use both and, in many cases, these are supplemented by their own correspondents. Network affiliates are aided by "hot lines" through which they are alerted whenever an important story is breaking. UPI maintains daily voiced news and actuality reports to some 300 radio stations. Spot news, commentary and features are supplied. A full-time staff of domestic and overseas correspondents is supplemented by special UPI newsmen on assignments around the world.

Too much dependence on the wire services restricts the coverage of local news. The radio station that does not send a single member of its news staff into the community on a regular beat misses one of its best chances to increase its circulation. The use of direct lines to police and fire departments and to the city hall, as well as the use of stringers, have their places in complete news coverage but they are not substitutes for regular first-hand reports by a member of the station staff. The practice used by some stations of inviting listeners to telephone news tips to the station is, to put it bluntly, foolish.

Even the local coverage of community events is no guarantee that anything worthwhile will be reported. Radio stations need newsmen who can discover news stories overlooked by people who are not trained journalists. A special kind of writing and editing for the *ear* is needed. Often, the journalist who has no training in broadcasting may be too well trained in how to write for the *print* media. He may also be ineffective as an air personality. What is badly needed is a new breed of radio personality who has training and/or experience in both journalism and broadcasting.

Mobile units, equipped with tape recorders and beeper phones have given radio news reportage a new dimension. In the larger metropolitan markets, cruisers and helicopters have been given regular details in the coverage of traffic conditions, informing commuters of highly congested areas and of street conditions during bad weather. Cruisers have been deterrents to crime in some instances as they have circulated on night beats through potential trouble areas of cities.

The radio station could and should produce documentaries dealing

with community problems. The undertaking could be one of the most exciting production experiences on the station. Radio documentaries are relatively inexpensive in comparison with costs in live television or on film.

An understanding of the traditions of journalism and of journalistic
integrity is needed. Proper recognition should be given to news programming and to the people who prepare it and air it. A good newsman may
rebel occasionally against some of the traditional rigidities of broadcasting,
including formats and time segments. He may raise havoc with some established station practices. On the other hand, he will believe in the importance
of news seven days a week. He also may supply a kind of enthusiasm that
could be contagious throughout the station and that may hopefully infect
other station employees.

Drama Programs

Condolences were expressed for all radio drama after the demise of
the soap operas. Back in the dark ages before television, the dramatic presentation has been one of radio's staples. Then there were years of an almost
complete absence of drama in the medium. The syndication services
brought about its revival.

All varieties of drama are now offered to stations by the syndicators
and they have found general acceptance. Many of the availabilities are recorded shows of the '30s and '40s that have been taken out of the vaults,
dusted off and dubbed.

Regretfully, as yet, there is no sign of a revival of locally produced
drama on radio stations. Most stations built since dramatic creations were
dropped by radio are not equipped with adequate space and facilities to
produce such programming. Those that are so equipped might find some
unusual gratifications in dramatic production, particularly if they are near a
college theater, a civic company or a summer drama group. Much of the
talent on local levels today is far superior to that which was available in
those areas in the earlier and greatest days of radio drama.

Community Centered Programming

Some of the greatest satisfactions in local radio can come from the development of the community centered programming, particularly when the
voices of the people who live in the area are featured. Such development
can build a position of solid respect in the community.

As much care should go into the public service community program as
goes into any other locally originated program on the station. Public service
programming efforts should be regarded as station investments in the future
growth and welfare of the area.

The station should be known as a champion for civic improvement and for the promotion of public safety, racial and religious understanding. Always it should take a strong stand in support of constructive projects and it should regularly expose any community evils which come to its attention. Mere notices, brief announcements, colorless paragraphs sandwiched in the day's schedule are not enough. Whenever the station reaches the stage where it is a true mirror for the community, then the man who has guided it to that accomplishment can take pride in this achievement. The station will enjoy acceptance and approval.

FM RADIO

The future of FM programming remains unclear. FM stations independent of AM ownership tend to stress high-fidelity or stereo programming. Some of these stations provide specialized music service. Others broadcast a variety of music categories. Those FM stations that are a part of AM operations often duplicate varying amounts of programming primarily designed for the AM audiences. No consistent pattern of FM programming has emerged as yet.

Hopeful signs for the future of FM include: steady annual increases in FM set sales; a growing number of FM sets in automobiles; and a steadily expanding list of applicants for FM licenses.

Unduplicated FM stations quite generally have provided vital and important additional radio services. Their program schedules show good balance between music and talk and there is much variety within each category. A few stations in metropolitan markets have successfully programmed a predominance of classical music but the majority have offered a wide range of programming.

We find much excellent production in the individual programs on most of the unduplicated FM stations. The low-key emphasis is consistent in the conversational approach of the announcers, in the soft-sell commercials and in the structure of the programs. Apparent efforts are made to avoid the strictly background or "wallpaper" kinds of offerings. Good balance is achieved through the avoidance of excesses of any single program type. The capitalization on the opportunity to broadcast in stereo undoubtedly has added much to the appeal of the stations.

FM appears to be here to stay after having experienced a particularly hectic youth. Programming should be the least of its problems of the future. Its earning potential remains the big question.

NEW ALLOCATIONS RULINGS

A freeze on all applications for new AM stations as well as for major facilities changes was imposed by the FCC in 1962 to allow time for the consideration of revisions in allocations policy. It was terminated two years later with the adoption by the Commission of its plan for future AM and FM allocations. The ultimate effects of governmental policies are still in the future. We may not, however, assume that all future AM assignments will be granted on the basis of rigid engineering standards. There are advantages and disadvantages inherent in the ruling.

The net effect of the new allocations system on the future of AM radio was the encouragement of new stations in markets that had inadequate service and a sharp curtailment of the number of new stations in the large markets. At last, some order has begun to emerge in the chaotic over population problem of AM radio.

Music Licensing

One of the major operating-cost items in broadcasting is the music license fee. This is an expense factor in both radio and television but it is particularly high in radio because of the extent to which music is played. The license fee is for performing rights. Close to a $60,000,000-a-year business, music licensing is controlled in the United States by three organizations.

The American Society of Composers, Authors and Publishers (ASCAP) is the largest and oldest. It was formed in 1914 and now has a repertory of around a million titles. ASCAP collects almost two-thirds of the annual payments made wherever music is played for profit. Initially, its revenues were collected from restaurants, hotels, dance halls, etc. Then motion pictures became a prime source. Today, broadcasters account for about four-fifths of the annual receipts.

Broadcast Music, Incorporated (BMI) was created in 1940, at a time when broadcasters were restricted from playing any music not in the public domain. An increase in fees by ASCAP was deemed too high by broadcasters. Hence, when their station contracts with ASCAP expired at the end of 1940 and were not renewed, stations had to program the old tunes. BMI was created as a source for new compositions. It was industry-financed. The difficulties between broadcasters and ASCAP were resolved after some ten months. By that time, BMI had become a going concern. It now has some three-quarters of a million titles.

The Society of European Stage Authors and Composers (SESAC) is relatively small by comparison with the other two. Although originally representing European works, SESAC is now based in the U. S. and its repertory includes American creations. It is a privately owned organization, formed in 1931.

All three licensing organizations have found themselves in conflicts with broadcasters extending into 1967. ASCAP was yet to settle a dispute over a proposed rate increase which had been requested two years earlier. BMI reached agreement with an All Industry Radio Station Music Licensing Committee on its first increase in station rates in its twenty-six-year history. SESAC agreed to publish a catalogue of its compositions after the Federal Trade Commission had the company under investigation.

So licensing matters stand at the moment. It would be injudicious to say here they rest.

PROGRAM REPORT FORM

In August of 1965, the FCC ordered the use of new AM-FM program forms for all applications for new stations, for license renewals, for requests for changes in facilities and for transfers and assignments of control. New program-logging requirements were also issued.

Broadcasters were cautioned by the Commission that it is their responsibility to notify the FCC whenever "substantial changes occur" in programming and in commercial practices.

The new (1966) AM-FM report forms contain three basic changes. The first alteration is really an addition since it had not been a formal part of previous forms. This is a requirement that the broadcaster submit a statement of: (1)" . . . the methods used by the applicant to ascertain the needs and interests of the public served by the station"; (2) ". . . the significant needs and interests of the public which the applicant believes his station will serve during the coming license period, including those with respect to national and international matters"; and, (3) "typical and illustrative programs or program series (excluding entertainment and news) that applicant plans to broadcast during the coming license period to meet those needs and interests."

The second major change concerns the categorical breakdowns of station programming. A new category of "Instructional" programs is added. Here the programs that are of an instructional nature but are not necessarily "presented by or in cooperation with an educational institution" may be included. There are also new categories for the designation of time devoted to three program types: station editorials, political programs and educational-institution programs. The complete categorical listing of program types now includes: agricultural, entertainment, news, public affairs, religious, instructional, sports, "other," editorials, political and educational-institution programs.

The last major change pertains to commercials. Where previously reports were requested concerning the *numbers* of commercials in the composite week, the new form calls for an expression of the total commercial time in hours and minutes.

Unquestionably, the addition of the statement concerning audience needs and interests is the change of greatest consequence to broadcasters. More than ever, it becomes imperative that the manager of a station establish regular two-way communication between his station and the public it serves. No longer can programming be designed by intuition. It must be keyed to the *actual* needs and interests of the people.

The change also forces the manager to engage in long-range planning whether it has been past station policy or not. The requirement that "typical and illustrative programs or program series" be submitted makes such planning inescapable.

As usual, broadcasters resent being ordered by the FCC to submit this additional data. Also as usual, had there been sufficient evidence that stations were conducting inquiries of this nature there would have been no need for the government order.

If it is fair to say that station management has been irritated by program-data requirements, sometimes seemingly overdetailed and irrelevant, it is also fair to say that management has, in many cases, been enlightened by its own listing of the very details required for program summarization. Shortcomings have a way of showing up in station statistics. Vague and comforting impressions to the effect that a station is doing a bang-up demographic job may be subject to drastic reassessment once the actual programming output is factually examined. Management may, of course, dispute endlessly over categories. For the most part, such disputation is futile. Giving make-do or lackadaisical programming lofty classifications under public-service categories is foolish as well as deceptive. What is worth transmitting is worth doing well. All excuses are poor excuses for feeble concepts and poor performances.

PROGRAM ISSUES

Four specific issues in programming affect radio and television managers. They deal with vital aspects of freedom of speech in broadcasting. In order of discussion, these are the issues of equal time, the fairness doctrine, editorializing and equal access to courtrooms and governmental legislative sessions.

Equal Time

Section 315 of the Communications Act of 1934 relates to the use of broadcasting facilities by candidates for public office. Under its provisions, radio and television stations are not obligated to carry political broadcasts but if any "legally qualified" candidate does use the facilities of a station, all other candidates for the same office must be provided equal opportunities.

There have been only three changes in Section 315 since it was adopted as a part of the Communications Act. Two of those were permanent changes by amendments; the other was temporary.

In 1952, Congress added an amendment making it illegal to charge more for political broadcasts than the normal cost of time on a station for other purposes.

The second amendment grew out of a case in Chicago in 1959. In the spring of that year, several ex-officio public appearances of the mayor were filmed and shown as part of regularly scheduled newscasts. Since the mayor was a candidate for re-election the following November, Mr. Lar Daly, a declared candidate for the same office, asked the FCC to rule that he should be given equal time. This was the first instance of a request for equal time on news programs. The FCC ruled that equal time must be granted. Broadcasters vigorously protested the ruling, claiming that it would be next to impossible to administer. As a result of the complaints, Congress amended the Communications Act in 1959 to exempt newscasts, on-the-spot coverage of news events, news-interview programs and certain news documentary programs from the "equal time" requirements of Section 315.

In August, 1960, the equal-time requirements were temporarily suspended for the offices of President and Vice-President during the 1960 political campaign. This suspension led to the now historic "great debates" between John Kennedy and Richard Nixon. The networks offered time for as many as eight debates; four were held.

The debates were of unquestioned benefit to the American public. Audiences never were less than fifty to fifty-five per cent of the adult population of the United States.

There was no suspension of the equal-time rules during the 1964 campaign. There were controversial challenges, as might have been expected. The President's annual appeal for contributions to the United Community Fund was ruled by the FCC as a broadcast obligating broadcasters to supply equal time to all other Presidential candidates. Later, the Commission interpreted that the broadcast coverage of Presidential news conferences would entitle all of the candidates for the Presidency to similar claims. However, when President Johnson delivered a speech dealing with the international situation in mid-October, carried by the three radio-TV networks, the Republican candidate asked for equal time and was refused by the FCC. The President's speech was labeled a bona-fide news event, bound up with the nature of his office.

It should not be forgotten that political broadcasting is big business for radio and television. The 1964 campaign established a new high for political expenditures in broadcasting. Most of the total of $34,600,000 went to stations rather than networks. Sustaining time on the networks amounted to a total of four hours and twenty-eight minutes in 1964 as compared to a total of thirty-nine hours and twenty-two minutes in 1960 when the equal-time rule was suspended. Ninety-four per cent of the nation's television stations carried sustaining political time in 1964 but only forty-three per cent of the radio stations did so.

Most station managers, if given the power of decision, would prefer to have Section 315 repealed. They argue that its nuisance value whenever there are multi-candidates for an office, each having the right to request "equal time," creates problems greatly outweighing its benefits.

The assumption at law is that all candidates for the same office are equal. Obviously, this is a false assumption. Various fringe-party candidates reported by the press on the back pages can and do claim broadcast time in radio and television equal to the candidates of the major parties. Yet, in the elections that follow candidates of minor parties, or of no party at all, almost invariably receive an insignificant percentage of the vote.

In the 1962 election, the legally qualified parties with candidates on the ballots in the various states included: Republican, Democratic, Prohibition, Socialist-Labor, Socialist, American Labor, Constitution, Christian Nationalist, Liberal, Independent, Socialist Worker's American, America First, American Vegetarian, Greenback, Four Freedoms and the Poor Man's Party.

The complexity of the problem of granting equal time to all candidates for the same office becomes overwhelming when extended to all of the various offices that appear on the ballot, including state legislators, mayors, councilmen and all of the various other state, county, district and local offices. It can become ludicrous, as in a case cited by Commissioner Robert E. Lee of the FCC. In that instance, a legally qualified candidate of the Progressive Party demanded equal time from a local station in behalf of his candidacy for the office of governor of a state. The station tried to comply with his request but had difficulty in rigging a line to the candidate's place of residence—a Federal penitentiary! [2]

A particularly vexing provision of Section 315 is the "no censorship" clause. Under this provision, licencees of radio and television stations do not have the power to censor material that the various candidates broadcast. Even if, in the judgment of the station officials, the material is libelous, censorship of the material, in the case of political candidates, is prohibited. However, should the candidate make either libelous or slanderous remarks on the air, the station cannot be held liable provided it does not directly participate in the libel or slander. This position has been upheld by the United States Supreme Court. The protection for the stations applies only to "legally qualified" candidates and does not apply to supporters of those candidates.

What is a legally qualified candidate? The following is the definition of the legal department of the NAB:

In general, a candidate is legally qualified if he can be voted for in the election being held and, if elected, will be eligible to serve in the office in question.

Thus, if the state law permits write-in candidates, an announcement that a person is a candidate for re-election would probably be sufficient to bring him within Section 315. In some states, however, a person is not a legally qualified candidate until he has complied with certain prescribed procedures—such as filing a form or paying a fee entitling him to have his name printed on the ballot.[3]

Some of the bewildering difficulties attendant upon political broadcasting are briefly indicated:[4]

Identification of Sponsorship. Under Section 315, a licensee of a station does not fulfill his obligation under the Communications Act by merely announcing that "this has been a paid political broadcast." The announcement must state *by whom* the broadcast is sponsored. It may be either a visual or an aural announcement. If the program exceeds five minutes in length, an announcement is required at both the beginning and the end of the program.

Records of requests for political time. All records of requests by candidates or made in their behalf, together with notations showing the disposition of the requests and the charges made, must be kept by the station for public inspection for a period of two years.

Equal time for Communists. This is an exception where the equal time rules do *not* apply.

Kinds of programs not applicable. Section 315 has been amended to exclude the equal access obligation in certain kinds of programs where candidates may appear. These are: (1) bona-fide newscasts, (2) bona-fide news interviews, (3) bona-fide news documentaries, and (4) on-the-spot coverage of bona-fide news events, including political conventions.

Person speaking for or on behalf of a candidate. The rule does not apply.

Charges for one candidate; free time for another. Not permitted. There can be no discrimination of any kind. The time segments must also be equally desirable for all candidates for the office.

Station advising of opposing candidates of equal time availabilities. Not necessary. The initiative for making the requests is encumbent upon the candidates.

Network appearances carried on local stations. Should a candidate be carried on a network-affiliate station from a network-originated source, other candidates for the same office are entitled to request equal time on the affiliate station if it is in the area in which the election campaign is being conducted.

National and local rates. A station with both sets of rates may not charge the national rate to a local candidate.

May a deadline be set for the use of equal time? Yes, so long as it is "reasonable."

Taped reports by congressmen. These are *not* exempt from the provisions of Section 315. If the congressman is a candidate, a station is under obligation to afford time to opposing candidates.

THE FAIRNESS DOCTRINE

Closely allied to the rules affecting broadcasting by candidates for public office is the FCC fairness doctrine which is incorporated in Section 315, and, since July, 1967, in the FCC Rules & Regulations. The fairness doctrine says that broadcasters must afford reasonable opportunities for presentation or discussion of conflicting points of view on public issues. As with the equal-access rule, if a controversial issue is presented on a radio or television station then the station has the obligation to provide equal opportunities for opposing viewpoints to be presened.

Unlike the rules covering political broadcasts, the station licensee may be held liable for defamation, libel or obscene material in the broadcasting of controversial issues. It is, therefore, necessary for station management to exercise supervisory control over the materials that are broadcast. Censorship of those materials by the licensee is permitted.

One problem of application of the fairness doctrine is the wide range of interpretation of the term "fairness." What may appear fair to one person may seem unfair or biased or slanted to others. As a consequence, treatment of almost any controversial issues can open up any number of requests by individuals and groups for equal opportunities to be heard.

The problem becomes even more baffling when the individual or group says that it does not have the money to pay for broadcast time but still claims the right to make opposing views known. The broadcaster may attempt to sell the time for a response on an issue but, not being able to find a sponsor, he still has the obligation to present both sides of the argument.

The matter of propaganda is at the heart of many of the problems associated with the application of the fairness doctrine. Aware that the objection privilege exists, groups of all persuasions have become bold in their demands for equal time and clamorous in the manner and frequency with which they charge that they have been unfairly attacked.

The question for decision in the future would seem to be whether society is better served by an insistence that all sides be presented, no matter how divergent, or whether station management should be depended upon to use good judgment in the presentation of all important facets of all important problems. The basic difficulty is that while printed media are capable of indefinite expansion, and live speeches to live audiences may take place from the soap-box to the largest assembly hall, radio and TV transmissions are limited to the number of minutes in the hour and the number of hours in the broadcast day.

The very nature of electronic communication would seem to require the adoption of new procedures.

Most licensees feel that an all-out effort must be undertaken to challenge the constitutionality of the equal time rule and the fairness doctrine. At the time of this writing, the fairness doctrine is being tested in two law suits, one before the U. S. Supreme Court and another before a U. S. Court of Appeals. These suits may be long and costly, but the advantages to broadcasting are well worth the effort.

Editorializing

The issue of editorializing in radio and television began with the famous *Mayflower Case,* which resulted in a 1940 decision by the FCC. The decision read in part:

> . . . under the American system of broadcasting it is clear that responsibility for the conduct of a broadcast station must rest initially with the broadcaster. It is equally clear that with the limitations in frequencies inherent in the nature of radio, the public interest can never be served by a dedication of any broadcast facility to the support of partisan ends. Radio can serve as an instrument of democracy only when devoted to the communication of information and the exchange of ideas fairly and objectively presented. It cannot be used to advocate the causes of the licensee. It cannot be used to support the candidacies of his friends. It cannot be devoted to the support of principles he happens to regard most favorably. In brief, the broadcaster cannot be an advocate.[5]

In June, 1949, the Commission issued a report saying that broadcasters might editorialize provided they allowed air time for opposing points of view:

> If, as we believe to be the case, the public interest is best served in a democracy through the ability of the people to hear expositions of the various positions taken by responsible groups and individuals on particular topics and to choose between them, it is evident that broadcast licensees have an affirmative duty generally to encourage and implement the broadcast of all sides of controversial issues over their facilities.[6]

The "affirmative duty" reference was interpreted by the FCC to mean the "seeking out" of opposing points of view whenever one side of a controversial issue was presented on a station.

In spite of the fact that some broadcasters had worked diligently through the 1940s to acquire the right to editorialize, very few of them exercised their newly won right during the 1950s. The obligation to "seek out" opposing points of view may have seemed burdensome, injudicious or distasteful. In 1959, the Commission tempered its earlier interpretation and adopted a "fairness" obligation on the part of the licensee in place of the obligation to "seek out." Then came a 1963 policy statement by the FCC which, although intended as a clarification of the fairness doctrine, confused the broadcasters who were undecided about editorializing. The right to editorialize was plainly conferred, and the practice urged, but most radio and television people held back. They still do.

There do appear to be tangible benefits from station editorials. Stations that have broadcast editorials of meaning and significance have not found negative reactions from either state and city government sources or from advertisers. There is a growing tendency for those stations to grow bolder in their editorials as expected reprisals do not occur. The increased stature of these stations in their communities has become commercially beneficial. Some stations are even using their editorial success stories as evidence of the power of their broadcast operation to influence people.

Broadcasting, a trade publication, editorialized on broadcast editorializing. This would seem to be a well considered judgment:

> . . . Editorializing, a key instrument of leadership, is thus becoming more than a broadcast right; it is moving more and more in the direction of being a broadcast obligation. . . .

> It falls to the lot of those broadcasters who can afford to editorialize to do so industriously and with all the professionalism they can muster. The fairness doctrine will be defeated only if broadcasters continue to expand and improve their presentation of controversy—and stand prepared to defend themselves against the inevitable challenges to their performance.[7]

The editorial must be regarded as management's voice and it must represent station policy and point of view. The choice for air spokesman should be someone who clearly represents management, who embodies authority and believability and who conveys the management image.

In order to protect the separate editorial image, it is advisable to schedule news and editorials apart from each other. This can be done in radio simply by airing the editorial at a time completely removed from the news block. It is not so easy to accomplish in television due to its rigid program structure. The person who delivers the editorials on television should be someone who is not seen at any other time during the day.

A full-time editorial man who conducts all of the research and writes the editorials could be the logical person to broadcast them. The responsibility is great and if radio and television editorials are to command the same respect as do newspaper editorials, a basic investment in time, effort, research and talent is imperative.

The point must be stressed that only those stations that are qualified should attempt to editorialize. We shudder when we think of the damage to society and to broadcasting if the air should suddenly become rancid with ignorant and bigoted or simply fatuous editorials. If a station manager truly wants to be an influence for good in his community through editorials of real social significance, then it is his obligation to hire qualified manpower and allocate sufficient time for research. Then the station can be in a position to become one of the most significant forces in the community.

The opportunity for the radio or television station to editorialize indicates one of the most important future directions of the broadcasting industry. All broadcasters must realize that it is only a matter of time before they must accept this mandate of public service—accept it with its attendant responsibilities.

The Right to Equal Access

Equal access has been defined by broadcasters as the right to take microphones, cameras and auxiliary equipment, "the tools of the trade," wherever the press takes its "tools" of paper and pencil. Broadcasters have argued that they are entitled to this privilege under the guarantees of freedom of the press as stated in the First Amendment to the Constitution of the United States.

Access to the Courts

In the case of broadcasting's access to the courts, Canon 35 of the Canons of Judicial Ethics of the American Bar Association has served as a restrictive force. Canon 35 forbids the broadcasting of courtroom proceedings or the taking of photographs during court sessions or recesses. It was passed in 1937 as a reaction to an inept and overly sensational treatment of the radio coverage of the Hauptmann trial in the Lindbergh kidnaping case in 1932. The Canon was amended in 1952 to add the words "or televising."

The effect of Canon 35 in banning radio and television from the courts has made the problem of equal access one of the great issues of the broadcasting industry. While there has been considerable argument for a modification of the Canon, the original restriction has held over the years. The progress made in getting microphones and cameras into the courts has been negligible. For all intents and purposes, this remains one activity of modern society that is "off limits" for most of the electronic media.

Various arguments have been advanced against the admission of microphones and cameras to the courtroom. We cite them here as essentially trivial and as instances of a blind reliance on views no longer pertinent. It has been held that broadcasting is basically an entertainment medium, hence not covered by the guarantees of freedom of speech in the First Amendment to the Constitution. Yet, the United States Supreme Court has ruled that broadcasting is entitled to the same guarantees as other media. It has been argued that broadcasters would use access to the courts not in a spirit of public service but in a spirit of entertainment. Still, on the basis of several cases where microphones and cameras have been admitted to trials, judges and attorneys have commented that the coverage was handled in the best interest of all concerned, including the general public.

It has been said that some attorneys and judges would take advantage of broadcast coverage to engage in "show-off" performances in order to get publicity for themselves. However, where trials have been presented by the electronic media, the judges have shown that they were able to keep proper order in their courts. It has been claimed that the media would violate the rights of privacy of all the people in the courtroom. Legal opinion has held that there is no law guaranteeing personal privacy in public matters.

It has been alleged that permission for radio and television to cover the courts would result in such confusion of equipment and personnel as would prevent orderly legal procedures. The fact is that with the development and miniaturization of cameras and accessory equipment, plus the demonstrated efficiency of pooled arrangements, facilities for court coverage without distraction are well known.

In those few instances, where exceptions have been made and where court proceedings have been broadcast, the reaction to the coverage has been largely favorable.

In what was called, "A majority of four and one-half," [8] due to the opinion of Justice John M. Harlan, Canon 35 was in effect written into a law by Supreme Court decision in June, 1965.

Broadcasters may find encouragement in Justice Harlan's opinion. In urging the court to "proceed only step by step in this unplowed field," Justice Harlan forecast the possibility of the time "when television will have become so commonplace . . . in the daily life of the average person as to dissipate all reasonable likelihood that its use in courtrooms may disparage the judicial process." [9] Justice Harlan, while voting with the majority, implied that he might shift his vote in another case of this nature involving different facts.

Eventually, as Justice Harlan has indicated, the radio microphone and the television camera may come to be commonplace in the courtrooms. The right will not come without a considerable initiative on the part of the broadcaster. The burden will be on him to produce evidence that the electronic media will not disrupt the process of justice in any way. Douglas A. Anello, general counsel for the NAB, sums up the sensible and, indeed, the only tenable view:

It is up to us in the broadcasting profession to demonstrate that our conduct in courtroom proceedings can be as decorous as it has been on so many other equally important public occasions.

If and when the opportunity to broadcast any part of a judicial proceeding is presented, it is incumbent on all of us to do so with the utmost dignity. Ground rules should be agreed upon in advance by all concerned and should be strictly adhered to throughout the proceedings.[10]

Access to the Federal Government

The impression might be gained from daily Washington broadcasts that radio and television have equal reportorial access to affairs of the Federal government. True of the executive branch, it is far from true in legislative and judicial areas.

Sessions of the U. S. Senate are closed to broadcasters. Committee hearings of the Senate can be covered by special permission of the chairmen and ranking minority members. Prior permission, however, is no guarantee of coverage. Access has been granted, refused, limited and arbitrarily expanded and restricted.

Usually, broadcasters have been better treated in Senate hearings than in the House of Representatives, where no radio or television coverage is permitted of full or committee sessions. The only exceptions in the House are in the cases of special joint sessions of the Congress. The House makes (and unmakes) its own rules. There is no appeal.

In July, 1966, President Johnson signed a Freedom of Information bill into law. A legal principle is now established that Americans have the right to examine nonclassified information and may go to court to force a governmental agency to make it available. However, it must be understood that the law applies to the executive branch of the Federal government only. Understandably, certain kinds of information may be withheld, including information bearing on matters of national security, FBI files, and private or confidential records such as tax returns and financial statistics.

The attitudes of recent U. S. Presidents have been cordial toward all of the mass media. President Roosevelt held an average of two non-broadcast press conferences a week and became famous for his "fireside chats" on radio. President Truman, while often brusque with the media, held an average of one non-broadcast press conference a week. President Eisenhower's press conferences were recorded for delayed broadcast, thus allowing editing of the material. President Kennedy inaugurated live press conferences on both radio and television and President Johnson has continued the practice of permitting live broadcasts of his press conferences.

Access to State Legislatures

Regardless of, or indeed in spite of, argument, only thirteen states had officially permitted continued live legislative broadcasts by the end of 1963. Those states were: Alabama, Arizona, Georgia, Idaho, Illinois, Indiana, Missouri, New York, Oklahoma, Tennessee, Texas, Vermont and West Virginia.[11] There seems to be little rhyme—and no reason.

Access to City Councils

In attempts to cover city council meetings, broadcasters and other representatives of the mass media are sometimes the victims of a convenient maneuver known as the executive session. Many so-called executive sessions are in reality only closed meetings.

The business that may be conducted in an executive session has been defined by statute:

> *Executive Sessions.* A body may exclude the public when it is considering or acting upon any of the following matters:
> (a) The dismissal, promotion, demotion, or compensation of any public employee, or the disciplining of such employee or investigation of charges against him, unless the employee affected shall have requested an open meeting.
> (b) The hiring of any person as a public employee.
> (c) Matters which, if discussed in public, would be likely to benefit a party whose interests are adverse to those of the general community. This provision shall include but not be limited to consideration of the acquisition of land.
> (d) Matters which, if discussed in public, would be likely to affect adversely the reputation of any person, other than a member of the body itself.
> (e) Welfare matters where federal grant-in-aid requirements prohibit publicity.[12]

City officials who use the closed meeting for other purposes may not realize a very real denial of "public interest, convenience and necessity." Here would seem to be a ready theme for radio and television editorializing.

Mass Coverage of Events

The Joint Media Committee on News Coverage Problems is composed of representatives from five professional news organizations: Sigma Delta Chi, The Associated Press Managing Editors Association, the National Press Photographers Association, the Radio Television News Directors Association and the American Society of Newspaper Editors. This joint committee has issued a statement concerning "Orderly Procedures for Mass

Coverage of News Events." [13] Noting that many public events are covered by the press with disruptions, the report cites a lack of preparation and organization as the reasons for turmoil at some crowded events. The committee recommends careful advance planning for public events so that orderly newsgathering may take place. Even unexpected happenings could be covered in a more orderly fashion if governmental, civic, police and other authorities would "arrange measures by which the media can do their job in an orderly fashion and with a minimum of confusion." Local news executives are advised:

> On occasions where it is apparent that no adequate arrangements have been made and where a confused, disorderly situation could ensue, one or more of the senior news representatives in the area should take the initiative in proposing newsgathering procedures that will be fair and efficient. We believe that such an effort will not be taken as presumptuous or officious, but will be welcomed by all concerned.

The committee recommends that where space limitations exist, a pooling arrangement is more satisfactory than no plan at all. It is also preferable to any settlement upon the granting of privileges on a first-come basis. Let station managers take note, and station newsmen take heed.

The Challenge

In the fight for equal access, broadcasters do not ask for permission to cover all trials nor do they propose to cover all of the proceedings of legislative bodies. The commercial schedule would not permit such extensive coverage. What broadcasters do want is the opportunity to cover legislative and courtroom proceedings at times when the event reported is of special interest to the public.

When and if broadcasters achieve equal access to the courts and to governmental sources, no aspect of their programming will call for greater integrity and professional attitude. It will be no assignment for staff announcers who have little, if any, background in journalism. This coverage is too important for a reliance on microphones, tape recorders and cameras to transmit the whole message. The trained and experienced reporter's judgment will be an absolute necessity. To bring the promise of the judgment to bear in his own radio-television community is the duty and distinction of the responsible station manager.

5

Television Programming

Television is seen and heard in every type of American home. These homes include children and adults of all ages, embrace all races and all varieties of religious faith, and reach those of every educational background. It is the responsibility of television to bear constantly in mind that the audience is primarily a home audience, and consequently that television's relationship to the viewers is that between guest and host.

—from the NAB Television Code.[1]

IN JANAUARY, 1948, NBC bought full-page space in various newspapers to call the attention of the public to the "greatest medium of mass communications in the world—Network Television." At that time, the NBC television network consisted of four Eastern cities: New York, Washington, Philadelphia and Schenectady. Nine people out of every ten in the United States had never seen a television program. Nearly half of the television receiving sets were located in the New York area and there were only seventeen television stations in operation in the entire country. Call the advertisement a wild exaggeration if you like. Call it a mad prophecy. It turned out to be a rather sober projection of fact.

EARLY PROGRAMMING

What was the nature of the programming that caused people to be almost hypnotized by "the tube?"

Most of it was really televised radio. The program materials and the formats of popular radio shows were transposed to the new medium with little change.

Later, programs were developed that utilized the unique properties of the medium. The production techniques painfully evolved were later to have their influence on the film and theater arts. The significant experimentation and the discoveries of new dimensions in television were basically network contributions.

We noted in the preceding chapter that most of today's radio programming originates in local stations. In contrast, most of today's pace-making television programming originates from the networks. With few exceptions, American television has been network-dominated almost from the beginning. It still is, except for a few aggressive group-station owners dedicated to prestigious programming and a greater choice of program product.

NETWORK ENTERTAINMENT PROGRAMS

Three television networks provide more than 10,000 hours of programming a year. Most of it is classifiable as entertainment. The entertainment program has consistently attracted the largest audiences.

To call the roll of television entertainers is to list a shining company of folk minstrels and folk heroes. Milton Berle was a champion of the pioneer day, when the variety stage moved into the American living room. The names in theatrical lights became the names on the family set. Sid Caesar and Imogene Coca, Phil Silvers, Ed Wynn, Ken Murray, Herb Shriner, Ernie Kovacs, Red Buttons, Bob Hope, Jack Benny, Jackie Gleason, Danny Kaye and Red Skelton were household comics. Straight and singing emcees, who presided over various acts, have captivated huge audiences week after week, including such people as Ed Sullivan, Arthur Godfrey, Perry Como, Ernie Ford, Garry Moore, Frank Sinatra, Dinah Shore, Jimmy Dean, Andy Williams, Sammy Davis and Dean Martin.

Drama of one form or another has been well received over the years. Crime and suspense stories hit their peak of popularity in the early 1960s, then fell off sharply. Other adventure stories have maintained their ratings consistently well. Women's serial dramas were not seen on television until they had almost run their course on radio and did not appear on nighttime television until the 1964–65 season. The Western series, surprisingly, was also late in its appearance but has been popular ever since, although the ratings of this type of offering peaked in the 1959–60 season. Situation-comedy series have increased steadily in number and in popularity over the years.

Quiz and audience participation formats and game shows, borrowed largely from radio, were better liked in television's early period. The same can be said for most of the amateur talent programs.

Feature theatrical film began to be used as a major network attraction in prime time during the 1961–62 season and it has become increasingly popular as a network offering ever since.

Various musical-variety formats have attracted large, regular audiences. In this category are such widely different kinds of programs as *Law-*

rence Welk, Hullabaloo, The King Family, Shindig, The Judy Garland Show, Hootenanny and *The Bell Telephone Hour.*

Daytime network television abounds in entertainment but of a somewhat different variety. Here the dramatic serials, game shows, various talk formats and network re-runs are the staples, with some morning programs for pre-schoolers and a late-afternoon set of offerings for the in-school crowd.

There have been other forms of entertainment offered but by and large these have been the mainstays of the network entertainment types, year in and out.

Program mortality rates have been high. But, then, show business was always chancy. Casualties of new programs after one season on the air have averaged twenty or more each year since 1960. Partly, this situation is due to insufficient audience interests plus an abundance of offerings of the same types. It is due also to the selection of some programs that are not strong enough in concept to last very long. Who remembers *Haggis Baggis?* And how long will *My Mother, The Car* be discussed with fond memories?

An ancient, yet observant, show-biz maxim applies equally well to productions on the screen and stage. "It's always a bum season," some philosopher remarked, "for a bum show." Usually it is a short season for a slight show.

Those who criticize the networks for devoting the major emphasis of their programming to entertainment may do well to consider the intensively competitive nature of the medium. Television programming has evolved to insure performances requisite to survival. By the mid-1960s, there were few points of significant difference between network approaches. All networks appeal to the public in similar terms for approximately equal shares of the viewing audience.

The instant hit is not entirely uncommon in television entertainment. When it happens, even the program executives are at least mildly surprised. The hit series is, however, a stroke of luck which every producer hopes to achieve. In its quest, it is not uncommon to appropriate a format which has achieved success and add a few new gimmicks. It is not uncommon for the new venture to fail, either.

Occasionally, a special program will be so well received that the gears will start in motion for more of the same type. When *Death of a Salesman* received outstandingly favorable reactions, all three networks hastened to revive the experimental drama as a prime-time regular offering. Yet, here few works of comparable artistry are available. Probably, it is always a good season for authentic works of genius.

The "special" has always been reserved for the most lavish production methods and budgetary support. Once labeled "the spectacular," it has been just that in comparison with many of the programs that are offered on a regular basis. Advertiser interest in the opportunities for enhancement of corporate image through the prestige values of the specials has brought about a continuing increase in the number offered and in their quality.

The Hallmark Hall of Fame is one illustration of a prestige program that has appeared as a series of specials over a fifteen-year period.

Whether caused by a growing necessity to use post-1960 theatrical feature films, by an increasing amount of audience sophistication or by a maturation in the industry or by a demand for excellence, network programming grows steadily more "adult." Provocative themes and language that would have met mass resistance in television's early days are more frequently aired. There seems to be general audience acceptance of this change. Hopefully, a more adult audience is responsive to serious works of art.

NETWORK SPORTS PROGRAMS

Even though sports programs are a form of entertainment for most fans, the category has such dimension in network offerings as to deserve separate treatment. In any case, expenditures for cultural, informative and dramatic programs are relatively insignificant when compared to networks sports outlays for programs addressed to the mass audience.

Football

When the first Super Bowl game was arranged between the champions of the National Football League and the American Football League, the question of television coverage rights was involved. CBS owned the contract for the televising of all NFL games and NBC held the television rights to the AFL games. The problem was resolved by permitting both of the networks to carry the game for a fee of $1,000,000 from each network. CBS acquired sole rights to the game in 1968 and 1970 with NBC carrying the 1969 game exclusively. The rights to televise these three events cost $2,500,000 for each game. This amount represented a new high for the rights to a one-day sports event. This is typical of the way the bidding is going for exclusivity in the telecasting of football.

The rights to the professional NFL regular schedule had cost CBS $9,300,000 for the 1962 and 1963 seasons. In order to retain those rights for the 1964 and 1965 seasons, CBS paid the astronomical sum of $28,200,000. The rights to the 1966 and 1967 seasons, with an option to renew for 1968 and 1969, again became the property of CBS for the sum of $37,600,000. The NFL contract permits coverage of various regional games each week. CBS had the exclusive rights to all regular season games played in the conference over the two-year period. In addition, CBS paid another $6,000,000 for the rights to two championship games, two pro bowls and two playoff bowls. The network introduced an innovation in the scheduling of sports by instituting nighttime coverage of selected pre-season and regular-season games.

ABC had paid $10,000,000 for the rights for five years (1960–1964) to the AFL regular season and championship games. NBC, by bidding $36,000,000, received the AFL regular season rights for the five years 1965–1969, with the league's championship and all-star games sold separately.

The National Collegiate Athletic Association (representing amateurs, be it noted) as well as the professional National Football League advertised for competitive bidding every two years. CBS carried the NCAA games through the 1962 and 1963 seasons. NBC had them during 1964 and 1965. Then, without announcing any open bidding, the contract for 1966 and 1967 was awarded to ABC for $15,500,000, an increase of almost two and a half million dollars over the preceding two years. An option for a two-year renewal on ABC was retained by the NCAA.

The total which the broadcasting industry invested in rights to football games in one season (1967–68) was estimated at over $48,000,000. The figure includes local radio and television rights in addition to the network investments.

There was little difficulty finding sponsors who would pay as high as $75,000 per minute for game participations, $25,000 a minute for pre-game and $35,000 a minute for post-game shows. ARB found that football occupied the top eight positions of favorite programs of men in a poll taken in the fall of 1965.

Football has built-in appeal through its live action and its element of the unexpected. The use of the isolated camera, stop-action, slow-motion and directional microphones have added to the interest in coverage by television.

The NFL and AFL will merge into one league beginning in 1970 and the competitive bidding for the rights to those games may be intense. The trend is up.

Baseball

Football figures have been cited as illustrative of sports costs. The costs of baseball rights are on the increase, too. NBC's contract for the All-Star games and the World Series in 1967 and 1968 cost $12,600,000, a sixty-eight per cent increase over the same network's cost for those rights for 1965 and 1966. NBC also purchased the rights to the Game of the Week from the baseball clubs for an additional $6,000,000 each year for three years.

The first network venture into sports ownership occurred in 1964, when CBS bought the New York Yankees.

Efforts to move major-league baseball into evening prime time on the networks met with some success during the 1966 season, when night games were carried for the first time on selected holidays.

The Olympics

Every four years, the networks submit bids for the rights to cover the Winter and Summer Olympics.

The rights to both the 1968 Winter Olympics in Grenoble, France, and the Summer Olympics in Mexico City were awarded to ABC. Total cost for the televising of the Winter event was estimated at around $6,500,000, including $2,000,000 for rights. The Summer coverage on television was estimated to cost in excess of $12,000,000, including $4,500,000 for rights.

Other Sports

There are many golf series on television. In addition to coverage of all of the major golf tournaments, special golfing events merit special reporting.

Network television covers the Triple Crown in horse-racing, including the Kentucky Derby, the Preakness and the Belmont Stakes. On occasion, it also carries other scheduled racing events.

An investment of more than $1,000,000 is made for prize money alone in bowling series shown on television. The audience for these programs is estimated at some 7,000,000 regular viewers.

Basketball coverage for the most part is provided by a "specialist" in the field of network television. Big Ten and pro basketball are available through Sports Network, Incorporated. This network also provides coverage of the National Collegiate events in indoor track, swimming, diving and skiing; the national indoor tennis championship; horse racing; various PGA golf tournaments; and road games of major league baseball. The sports fan has a permanent seat in the television grand stand.

NETWORK NEWS AND PUBLIC AFFAIRS

As the differences in the nature of the entertainment offerings of the three networks tend to decrease, the image of each network becomes more reliant upon its sports contracts and on its offerings in the field of news and public affairs.

In retrospect, the season of 1963–1964 may have been the breakthrough year for the networks in the field of news and public affairs. It was the year the Roper poll first disclosed the information that television was the public's major source for news; it was the year NBC and CBS doubled the length of their evening newscasts; it was the year the three television networks committed themselves to spend $70,000,000 for the production of news and documentary programs for the season, prompting *Broadcasting*

magazine to editorialize: "Altogether the new surge of information programming is the healthiest trend to develop in broadcasting's recent history
It will do more than most others for broadcasting and for the country.'
Further, 1963–64 was the year the three networks averaged about six times
as much "hard" news coverage as they had in 1950 and about 100 more
hours of documentaries than they had carried as recently as 1959. It was
the year when over half of the documentaries were sponsored.

It was also the year, unfortunately, of the coverage of the events following the assassination of a President of the United States.

The Week-End of November 22nd, 1963

That awful week-end brought the heaviest possible challenge to electronic journalism. The cancellation of all regular programming and advertising, the thoroughness of the participation by the media and the dignity of
the coverage of all of the events were all indicative of the true coming of age
of radio and television as major news media.

The television audience on that week-end approached universality for
the first time in history: 96.1 per cent of all homes with television sets,
according to Nielsen, watched the week-end coverage on an average of
31.63 hours per home. The largest single audience of the week-end was
assembled during the requiem mass, which was attended through television
by more than 97,000,000 persons. Slightly fewer than 97,000,000 saw the
burial service. At no time during the entire week-end was the audience less
than fourteen per cent of all homes, representing more than 7,000,000
people.

The reliance of the people on television in those hours of crisis is
shown in the Nielsen report of the growth of the audience throughout the
afternoon and evening of the assassination. At 1:30 P.M. eastern standard
time, on Friday, November 22, the television sets were in use in approximately 23.4 per cent of American television homes. Fifteen minutes later,
after the first reports of the assassination, more than a third of the television
homes in the country were tuned in. By 2:00 P.M. the audience had increased to 42.2 per cent of the homes. Two and a half hours later, sets were
in use in seventy-five per cent of all homes. By 11:00 P.M. the people in
some 92.6 per cent of American homes had seen an average of almost six
hours of television coverage. But these figures are all but irrelevant. The
event surpassed cost accounting, surveys and statistics.

The senseless tragedy in Dallas, the moving rituals of mourning and
the outpouring of the nation's love and grief were unparalleled in the American experience. Men and women whose hearts marched to the slow rhythm
of muffled drums will long remember. That much of television can be trivial
and tawdry—as much of quite ordinary life can be trivial and tawdry—is
beyond question. But, let it stand also beyond question that in a tragic
time ours was a common dignity and a common greatness. In shock and

trial and bereavement, no people behaved more magnificently, no medium of communication served so selflessly and so well.

Other Special Events Coverage

Another sad event, the funeral of Winston Churchill, further enhanced the reputation of the networks for dignified coverage.

Television distinguished itself by its reporting of such events as the visit of Pope Paul VI to the United Nations and New York, the New York transit strike early in 1966 and the series of space projects and flights by the astronauts. Perhaps as much as any other single influence, television helped to bring about public awareness of the civil rights movement.

Political Coverage

In 1952, television had its first opportunity to provide coverage of the Republican and Democratic Conventions for a mass audience. The 1948 conventions had been televised but the audience had been limited at that time and the production efforts had been minimal.

An estimated $25,000,000 was invested by the three networks for the two weeks of coverage of the 1964 conventions. In addition, various network affiliated and independent stations covered the activities of state delegations for their home audiences. According to *Time* magazine, there were more people representing the three networks at the 1964 Republican convention (1825) than there were delegates (1308).

Pooled network coverage of the national political conventions may not be too far away. Mounting costs of television coverage and the disappointing size of the audience may force this development. At least one network in future years may continue to carry its regular programming during the conventions. Eventually, there may be a rotating system of coverage arranged by the networks themselves.

Starting with the Republican primaries of 1964, a new element of prediction was added to the coverage of election returns. CBS correctly predicted the winner of the New Hampshire primary just eighteen minutes after the polls were closed. NBC announced the winner of the Illinois primary fifty-five minutes sooner than either of the other networks and announced the winner of the Oregon contest twenty-two minutes ahead. CBS won by four minutes in the Maryland primary and then proceeded to name the winner of the California primary before the polls in some parts of the state had closed. Some question arose over whether such action represented responsible broadcasting. It is argued that in a close national election—the difference in time zones being a factor in the vote count—a prediction on a national broadcast could make the difference in the determination of the eventual winner. This would seem to be a fanciful objection. The answer to it would seem to be "So what?"

More significant, the buying of sampling and projecting services by the print media from television networks has already constituted a new departure in news reporting. Fred Friendly, then President of CBS News, called it "a milestone in American journalism." The sampling procedures developed by the networks have become too expensive for even the largest single newspapers to duplicate.

The Documentary

The documentary program is a relative newcomer to network schedules. During network television's first decade, the format was considered too specialized in its appeal to be able to attract a mass audience, which may be only a way of saying assemblers of documentaries didn't know how to do them well. The few documentaries attempted tended to prove both points. In those days, a documentary in competition with a program of pure entertainment almost always showed a discouraging rating. Sponsors, anxious to reach large audiences, considered the documentary a poor investment. The sponsors changed their opinions before the public did. By the end of 1960, there was considerable evidence of increased advertiser support for all informational programming.

Two important network decisions gave support to the growth of the documentary as an important format. Both of those decisions required much courage and foresight in the light of the previous undistinguished record in this kind of programming.

The first decision was to increase documentary budgets to permit more time, personnel and facilities to be devoted to their preparation. As a result, a type of program once dull and one-dimensional in its scope became exciting and as broad in treatment as it was possible to make it. Documentaries began to appear regularly in prime-time evening schedules. While their ratings still did not compare in size with the popular entertainment offerings, the size of their audiences showed as much relative growth as other kinds of programs.

The second network decision was to deal with certain controversial subjects previously judged too risky for presentation on national television. As a result, documentary units of the networks broke barriers of public sensitivity on various topics by bringing analyses into the open.

Some of the subjects examined on the air by network documentary units included: integration, poverty, urban development, campus morals, welfare inequities, unemployment, menopause, the population explosion, birth control, the bookies, the problems of adoption, the traffic in drugs, juvenile delinquency, abortion, cigarette smoking and cancer, and divorce. International issues were treated, including such problems as the Cuban crisis, the Berlin wall, the conflict between India and Red China, the Panama revolt, revolutions in South America and the Mid-East, the Kremlin, the Viet Nam and Laos situations, the common market and the emerging nations of Africa. Not all the documentaries dealt with serious subjects but even the lighter ones were used to inform, to broaden understanding and to stimulate thought. Some representative subjects of this type were: the decline of royalty, the American woman, the festival frenzy, the circus, the decade of the twenties and American humor.

A key factor in the success story of the network news and documentary units has been their insistence on independence from sponsor control. No other network program group has been so divorced from the advertiser's advice and/or restraint in the selection and treatment of controversial subjects. In a few cases, there have been threats of cancellation. In most instances, the networks have backed their documentary producers and have announced that the programs would be shown over their facilities with or without sponsorship. They usually have had sponsorship.

In spite of an increased emphasis on news and public affairs by the networks, the problem of securing the cooperation of affiliates was and is most difficult. Two programs that became Peabody Award winners in 1965 were refused by many affiliated stations when they were broadcast by the networks. *Profiles in Courage* was not seen on twenty per cent of NBC's outlets; *CBS Reports* was refused by forty-five per cent of the network's stations.[2]

A study in the Spring of 1966, showed that substantial numbers of network-affiliated stations had not carried news programs on the war in Viet Nam.[3] Specials on February 12 of that year were broadcast by forty-two per cent of the CBS stations and thirty per cent of the NBC stations. Fewer than half of the CBS stations carried a Viet Nam special on February 18 while sixty-five per cent of the NBC stations carried a similar special the same evening. The study found that sponsored evening newscasts may count upon affiliate acceptance but single, weekly public affairs programs are likely to be rejected or else carried on a delayed basis by a high proportion of stations.

It may be more profitable for the local station manager to schedule a local commercial showing of syndicated film in place of a network public affairs program, but it is a burdensome expense for the networks to develop these excellent offerings and the cooperation of affiliates in carrying them should be little enough to ask. It would seem proper for local stations to realize the changing nature of their medium.

The refusal of sizeable numbers of affiliates to carry public affairs programs from the networks may be a decisive factor in the reduction of the frequency of these offerings.

George Norton, advertising vice president of General Telephone and Electronics, advances a demographic reason of great cogency:

> Our research shows that news-documentary programs reach 27 per cent more professional and white-collar people than entertainment programs, 44 per cent more people with one or more years of college, 21 per cent more in the upper-income group.[4]

Network Film Programs

Films were little used in early network programming. Television was a new medium that seemed to demand live production. Old feature movies and varied short subjects hardly seemed appropriate, especially when they were re-runs of materials produced by and for a competitive form of show business.

Policy changes on the use of film were made after Hollywood began to produce and syndicate programming especially for television. Actually, the local television stations were first to schedule the bulk of the new availabilities. Then the networks began to see possibilities in the Hollywood product. By 1959, they were the primary markets for West Coast film production and before long most of the network schedule consisted of filmed programming.

By the 1965–66 season, almost eighty-five per cent of the prime-time programming of the three networks was on film. As recently as the 1962–63 season, the percentage had been around seventy. The film shows included most of the dramatic programs, the action and adventure series and the situation comedies. Most of the prime time variety and the quiz or panel programs were on tape. It became difficult for local stations to find syndicated film series which had not already been shown by the networks.

Almost twice as many off-network series were offered to stations in 1966 as were made available the previous year. Since most of them were in black and white, the increase in offerings may be attributed to a race against obsolescence as color programming comes more into demand.

The pace of film production changed considerably when the film companies became major producers for television. Previously accustomed to as much as a year and a half for the completion of a feature film for theater exhibition, film makers now find themselves turning out two half-hour films every week.

There are certain advantages to the film producer in selling his film to a network rather than to individual stations. He can recover his production costs sooner, his distribution costs are lowered, far fewer prints of the film are needed, and the costs of promotion of the film are usually absorbed by the networks.

Even with these advantages, the creation of a pilot film for a prospective series is a heavy risk. The cost of pilots, due largely to contract restrictions on talent and to overtime payments, runs considerably higher than the costs of subsequent programs in a series once it is sold. The investment in a half-hour pilot averages around $200,000. An hour pilot, usually involving on-location shooting, can cost well over $400,000.

Some twenty pilots that are created each year are not accepted by the networks. It should be understandable why many independent producers hesitate to invest such a sizeable amount of capital on a highly speculative risk. It should also be clear why so many producers who enter this competition tend to play it as safely as possible by developing programs similar in nature to those which have already been successful.

On the positive side, once a pilot is accepted, there are the prospects of sale of the remainder of the programs in a series, the possibilities of network renewals and off-network syndication for United States television stations and for the foreign market.

The growing dependence of the networks on the Hollywood production centers may lead to future problems. Increasing costs of turning out pilots on speculation and the high mortality rate of those products after they are accepted could have the effect of drying up a major program source. The signs are pointing to a need for a renewed emphasis on live programming by the networks.

Videotape has not, as yet, replaced film as a key source of programming due to its inflexibility in use. Producers, as well as talent, have come to rely on editing privileges before final approval of their product. Videotape is more difficult to edit than film and considerably more expensive; yet, further ease and facility of editing is but a short time removed.

During the 1966–67 season, feature films were on the networks on six nights of each week. This brought the proportion of total network prime time devoted to feature films to well over fifteen per cent. Television is consuming features faster than the movie industry can turn them out.

Neil Hickey notes that the backlog of Hollywood features dropped from 2,200 in 1961 to 875 in 1965.[5] If each network series needs thirty new features each year (assuming that two-thirds of them will be re-run), then six series will need 180. The total output of Hollywood feature production is now only some 130 to 150 features a year. Many cannot be shown on television. However, since viewers seem responsive no matter what film is shown, network financing of features made especially for television may be expected to increase.

THE COSTS OF NETWORK PROGRAMMING

The programs of the three networks in the prime nighttime hours alone cost millions of dollars every week. For the advertiser, the cost of a program is only a part of his total expense; the value of the time and the charges for network facilities must be added. Time and facilities charges vary with the time of day, the length of the contract, the number of stations on which the program is carried and other variables. The charges for prime time on a full network can readily exceed $100,000 an hour. Our concern in this section is not with time and facilities charges but with the costs of various kinds of programs and the effect of these costs on program decisions.

As a potential sponsor, the reader may ask himself whether he would rather buy an hour of *Lawrence Welk* at around $75,000 or *CBS Reports* at a figure of some $100,000, or whether he would prefer to sponsor one of the top hour-long variety programs at a cost of $175,000 to $200,000. If the ratings were comparable, the less expensive series might at first appear to be the better purchase. However, there are other variables to consider, such as the demographic characteristics of the audiences reached, the type of program in relation to the type of advertising, the competition on the other networks at the same hour and the prestige values of the program for the advertiser.

The ideal program purchase for any advertiser is the series that comes in at the lowest budget yet delivers the most people with the demographic characteristics the advertiser wishes to reach. This is no easy determination. Yet, this challenge to discover the ideal combinations is one of the reasons why commercial programming is such exciting work.

Network programming costs have risen steadily over a five-year period averaging about six per cent higher each year. Color telecasting itself calls for increasing expenditures for film, photography, sets, lighting, locations and costumes.

Nine significant additional factors causing network program costs to increase are: "(1) TV's phenomenal success, which has enabled it to pay more and its suppliers to demand—and get—more; (2) the demand for increased production values; (3) unions; (4) the changing economics of programming, and especially the change in the syndication market; (5) talent agents; (6) residuals; (7) the increased reliance on film product, primarily Hollywood-produced; (8) a widespread acceptance of the inevitability of continuing price increases; and (9) show business." [6]

All signs point toward further increases. The advertiser seems to expect the price to go up and the networks have yet to experience major difficulties in selling their programs.

The high costs of television programming have been a factor, however, in a shift away from program sponsorship to participation advertising whereby various commercial accounts appear within a program. Since 1960, the major amount of advertising in network television has been of the multiple-sponsor type.

The trend is away from single program or even alternate week sponsorship. This trend, as much as anything else, has made the use of feature film possible. The costs of such programming would be prohibitive for single sponsors but by dividing the costs of the program among several participating advertisers, a feature of two hours or more in length can be sold.

Production costs of filmed commercials have increased along with program costs. A one-minute filmed spot that could have been produced for $750–$1500 in the early 1950s would cost a minimum of $4000 today and some budgets run as high as $25,000 per commercial.

If he who pays the piper calls the tune, it would seem that he who pays the piper the higher fees will dominate the television song-and-dance. As a matter of fact, he does.

Up to this point in this chapter, we have discussed only network television programs. As we have said, the networks created most of the television as we know it today and they still continue to dominate the programming of American commercial television. The public is most familiar with the various network programs because these are what most of the people see most of the time. There are, of course, some outstanding locally originated programs available at various times of the broadcast day.

LOCAL STATION FILM PROGRAMMING

Aside from a network, a television station has two principal sources of programs: film and those produced locally by the station. Of those two sources, most stations draw upon film for the larger share of their locally originated programming. The film that is shown consists of both syndicated series and feature movies.

Syndicated Film

At one time, it was possible to operate a television station daily from sign-on to sign-off with nothing but film and not have to repeat anything that had been shown previously in the coverage area. The moment the major film companies began to concentrate on selling their products to the networks, first-run syndicated film for local station use became a scarce commodity.

In place of first-run syndicated film, stations now buy re-run rights to series that have been shown on the networks. The sale and distribution of these "off-network" programs is provided by syndication companies. Through careful selection, a station can present outstandingly popular programs of former seasons from all networks.

Syndicated off-network material for a local station should not be selected on the basis of its appeal to station personnel. The program manager, film buyer or whoever is designated to pass final judgment must evaluate all purchases on the basis of his considered opinion of probable local audience response.

It makes little sense to buy a film package because it may be the cheapest available. The same value judgments used in the approval of local live-production efforts should be applied to the selection of the station's film offerings. Insofar as all local originations, whether live or on film, blend into a planned design, the station image becomes clearly recognizable. A hodgepodge of program offerings, some of which fit into no overall pattern, can blur that image.

Action-adventure, comedy, travel, game shows, variety musicals—the range is as broad as show business. Somewhere in all this availability is the most effective combination for each specific television station.

But within the several categories, a wide range of quality exists. The most expensive packages are not necessarily the best. No syndicated or re-run material was created for the specific public of any local television station. Much of what is available can become popular locally. There is also much that can do little, if anything, to enhance the station's favor in the community.

Off-network re-runs, in general, have found favor with many audiences. Particularly is this true in the case of series that have had extended runs of two or more seasons on a network. Those network programs which have been scheduled against popular competitive offerings on other networks can make good possibilities for local re-runs. Actually, there should be favorable chances for any off-network series with particular appeal for a specific local audience even if the series has been carried on the same station previously as a network feed. Only some twenty per cent of the viewers see the average original telecast of any program in a series. Any re-run that the other eighty per cent can see is a new show as far as they are concerned.

It would be difficult, as well as unwise, to attempt to select most of the local film schedule from off-network availabilities. Only some of these programs should be chosen. Even in a single-market situation, a station should avoid becoming a completely second-run house.

In addition to the long-established film syndicators, all of whom have materials that should be considered, a relatively new source has developed. Several group-owned stations now produce a variety of offerings for syndication.

Can the local station look ahead to syndication of some of its own local production? With the growing need for program sources, it would seem that any series with good quality should be in demand. The sales organization necessary for the circulation of film or video-tape packages might prohibit the small market station from getting into syndication. Yet, the possibilities of fruitful program exchange with other similarly located stations or of participation in a group-station effort should be considered.

Feature Film

Feature film for television consists almost entirely of entertainment originally made for theater exhibition. It is desirable for station use because it fills large blocks of time and because of its popularity with the viewing audience. A feature film if properly promoted can often bring a higher rating to a station than any of the competing programs on other stations, whether network or local. After all, feature films are show pieces, many of them brilliantly conceived, splendidly cast and elaborately produced.

The value of feature films as a program product is amply demonstrated by their success on network schedules. No station's program offerings are well rounded and firmly entrenched for sales purposes without the benefit of feature film strength.

Most stations in large markets should purchase the rights for five to seven showings of feature film. Good-sized audiences can be attracted for each showing if there is an interim of six to eight months between each scheduling and if the feature is presented at different times of the day each time it is used. It is wise, also, to schedule the re-runs on different days of the week. In small markets, one re-run may be all that may be expected to pay returns to the station and the advertisers. One nighttime showing followed by a daytime re-run after a period of close to a year should be a profitable formula in the small market situation.

STATION PRODUCED PROGRAMS

If expert knowledge is needed in the selection of film offerings, it is even more necessary in the building and production of the station's locally produced programs. By and large, all networks stake equal claims on audience appeal. The local station, to achieve dominance in its market, must reach that objective through its local schedule, not by reliance on network affiliation.

If the local station turns to syndicated film and feature movies, it may find market dominance equally hard to achieve. Available film for television cannot be monopolized by any one station and the differences in appeal between any two stations' offerings cannot be anything but minimal. The only chance to acquire a clearly identifiable local image lies in the local production the station undertakes.

Before the networks provided extensive program schedules, when film was scarce and generally inferior, local stations had to produce most of their own programs. Much ingenuity was shown by local program departments, even with only one camera and no remote facilities. Today, with more knowledgeable personnel and far better equipment available, the same degree of resourcefulness should result in outstanding local programming. Yet, far too many stations do not take advantage of this opportunity.

The production of local live programs is not easy. It involves more personnel, more time and more expense than are needed to ride the network and transmit film. Sometimes, the return for all the extra investment seems hardly worth the effort, particularly if audiences are small and the ratings are low. Yet, anyone who manages a television station and who hires a program manager with a true dedication to the medium can never be satisfied unless he engages in the kind of activity that motivated him to enter this form of communication in the first place. The thrills of program creation, the discovery of new talent, the favorable comments from the audience, these are gratifications that should feed his ego. He should never be satisfied in merely supplying facilities for carrying the creations of other people. If he is truly of the show-business genre, he will *have* to be involved with production because it is a part of his way of life and the product he displays will have to be of professional quality or he will not be satisfied.

It has been difficult for the writers of this book to accept the almost unbelievable naiveté of some owners of television stations. Those owners with upward of a million dollars invested in each enterprise have entrusted their capital, in too many instances, to management that either does not understand creative programming and production or is not interested in it. There have been cases where owners have been advised by management that it is impossible for the station to appeal to local audiences with station-produced programs other than news. It is our opinion that these managers have conveniently used this argument to cover their deficiencies in the program area.

At some stations, whatever local programming does get on the air is hardly ever distinguished or even distinguishable. An example to be deplored may be found in the news-weather-sports format on many local stations. Here, in too many cases, is a public exhibit of the station's professional disabilities.

Usually, the news segment is presented first. An announcer reads the news from sheets of paper, making contact with the camera only intermittently. Occasional still pictures are picked up by the cameramen. The director calls for some unmotivated switching in order to give some semblance of variety to the chief visual—the newscaster's face and shoulders.

The weather segment departs from the use of script and, as a rule, the "weatherman" maintains a fair degree of contact with the camera. He is restricted to a stylized set that is shown in all seasons, featuring a map of the United States and a map of the local area, both with prepared weather markings. For some unidentifiable reason, most "weathermen" seem to feel an obligation to be clever and they try. Oh, how they try! Some stations have "weathergirls," who substitute pulchritude for humor.

The sports announcer comes on strong and in a masculine manner provides the sports headlines of the day, followed by a reading of the scores of whatever sport is in season. Since the networks give little attention to this service, most of the scores and other sports information is of a national, rather than a local, character. Visuals on this segment consist of a scoreboard, an occasional still photo and, sometimes, some silent-film footage.

The three segments are usually sponsored separately, necessitating an opening and a closing for each segment. The time needed to open and close together with the time for commercials within each segment leaves little opportunity to give much more than highlights of information. The programs give the impression of fast pacing, often to the point of confusion. Standard sets and substandard lighting are used.

It is true that there is a wide variation in the abilities of stations to

create local programs. The metropolitan station obviously has far more resources available to it than does the small market station. The comparative
differences, however, should be in terms of quantity of output, not necessarily quality. In local production, resourcefulness is a far more important
commodity than a huge budget.

It is advisable to develop one or two local program formats at a time
and then concentrate on their improvement before attempting additional
efforts. One outstanding daily local show with general audience appeal in
addition to one well produced daily news show would be preferable to a
number of mediocre programs.

Many stations have not realized the potential for audience popularity
in the locally produced daytime program. Robert Mortensen, General Manager of Station WIIC-TV in Pittsburgh, has said:

> Many stations go to their film libraries during the daytime hours be-
> cause they feel it may be more economical in the long run. We've
> found that local live programming, featuring staff talent, staff material,
> production and equipment is not only cheaper than running some of
> the dog-eared oldies that come in most of the film packages, but is one
> of the finest methods available for a station to interest new local ad-
> vertisers in using the station as a selling medium.

> This is one area of local television that has so much to offer from an
> economic standpoint as well as from a public interest angle that I'm
> surprised more local stations haven't dumped their films for local per-
> sonalities and live shows. It's done far more for us in prestige and
> profit than any network or syndicated offering could ever do.[7]

There is evidence of sufficient interest in good locally produced programming to warrant experimentation with new ideas and new techniques.
Two examples of local programs with a great deal of originality and creativity may give the reader some ideas concerning how new and different programs can be originated.

WBBM-TV in Chicago handed out some 11,000 ballots to home-
bound commuters, telling them that a program on transportation problems
in Chicago would be broadcast that evening and requesting them to watch it
and mail their ballots to the station. More than 2500 ballots were returned.
This was but one of the series of excellent programs on the station using
audience participation.

Surveys, opinion polls, local responses to local questions may be the
basic ingredients of good—and pertinent—program material. Telephone
questions and conversations can interest a community. As a variation, studio guests can speak on selected problems during the first ten minutes of
each program, then the viewing audience may be invited to ask questions.

A case history of Station WWJ-TV in Detroit, as presented as a part of a survey of local station programming in 1966 by *Television* magazine, presents a convincing argument for local production. The only syndicated film used on WWJ-TV consists of one daily five-minute show and some cartoons used on a children's program. A travelogue, a traffic court, a hunting fishing outdoors program, a zoo visit, a women's interest feature, an exercise show, personal advice, actual religious services, a project in woodworking, helpful hints on country and suburban living, an information series on homes in the area and a news-weather-sports telecast—all these are locally and rewardingly produced by the station.

Children's shows must be well—not necessarily expensively—done or not at all. Children are loyal viewers but merciless observers.

More stations place local news programs in their top-rated local category than all other types combined. Few stations, however, give them top talent and production status. Every station should budget as high as it can afford for news because costs can be covered through sponsorship. Mobile units are a "must" in any area where significant news is made daily. Helicopters have proved advantageous in large markets for reports of traffic conditions and for special spot news events.

Adequate equipment is nice to have. Adequate people are a necessity. The program man who greatly relies on stills and silent films, too frequently also relies on a still mind and a silent, not to say utterly secret, power of enterprise and invention.

In the creation of local programming, many stations have discovered that the greatest opportunity to be different lies in the public affairs field.

The aims of the local public affairs programs should be to inform, to broaden understanding, and to stimulate community thinking. In television, reality exists side by side with the illusions of show business. Whenever a public affairs program is presented, the public needs to have it made clear that they are witnessing truth rather than the fiction which may be seen at other times. The station has the responsibility to make the distinction clear by eliminating the elements of make believe whenever it presents the factual.

Every television property should have one individual (even on part-time assignment) designated to handle all public affairs programming. The function should not be assigned to a group of individuals nor should the duties be passed from one person to another over a period of time. Public affairs programming is too vital to be given casual treatment.

Unfortunately, many stations have taken the easy way out by giving lip service and time allotment to a public affairs concept and failing to interest or alert the public to a genuine community problem.

A good public affairs program need not be divorced from entertainment. These programs should be produced with all the skill, verve, and appeal of commercial programming. If they are well done they can appeal to a long list of local advertisers. Qualities necessary for sponsorship are:

importance of subject, imaginative presentation, good production-direction-writing, wide viewer appeal, timeliness and news worthiness. In other words—good television.

COSTS OF LOCAL PROGRAMMING

The economics of local programming can be frightening when the need for live studio facilities, engineering, production and all other required elements are considered. Some stations' program expenditures (total, including all programming, film and live) are less than twenty-five per cent of their total operating costs. This is incredibly low and it usually reflects a lack-luster programming effort or a weak competitive situation, or both.

The average television station should expend about thirty-five per cent of its total station-operating budget for programming. Stations that are not affiliated with an interconnected network may expect costs for programming to go as high as fifty-five per cent of the overall expense.

The most effective means of program cost control in a well operated television station is through long-range planning, especially insofar as film programming is concerned. Any station involving itself in one crash film program after another in an attempt to find winners from the available syndicated half-hours and features will probably serve an unhappy audience and an unhappy auditor.

The overall cost of the film product depends upon the type of station and upon the competition for filmed shows in the market. Obviously, in a seven-station market, such as Los Angeles, there is a far greater competitive struggle for all film availabilities than is true in a three-station market such as Cincinnati or Atlanta. There is little uniformity of policy in film pricing. There are few guide lines.

Although there is no standard asking price for syndicated film, the average seems to run about $125 for each half hour for a station in a medium-sized market. For three to four additional re-runs over a five-year period, a manager should expect to spend another $300 to $350. A station in a small single-station market might be able to lease the same film for one showing for $15 to $20 per half hour.

The smaller the market, the greater is the chance that the cost of live production could exceed the cost of film rental. In a medium-sized market, both the costs and the drawing power of live production and film are somewhat comparable. Here, the rental of a syndicated half-hour film might be around $125 and the investment in a local production of a half-hour studio square-dance or polka party, with, say, five musicians and four dancers, could average between $150 and $200 per show.

The expenses of local production in proportion to film costs can be kept under better control in stations in major markets. Even here, a decision between local live shows and film programming is difficult because of the risk involved in popular acceptance of the local production when the popularity of film is to some degree predictable.

Feature film production, as we noted earlier, has not kept pace with the use of those features by television. Prices for their use have skyrocketed. Costs of film features have increased greatly during the past decade in the large markets, more moderately in the medium-sized markets and only slightly in the small markets.

Financing a film program usually interests the manager but such other aspects of the film department as editing, shipping and receiving, keeping of records, screening, cueing and filing far too often receive inadequate recognition. These are highly important parts of the job and they need to be done if the film that the public sees on the air is up to the standard that the station wishes to maintain. Competent personnel can become dissatisfied because of the details of the job and they can lose their pride in accomplishment if there is no direction or sign of appreciation from management. Eventually, a great part of film programming may be automated but until that time arrives the people who work in film deserve more recognition than they have received in the past.

There is a distinct advantage in the involvement of the general manager, the program manager, the sales manager and the head of the film department in the decisions that affect the nature of film bought for the station. Each of these executives has a different kind of interest in what is selected. An interaction of ideas at this point in a group-decision atmosphere can pay dividends to the station.

COLOR TELEVISION

All around us in the world is a sea of color. Yet, television, the medium which should be able to make the most effective use of this dimension, was exceedingly slow to adopt it.

Several factors accounted for the slow development of color television and all of them were interrelated. An early reluctance of set manufacturers to enter the field and consequent dealer passivity, an indifferent attitude of the public due to the cost of the television receiver, weak advertiser support and the relatively few programs which were transmitted in color, all held back development.

Without going into a complexity of technical and psychological reasons, in 1965 a large part of the American public finally became excited over color television. Practically the entire NBC evening schedule, some ninety-six per cent, was offered in color during the 1965–66 season. CBS telecast half of its evening programming and ABC over a third in color. The following year, all prime time programs on all three networks were in color.

It has been estimated that up to January 1, 1966, some $80,000,000 had been spent on color by the networks, another $55,000,000 by television stations and around $25,000,000 by production companies, for a total of approximately $160,000,000.[8] The heaviest expenditures, however, were made by the general public, which by that time had invested around $2.8 billion. It was predicted that the number of color sets purchased would increase from three million in 1965 to twenty-three million by 1970.[9]

It is apparently only a matter of time before audiences will expect all stations to provide local programming in color. A station that carries network color and then shows its local programs in monochrome may begin to lose sizeable numbers of viewers to its competitors who provide color all the time.

Color adds to the emotional impact of entertainment programming as well as to commercials. How desirable it may be in information programming has yet to be determined. Certainly, much historical footage that exists only in black-and-white film and tape will continue to be used. It may be that in certain discussion and public affairs presentations, where emotion could be a deterrent to a concentration on facts, black-and-white telecasts will be preferable. Some combinations of color and non-color may emerge for such programs after a period of experimentation. For several years, however, it may be expected that every kind of program, whether improved by color or not, will be shown in tint.

Given something like total color television saturation, the novelty factor will diminish. Then, it will be fully realized that color alone will not save a second-rate program. Once again, a search will begin for new program ideas and fresh approaches.

UHF and the All-Channel Sets

In 1952, the FCC opened seventy new television channels in the ultra-high-frequency portion of the radio spectrum. Within a year, there were some 120 UHF stations on the air. Except in a few all-UHF markets, the "U" stations had rough going. Most people could not receive their programs and, with minimal audiences, it was next to impossible to get advertising revenues to keep the stations operating.

There was, however, no question about the need for the added channels. Only 650 stations could be accommodated in the VHF band. By 1960, most of those were assigned and the channels that remained were in areas of sparse population. The UHF channels (14 through 83) could permit from 1600 to 3000 additional television stations but they were not particularly attractive until such time as potential viewers had the equipment to receive them. Once UHF reception was proved practicable in actual telecasting, the FCC set out to assure its being built into future sets.

The all channel receiver law, passed by the 87th Congress and signed by President Kennedy in July, 1962, gave the FCC the power to require that, after a determined date, all television receiving sets manufactured and shipped or imported for sale in the United States be capable of receiving all VHF and UHF channels. That date was later set as April 30, 1964.

Programming is a key problem for UHF operations. Stations, particularly the ones located in metropolitan areas, have had to operate without the strength of network programs. They have had to compete with established and prosperous stations in bargaining for feature and syndicated film. People in the audience have formed habits of tuning to VHF stations. Many people either do not realize they have UHF selectivity or they do not understand what it is. Still, every new set bought represents a potential UHF viewer. In consequence, UHF stations will enjoy the audience their programs can command.

The most logical programming for the UHF station under present circumstances has seemed to consist of a kind of service that neither the competing stations nor the networks provide. Specialized stations concentrate on one kind of programming, such as sports, or on specifically segmented audiences. In spite of a considerable amount of ingenuity by UHF operators, the substantially different success format has not yet appeared.

UHF has been aided by the new interest in color as well as by an increase in the purchase of portable sets. These, of course, are equipped with UHF channels. It has been predicted that about ninety per cent of American homes should be able to receive UHF by 1970 or shortly thereafter. Since multiple-set homes are on the increase, it may be sooner. The rate of increase of UHF stations may be dependent upon a resolution of the issue of community-antenna television (CATV).

CATV

Community Antenna Television originated for the purpose of bringing reception to rural or other areas which were poorly served by reason of the inadequate signal strength of existing stations. As the idea grew, it was generally confined to areas without adequate television service. Usually, a tall antenna was erected by the owners of a CATV system and subscribers' homes were connected with the antenna. A monthly fee was charged.

CATV, in its original form, could hardly be called big business. Its revenues were small, from relatively few participants. Then the original concept of service to isolated communities changed. The new function of CATV became directly competitive with regularly licensed stations. No longer were the small communities of very great interest. The larger metropolitan centers became attractive, especially when the programming of key stations in those cities could be extended to other places by micro-wave or cable. Loopholes in existing law made such an extension possible. The new CATV had one primary goal and that was to make money.

It takes little capital to introduce competition by wire. It would be financially prohibitive to match it on local station budgets. The costs of installation of CATV systems average some $150,000 for service to 1000 homes, around $400,000 for 5000 subscribers and $800,000 to serve 10,000 homes.[10] Fees per home average $60 per year plus an initial installation charge. It is not difficult to pay off a sizeable loan and realize an appreciable profit within five to six years with fifty per cent or more subscribers in an area. The only key personnel needed are a chief engineer, a technician, an office girl, a lineman and a manager who is a combination salesman, public relations man and executive. The economics of the CATV competitive advantage should be obvious.

CATV operators are able to circumvent the multiple-ownership rule. While the number of television stations per owner is restricted by the FCC to seven, of which not more than five can be VHF, there is no limit to the number and influence on regional and local receptions a CATV-installation owner may have.

There is little argument over the positive benefits that CATV produces for the public and for the television industry as long as it concentrates on bringing more choices, without duplication of programs, to markets with no service or with one or two stations. In the multi-station market, broadcasters found a different story. There, additional channel activation resulted in additional segmentation of the existing audiences.

Broadcasters, sensing that the problems had grown beyond their control, sent up a cry for Federal regulation of the CATV's. Not all broadcasters, however, joined in that chorus. Some were already investors in CATV, having joined forces with this potential challenger to the established system of television. Thus, broadcasters became divided over the CATV issue. This division may be as important a factor as any other in the nature of any settlement that ultimately will be reached.

The FCC, already overburdened with its workload, responded to the broadcasters' cries for help. It proceeded to bring CATV under its jurisdiction even though the additional paper work called for manpower not provided for in its budget. The first action was to issue a formal order in April, 1965, bringing some 400 CATV systems using micro-waves under its control. Then, in February, 1966, the Commission publicly announced that all those using cable, around 1200 systems, were also to be FCC-regulated. At best, FCC action has been ameliorative and temporary.

Subsequent action by the FCC included a formal request to Congress that legislation be enacted to clarify and confirm the Commission's assumption of jurisdiction over CATV. The FCC asked that the legislation be prohibitive to the extent of denying any program origination rights to CATV. It also asked for consideration of the question as to whether the systems should be classed as public utilities and whether they should be required to obtain the consent of stations before retransmitting their signals. Then work began on the preparation of an information reporting form for the filing of required data by CATV operators.

In June, 1966, the House Commerce Committee, after a month of closed-door meetings, reported out a bill to confirm the authority as exercised by the FCC. It would grant in essence the provisions the Commission had requested. The bill contained a ban on all program originations except for limited types, interpreted to include news, weather and time services. Somewhat the same blackout provisions as adopted by professional sports were made to apply to CATV.

A Senate Judiciary subcommittee on Patents, Trademarks and Copyrights conducted hearings on the CATV aspects of copyright revision during the Summer of 1966. A House Judiciary subcommittee had held earlier hearings. The settlement of the copyright issue could be crucial to the future of CATV.

The issues are manifestly too technical and legalistic to be more than merely indicated here. Ultimately, under the American system, FCC rulings in these matters must be tested in the courts. Whatever legislation is enacted must also be reviewed by court decision. The law will take its course.

Any eventual settlement will either need to reaffirm or redefine the American right of free enterprise. Questions of prior rights and simple ethical business practices are involved. Certainly, CATV is a programming issue as far as the general public is concerned because its ultimate solution will determine the nature and cost of the offerings the people will get on their home television receivers. As much as anything else, the instances of vacillation and bewilderment on the part of so many broadcasters point up the serious need of a basic philosophy for the electronic media. At no other time since broadcasting began has that need been so obvious.

PAY-TV

Early attempts to establish pay-TV systems met with little success. In 1951, pay-TV was tried in Chicago and, in 1953, it was begun in Palm Springs, California. Little progress was made in either of those cases.

The first experiment to receive much attention in the United States was one tried at Bartlesville, Oklahoma, in the late 1950s. The Bartlesville system confined its programming to current motion pictures. For that service during eleven hours a day, customers paid flat fees of $9.50 a month. Only some 500 families in the town of 30,000 population were attracted as customers and the experiment failed.

A pay-TV system was started in Etobicoke, a suburb of Toronto, in 1960. This system used three channels, giving the subscribers a choice of types of programming. In 1961, it came under the control of International Telemeter Corporation, a subsidiary of Paramount Pictures Corporation.

The system was a pioneer in the use of leased cables. It closed its operation in May, 1965, after five years of programming. The reason given for its closing was that all of the information it needed had been obtained. Its subscriber list, initially numbering 5500, had dropped to around 2500. Possibilities of moving the system to Montreal were explored after the closing.

During its period of operation, current movies and sports had been the most popular offerings. There had been no discernible adverse effect on commercial television viewing. Its attractions had appealed to "selective tastes" and the amount of expenditure per home varied according to the "quantity, caliber and diversity of programming" that was offered. It was reported that revenue from subscribers, which had been expected to reach ten dollars per month, averaged some two dollars.

Two pay-television systems have been in operation in the United States in the 1960s. One is a broadcast system, WHCT, on UHF Channel 18 in Hartford, Connecticut. The other was a wired system, Subscription Television, Incorporated, (STV) in Los Angeles and San Francisco. As a broadcast system, WHCT comes under FCC jurisdiction. STV did not.

The Hartford Experiment

Pay-TV in Hartford began in June, 1962, as a three-year experiment, licensed by the FCC. The license was granted to RKO General for a system broadcasting coded or scrambled signals that are decoded by an attachment in the subscriber's receiving set. The system is called Phonevision, a technique developed and patented by the Zenith Radio Corporation. Subscribers pay for the installation of the decoder, a monthly rental fee and a fee for each program they choose to watch.

The Hartford license was renewed by the FCC in May, 1965, for another three-year period. There were several conclusions from its first period of operation. Its appeal had been chiefly to middle and lower income families. The average annual expenditure per family was slightly more than sixty dollars in addition to the decoder rental fees. Motion pictures constituted the most popular regular program fare. Only championship boxing matches drew larger individual audiences. Subscription-TV viewing occupied only about five per cent of the hours the people devoted to television. Charges for programs varied from twenty-five cents for some of the educational features to three dollars for a world-championship boxing match. The average amount charged for motion pictures was one dollar, for operas and ballets it was $1.50 and for sports events an average of $1.37.[11]

Zenith Radio Corporation and its subsidiary, Teco, Inc. filed a petition with the FCC in March, 1965, for a rule to authorize pay-television on a national basis. The announcement of the FCC in inviting comments indicated that the Commission was not opposed to such authorization.

West Coast Pay Television

Subscription Television, Inc., was the most ambitious pay system yet attempted in the physical coverage which it embraced, the program service which it supplied, and the $21,000,000 stock offering it made.

The STV operation in California was forced to suspend operations in November, 1964, when the voters of the state passed Proposition 15 outlawing pay television.

The proposition on which the citizens voted was declared unconstitutional early in 1966 by the California Supreme Court. The majority opinion, in a six to one decision, stated that it abridged the freedom of speech and was in violation of both the First and the Fourteenth Amendments. An appeal was filed by the State of California asking the U. S. Supreme Court to reverse the decision of the state court.

WHAT NEXT?

The issues of CATV and pay-television can be solved in a fashion by government edict. The broadcasters of the country, however, could and should have anticipated these crises before they developed. The warnings of the consequences of the industry's delay were sounded in sufficient time.

The prospect of relief from government intervention into television programming may not be on the immediate horizon. It is not too late, however, for broadcasters to prove that they are capable of handling their own affairs. That desired state of existence cannot be achieved by a dependence on Uncle Sam to settle problems after and not before they arise. True maturity in broadcasting will come when industry self-regulation is proven to be the best solution in all kinds of cases. We will have more to say on this subject in a later chapter.

6

Broadcast Engineering

BOTH RADIO AND television began as scientific and engineering phenomena. Essential advancements were made in the broadcasting process before the media were used, first by talent, second by sales and business management.

Most of the marvels of broadcasting that continue to amaze people even after they have acquired a fundamental knowledge of its process were developed by members of the engineering fraternity. Those who work in broadcast engineering today have inherited the traditions established by the great inventors and innovators from Hertz to Marconi, from de Forest to Zworykin.

The image-orthicon camera, the Zoomar lens, audio and video tape, electronic color and the relay satellites are engineering accomplishments that might conceivably have been discovered and applied regardless of specific informational and commercial usage.

Talent, programming, sales and management people were brought together through the evolution of broadcasting. They learned to respect mutual interests growing out of the regular communications system that is the vital medium as we know it.

The engineering world is necessarily technical and apart. The engineer is not subject to the public criticism that is often directed at programming and advertising. In his unobtrusive way, he makes his contributions to the broadcasting process without fanfare. Few outside his own department, including the station manager, understand engineering work and motivations or are able to comprehend much beyond the simplest basic procedures. On the other hand, the engineer may be inclined to dismiss programming and sales considerations as having very little appeal for him. Even so, friction between the engineering and other departments is more often due to poor communication than to a lack of proper understanding and mutual good will.

Once radio took on an air of maturity and sophistication in the early 1930s, the close ties between engineering and management that had prevailed in the formative years eroded in all too many cases. This division of technical and persuasional interests was not restricted to the local station level; it included networks as well. The breakdown of close collaboration between the work of the engineering department on one hand and administrative projects on the other reflected an increasing lack of a common language and the lapse of a common concern.

THE STATION MANAGER'S RELATIONSHIP TO ENGINEERING

It is hard to overstate the perils of estrangement. Most station managers are mere neophytes in engineering and rely heavily on chief engineers to supervise the technical affairs of their stations. They often run risks because of their paucity of technical knowledge in everything from the purchase of equipment and details of operations to the attitudes of the engineering personnel. Engineers, too often sketchily or arbitrarily informed (or ignored), sometimes miss opportunities to advance proposals that could have real benefits to the organization. With management playing superior and engineers playing canny, both may find themselves overspending on proposals of facilities or equipment and underachieving in broadcast potentials.

FUNCTIONS OF THE CHIEF ENGINEER

The chief of the engineering department has varied functions. He must maintain a balanced loyalty between management and the station engineers. He must sometimes assume the duties of an executive and, at other times, direct specialists in various phases of studio and station operation—studio control, short-wave remote relays, video-tape recording and broadcasts, transmitter work and the maintenance of equipment. He must take full responsibility for all regular maintenance checks and usually he is charged with building supervision and maintenance.

Management expects that the chief engineer will maintain proper liaison and provide all needed assistance to each of the departments of the station. More and more, his services are becoming vital to the manager on the Washington scene. He must be skilled in his relationships with the unions. His participation in community affairs is expected. He must be abreast of current trends and probable future developments in broadcast engineering and be able to make recommendations for the station so that it will keep pace with those advancements. No small part of his many functions is the obligation to help the station manager acquire a greater understanding of the work of the engineering department and to keep the manager advised concerning its problems and its achievements.

In short, the chief engineer, no less than the station manager, usually finds himself in an assignment which is somewhat different from the sort of career he once anticipated when he started his work in the broadcast industry. Generally, he finds that many adjustments are necessary. Given the man with the rich background in engineering who discovers the gratifications in leadership and given the manager who has the proper intellectual curiosity about the engineering department, the station has achieved one of the most important working relationships in broadcasting. The ideal is a station manager-chief engineer relationship so strong that the individuals operate in mutual understanding and mutual respect.

Balanced Loyalty

Historically, the engineer in broadcasting has not been inclined toward the business view. Yet, the chief engineer is expected to become a part of management's team. With the program manager and the sales manager, he becomes a member of a triumvirate indispensable to the station manager. Men who work in the engineering department expect their chief to represent their interests. The double existence the chief engineer is compelled to live, with his principal work in a field which is somewhat foreign to the manager and his duty to be loyal to corporate policy, is confusing to one who would prefer to find his satisfactions in his own creative way and not be bothered with the details expected of an administrator.

In a sense, too, engineers form a closed fraternity. They can be jealous of their skills and prerogatives. Management may seem remote and indifferent to the men on the cameras or at the control panels. It is, therefore, doubly important that the engineering leader understand and communicate company policy to his department. Shared knowledge makes for mutual interest and cooperation. In a well run broadcasting establishment, the chief engineer is conversant with the what and why of the overall operation.

Even then, conflicts are likely to arise. The matter of control of overtime costs for the company at the expense of extra income for the men on the engineering staff is one problem. The question of priorities in cases where the engineers want more equipment or supplies than the manager says the station can afford makes for friction between management and the chief engineer and the men on his staff. The need to sharpen engineering awareness of a station's needs for cleanliness and good housekeeping when individuals seem to get more satisfaction from their own system of equipment care creates minor irritations. Perhaps the hardest task for the chief engineer—or for any administrator, for that matter—is to keep a flow of communication accurate and complete from management to the men in the department and from the men to management. This is a function of a good administrator and the chief engineer, not being disposed toward administration or communication to begin with, often has to be reminded that this is important.

It is no easy task to maintain the balance needed between the interests of the people in this department and the manager's office, especially when so much may be lost in translation, so to speak, unless communication is clear. It applies both ways. Managerial directives may be misunderstood. The technical language of the engineer often has to be explained to management in words of low wattage.

Equipment Maintenance

One of the most important areas of administration for an engineering executive is in the field of maintenance. It has been proved in many operations, especially since the advent of television, that the finest properties with the best engineering personnel cannot do justice to certain technical repairs and still perform their other assignments efficiently. In many cases, therefore, it is efficient and economical to send cameras and other equipment to their factory of origin for overall repair and updating.

A well managed engineering department will get the maximum life out of all the major equipment in the station. It will run equipment checks oftener than is expected and it will take special pride in the performance of all equipment. It will have various functional charts for troubleshooting, whether of studio, transmitter or remote gear. It will submit discrepancy reports for every malfunction, no matter how small. The efficient engineering department will prepare an operations manual and will keep it up to date. All station equipment should be checked thoroughly at least four times a year in addition to the regular measurements for proof of performance.

Some engineering staffs have found that efficiency results from a rotating system of assignments among studio operations, transmitter duty, maintenance and remote work. Other stations have preferred to assign specific members of the engineering staff to specific functions. The latter policy makes good sense in those cases in which certain men prefer to work in studio production while others are better suited to assignments as far away from production personnel as possible. Assignments should be made by the chief engineer. They should be based on the need to achieve maximum efficiency in terms of the special intersts and skills of his men.

Building Supervision

It is advisable to vest in the chief engineer the responsibilities for building supervision both in the studio building and the transmitter. In a business that is keyed to electronics, almost every phase of the building unit needs the chief engineer's guidance and supervision. There is very little of a physical nature in a broadcasting operation that cannot benefit directly or indirectly from the professional supervision of the chief executive of the engineering department.

In smaller operations—and this will become increasingly true as more small communities have television stations in addition to radio properties—there should be most careful planning by the chief engineer regarding the location of a combined transmitter and studio site. With the exception of stations located in our very major cities, there is little reason why studio facilities should not be contiguous to the transmitter. While many stations in small to medium sized markets still maintain divided facilities, it is almost certain that combined operations will become more and more feasible in most locations in the future.

Relationship with Other Station Departments

The chief engineer must regard his role and that of his staff as a service arm of the radio or television station. While peak efficiency and specific cost control are demanded of engineering management, the programming of the station must be done by the programming department and not by an engineering entity. In short, the engineering department is there to furnish the technical guidance and operational know-how to stage the station's programming.

A good chief engineer must work with the sales and program departments in sales and program development. He should demonstrate what can be done with videotape and with audio facilities in the studio and on remote locations. He should assist sales and programming on ideas which are on the drawing boards for future implementation. In most cases, the chief engineer of any radio or television station can be a willing colleague in this area but he needs to be invited to participate. Once he realizes that his suggestions are wanted, he usually makes valuable contributions to the sales and/or program departments. The command function must abide in the front office.

FCC Liaison

Every broadcasting operation relies upon its chief engineer for liaison with the FCC. In fact, in many stations the only person who is truly qualified to handle many FCC matters is the chief engineer. While this may not be an ideal situation, it does exist. In this regard, the chief engineer must be aware not only of his own abilities but of his shortcomings as well. He should call upon Washington engineering consultants whenever necessary to protect the company's interests in matters before the FCC. There are a few engineering executives at the station level who can handle all phases of their Washington activity without need for outside engineering-consultant aid. Today's engineering executive must be prepared on the Washington front, as well as at home, for today it is not only difficult to add to or modify station holdings, it is difficult even to retain what one has unless the chief engineer is able to keep management posted on developments of a technical nature.

Liaison with Unions

The chief engineer must carry the major responsibility for liaison with the union men who operate under him. This is true even of companies which are large enough to have their own directors of industrial relations. There must be the closest association with the union shop steward and with the president of the local, as well as with the national and the international offices of the union. Costly hours, days and weeks of negotiation and work tie-ups can be prevented if the proper rapport exists.

The chief engineer should not wait until just before union negotiations start or until they are well under way to explain to his men why certain steps must be taken or why particular approaches cannot be implemented. Those explanations should be an ongoing process, taking place every day as a part of the interpretation of corporate policy.

The increased cost of doing business in broadcasting is a constant concern to management but this very economic fact could prove to be the catalyst bringing engineering and management closer together than they have been in the last forty years. Engineering needs to be made knowledgeable of the problems and the concerns of management. Management, in turn, should explain to all of the technically trained personnel what the requirements are for the immediate and the long range future. The road to management-labor relationships can be fraught with disaster unless all labor-saving possibilities are investigated. This does not mean that the engineering payroll should be slashed out of hand. But the industry is now at the point in its development when planning for the future must take automation into account, and this for every operation, regardless of size. The economic facts of life make this inevitable. Technical personnel should be apprised of the situation and the reasons for it.

With proper planning, automation not only may bring about sizeable savings, but it can gradually replace costly manpower without visiting undue hardships on individuals involved. Well operated stations with forward-looking management can, if sufficient advanced planning takes place, absorb into other phases of their radio and television operations all—or almost all—manpower affected by the introduction of automated devices. Technical personnel should be told exactly why automation gear, well conceived, well installed and knowledgeably employed, can eliminate many of the human errors that constantly recur and which pose so many sizeable losses for each property over a period of time. But the personnel should be taken care of and they should be given the opportunity to help to decide what their future contributions to the station may be.

Participation in Community Affairs

The chief engineer should be expected to take part in community affairs, but not necessarily in the same manner as other members of the staff.

Not always will he be qualified to serve as a speaker before clubs and organizations nor will he usually be interested in this kind of assignment. But he can be highly effective as a member of organizations. Often, as a member of a church or as a counselor to various charity and educational organizations or as an advisor to the Boy Scouts or to various sports groups involving youngsters, he can be a better representative of the station than many others on the staff.

Engineers, as a group, are not much inclined to public speaking, but they should be encouraged to appear before technical groups to address themselves to developments of the art. Many engineers are capable speakers but have a reluctance to appear publicly. Certainly, with the growth in every area of responsibility of engineers and with the reliance that management places upon them, this reluctance should become a thing of the past.

Future Planning

A good engineering executive looks to the future and plans all technical requirements well in advance. He stays ahead of developments in the industry and plans steps that he can take in the future to provide better performance and, if at all possible, at less cost than in the past. A good engineering executive plans now for eventualties, even for revolutionary changes. His planning must be sufficiently in advance so that if a change, say, should be five years removed, he can make arrangements to absorb within either his department, or in other phases of the station's operation, all of those personnel who would have to be relieved of their current duties due to the change.

So rapid has been the evolution of television that it is idle to lay down rules for station housing, equipment, location and design. It is as if we were to cite road maps for yesterday's prairie schooner in the planning of a tour by today's station wagon. At best, the present day builder will inform himself as to the basic functions, costs, probable needs and future expansion of his installations. Beyond that he will be well advised to hire the best architects he can find to consult with top programming, sales and engineering people. Once the basic requirements of a television installation are clearly visualized, details of design and construction can be worked out. In general, form will follow function.

Recruitment

Engineering recruitment is of paramount importance to radio and television stations for they have never been able to recruit engineering personnel on a satisfactory basis. A good source of supply for many stations is the large technical high school. Broadcasters need to make much more effort to recruit well educated engineering personnel and the chief engineer should be qualified to perform this function after making contact with accredited schools and colleges.

Relationships with the Station Manager

Regardless of his engineering knowledge, the chief engineer cannot be truly effective unless his training in the broadcast industry has been broad enough to make him an important factor in the successful administration of the station. In addition to the intelligent scheduling of manpower with efficiency and cost control constantly in mind, the chief engineer's obligation to management is to seek every possible means of improving the technical performance of the radio or television station.

Never let anyone tell you that there is not a difference in the *sound* or in the *look* of well or poorly supervised broadcast properties. There *is* an engineering difference that is achieved sometimes by superior equipment and facilities. More often, it is due to well trained and interested personnel. For example, in the case of color television, on one station in a market, the quality of color broadcast can be a thrilling tribute to this great new dimension in television and, on another station in the same market, it can be the most amateurish tint transmission that one has ever seen since the old field-sequential system.

Every station manager should take the time to become familiar with electronics gear now on the market or sometimes still on the drawing boards of the nation's major suppliers. Serious investigation of exhibits of equipment at the annual Spring conventions of the National Association of Broadcasters is a must for any station manager who wants to avoid getting caught in the quicksand of surging expenses. Managerial knowledge of the field of engineering and of its equipment can make a difference in profit and loss for the future. There is no more useful pursuit for station managers than the spending of an hour or two each week over a period of six months or more acquiring at least a familiarity with the engineering field, its equipment and attendant problems.

Thus far in this chapter, we have stressed the interdependence of the chief engineer and his department with the general administrative routine of the station. While it may seem incongruous to find front office personnel delving into matters of engineering and certain engineering experts becoming interested in finance and general business activity, this bit of "chemistry" is long overdue in broadcasting.

EQUIPMENT PURCHASE

Managers of established stations must purchase new equipment. Replacement is necessary for equipment that is becoming outworn or outmoded. Sometimes, however, there is a tendency to postpone equipment purchases or the remodeling of plant or building in order to improve the condition of the annual financial report. This policy may have certain immediate gains, but it only postpones the day of reckoning. A manager, who moves wisely in these matters constantly, strengthens his station's advantages over his competition and thereby improves his station's profit position. Many managers may not equate eventual increase of profit with the purchase of a new piece of equipment. They would change some of their buying practices if they did.

There are still some radio stations without mobile units for the coverage of community affairs. There are still a few television stations lacking video tape facilities. Others, as we have noted earlier in this book, have not installed color transmission equipment. What's more, some stations have not improved basic equipment in their studios, transmitters or offices for years and they give the appearance of poverty when seen by visitors. At the other extreme, many managers have acted on the recommendations of their chief engineers and have continued to show admirable profit margins while engaging in regular expansion of facilities and equipment. These men have proceeded on the sound management belief that one has to spend money to make money.

Parallels may be found in other businesses. The old-fashioned drugstore or restaurant, for example, which resists modernization, finds that a great part of its business goes to those other drugstores or restaurants that do spend the money to improve their plants. Some businessmen seem to believe they can be successful by keeping the costs down and operating on a narrow margin between income and outgo. But the margin soon becomes only enough for survival and eventually, if the narrow view persists, even survival becomes questionable.

In broadcasting, the rate of technological change is rapid and constant. In order to maintain an improved profit position in radio or television and in order to achieve regularly improved standing among those with whom radio and television do business, outmoded facilities and equipment are not assets. The purchase of additional or replacement equipment and the improvement of building or plant should not be determined by obsolescence. Outlays should be weighed against contributions to profit which the expenditures can make. Decisions to spend are not easy decisions. Only the manager with an alert and informed engineering department can make them wisely.

Because of the many factors that may influence the purchase of equipment, it is difficult to estimate the amount such expenditure should be at any particular station for any particular year. Annual equipment purchases for television stations may range from $6000 to $500,000 and more. The total equipment bill for all of the nation's television stations may be conservatively estimated at $35,000,000 each year, exclusive of maintenance costs and engineering payrolls. Looked at in one way, that's a lot of money. Looked at in another way, it's a lot of progress.

FCC Rules Violations

The Engineering Department of the NAB compiled a list of the most frequent violations of Part 73 of the FCC rules for the six-month period, July 1-December 31, 1965. Logging failures accounted for the largest number of FCC citations of error in the case of AM, FM and TV stations. The most general violations of the rules by AM stations are shown in Table I. Tables II and III show a listing of the most common technical errors by FM and television stations, respectively. It may be noted that the proportionate violations by radio stations far exceeded those of television stations, even when the greater number of radio allocations is taken into consideration.

Table I [1]

Most Frequent AM Violations

Section	Number of Violations	Item
73.111	211	Log requirements, general
.114	192	Maintenance logs (73.114(e) Failure to make or log required five days a week inspection of transmitting equipment)
.39	139	Equipment—Indicating instruments (73.39(d)(2) Remote ammeters, calibration)
.47	132	Equipment performance measurements (73.47(b) Failure to make, or keep measurements on file)
.57	86	Operating power (73.57(a) Maintenance of)
.40	77	Transmitter (73.40(b)(3)(iv) Fencing around tuning house or antenna base)
.93	73	Operator requirements (73.93(a) Failure to have first-class operator on duty)
.113	72	Operating logs (73.113(a)(3) Failure to make or record half-hourly entries)
.56	69	Modulation monitor (73.56(a) Defective)
.112	47	Logs, Program

TOTAL 1098
All other rule violations ... 305

TOTAL Violations 1403

Automatic Logging Rules

In 1961, the NAB requested a rule-making procedure of the FCC on the subject of automatic logging devices to record information that was then entered manually in station operating logs. The FCC issued a rule-making procedure followed by a Report and Order and new rules became effective on July 19, 1963.

TABLE II
MOST FREQUENT FM VIOLATIONS

Section	Number of Violations	Item
73.284	103	Maintenance logs (73.284(e) Failure to make, or make record of tower light inspections)
.254	63	Transmitter performance (73.254(c) Failure to make or keep equipment performance measurements on file)
.267	63	Operating power (73.267(b) Maintenance of)
.265	59	Operator requirements (73.265(a) Failure to have operator with first-class license on duty)
.281	51	Logs, general
.283	36	Logs, operating (73.283(a)(3) Failure to make or record half-hourly entries)
.275	24	Remote control and monitoring equipment, installation deficiencies
.295	21	Subsidiary Communications Authorizations—Operation (73.295(e) Logging)
.317	20	Transmitter and associated equipment (73.317(a)(14) Spurious emission)
.264	18	Station and operator licenses posting (73.264(a) Station license posting)
.282	18	Program logs (73.282(a)(3) Public Service Announcements)

TOTAL 476

All other rule violations 133

TOTAL Violations 609

TABLE III
MOST FREQUENT TV VIOLATIONS

Section	Number of Violations	Item
73.672	72	Maintenance log (73.672(e) Failure to make, or make record of tower light inspections)
.689	43	Operating power (73.689(b)(1) Maintenance—Visual transmitter)
.669	42	Logs, general
.682	32	Transmission standards (73.682(a)(13) Reference white level)
.668	19	Off-Frequency (73.668(b) Aural)
.687	15	Transmitters (73.687(b)(7) Aural transmitter)
.691	14	Modulation Monitor
.699	11	Synchronizing Waveform
.670	9	Program log (73.670(a)(3) Failure to indicate sponsor)
.690	7	Frequency Measurements

TOTAL 264

All other rule violations 20

TOTAL Violations 284

FCC rules now provide permission for AM, FM and TV stations to use automatic logging devices to keep operating (transmitter) and program logs. A third station log for maintenance is mandatory. Daily inspections are required at AM and FM stations, whether or not automatic logging devices are used.

Under the rules, a decision on the use of automatic logging devices for operating logs is voluntary on the part of station management. If a decision is made to use the automatic devices, several conditions must be met. The Engineering Department of the NAB has itemized the general conditions of use as follows:[2]

1. The use of automatic recorders must not affect the accuracy of the basic indicating instruments.
2. The automatic logger must have an accuracy equivalent to that of the basic indicating instrument.
3. Calibration must be made at least once a week and appropriate results noted in the maintenance log.
4. Aural alarm circuits must be provided.
5. The automatic device must read each parameter at least once every 10 minutes.
6. For remotely controlled transmitters, the automatic logger must be located at the remote control point. For manually controlled stations, the logger must be located at the transmitter.

In addition, it is required "that all manual readings be taken prior to making any corrective adjustments and all readings, whether manual or automatic, must be taken during the absence of modulation. Arbitrary automatic logger scales may not be used. The logger need not be directly in the operator's view."

Operating logs, whether kept manually or automatically, must show final stage plate voltage and plate current, antenna current and frequency monitor readings. Antenna base current must also be logged once each day under any of three conditions: (1) when the remote ammeter is defective, (2) when specified as a part of the station license for directional antenna operation and (3) whenever a station operates a directional antenna by remote control. Momentary interruptions of the carrier wave do not have to be logged if there is automatic restoration; if restoration is not automatic an entry must be made describing the cause and length of the interruptions. If the operating log is kept manually, entries must be made at the start of each day's operation and at thirty-minute intervals throughout the day.

The *maintenance* log requires information on meter calibration, inspections of tower lights, reports on inoperative equipment, reports on equipment tests and, in the case of AM and FM stations, a five-day-per-week inspection report of transmitting facilities that must be made by a holder of a first class license. At the conclusion of each inspection, verification must be made by an entry in the maintenance log. Such entry must include the date and the actual time spent making the inspection, with starting and completion times noted. Travel time to and from the transmitter is not included. Notations must be made certifying that the inspections have been made and descriptions of any repair or maintenance work must be given. Any defective equipment must be described and reasons for failure to make repairs must be given.

All program, operating and maintenance logs must be available for inspection on request of any authorized representative of the FCC.

RADIO REMOTE CONTROL TRANSMITTER OPERATION

In 1953, the FCC authorized all non-directional AM and FM stations using 10-kw power or less to operate their transmitters by remote control. The privilege was extended to all AM and FM stations, regardless of power, in 1956. There was a reservation that the operators of stations in excess of 10 kw were required to prove the performance and reliability of their transmitters over a twelve-month test period.

It is expected that this restriction may be removed sometime in the future. NAB has so petitioned the FCC on the basis of increased reliability of transmitting equipment due to technological advances.

The 1956 expanded remote-control privilege did not give operator relief to any AM directional stations, nor to those AM non-directionals with an excess of 10 kw. These stations are required to keep a first-class radio-telephone license holder on duty at all times when the stations are on the air. Non-directionals under 10 kw and FM stations with less than 25-kw power were permitted as of April, 1964, to employ persons holding third-class radio-telephone operator permits, endorsed by written examination, to conduct routine transmitter operations. These stations may, under certain conditions, employ on a part-time contract basis a supervisory engineer with a first-class license.

Most college graduates, who have majored in radio and television, should be able to take the examination and qualify for the third-class ticket. Testing normally covers three elements of FCC-examination content: (1) basic law, (2) basic operating practice and (3) basic broadcast, which is Section 9 of the FCC examination. Applicants who contact the nearest FCC field office are given a time and location for the test. They are requested to fill out an application (FCC form No. 756) and to submit the license fees prior to the taking of the examination. Most radio and television stations, as well as most departments of radio and television in colleges or universities, have NAB study guides for the third-class license on file. These may be helpful in studying for the examination.

It is recommended that a first-class engineer, who is employed on a part-time contract basis, be regarded as an independent contractor and that this designation should be so specified in writing. Other contractual items should include a statement of the engineer's specific duties, the rate of payment, a specification that he will supply his own tools and testing equipment, the policy in regard to the purchasing of supplies and equipment, a non-disclosure of station information clause and a statement of the length of the contract with termination and renewal conditions.

Again, it would be desirable if all differences in transmitter regulations based on amount of station power and nature of antennas might someday be removed. The NAB has worked on the development of equipment capable of taking samples of the electronic condition of any station's transmission system and of alerting station personnel to any deviations from allowable tolerances. When such equipment becomes available, it is hoped that there will then be no need for a continuance of the first-class operator requirement.

The NAB also has filed a request with the FCC asking for an amendment of the remote control rules so as to allow VHF television stations to operate their transmitters by the use of either a DC wire-line system or a multiplex off-the-air system. UHF stations are permitted the use of wire-line systems.

STANDARDS FOR COLOR TELEVISION FILM

Quality control in the processing of color film for television is necessary in order to prevent color tones in receiving sets from varying. In switching from one station to another or when the local station runs a filmed color commercial during a color program on film, the variations in color standards may be annoying to the viewer.

ALLOCATIONS TABLES

The FCC adopted a new FM allocations table in 1963. Supplemental action was taken a year later to permit

> . . . existing stations which were licensed under the previous rules to increase their facilities and improve service in those cases where the previous rules would have permitted such increases and in some other cases where the public would benefit.

The change in the rules enabled FM stations, in accordance with co-channel and adjacent channel separations considerations, to apply for increases in power and antenna heights. In some cases, the maximum permitted for the class of station could be allowed.

The maximum power allowable for Class A FM stations is 3 kw; antenna height is 300 feet. Maximums permitted for Class B stations are 50 kw in power and 500 feet in antenna height; for Class C stations, maximal power is 100 kw and maximal antenna height is 2000 feet.

A new UHF allocations assignment plan was issued by the FCC in 1966. A previous table, announced the previous year, was declared inoperable because of errors in the programming information that had been fed into a computer. This was the first time that the Commission's computer had been used in the drafting of an allocations table.

The 1966 allocations made more low-numbered UHF channels available, although they were not in areas of heavy population. The total number of UHF channel assignments 1098, of which 590 were made available for commercial television.

At the time of the announcement of the UHF allocation table, a further notice of rule-making was issued by the FCC, proposing that channels 70 to 83 be set aside for a new class of 10-kw, low-power television stations to serve small communities.

Generally, the UHF table establishes six or more unreserved channels in each of the twenty-five largest markets, five or more in markets 26 through 75, four or more in the markets from 76 through 100, and three or more in the 101st to the 150th markets. In most cases, those markets under 150th in size were assigned two channels. No commercial channels were provided for markets under 25,000 in population. At least one ETV reservation was made for each state and most major population centers were given two ETV channels.

Pressures continue to mount for more frequency availabilities for landmobile communications use. Such users of the spectrum as police, fire and other governmental services, as well as trucking firms, taxi companies and others who communicate with vehicles, have expanded significantly in recent years. With that expansion has come a need for more frequencies. UHF channels 14 and 15 were requested by the National Association of Manufacturers for land mobile use as early as 1963.

The Joint Technical Advisory Committee, representing various landmobile interests, would like a part or all of the existing AM radio band and the existing VHF set of frequencies to accommodate the declared need for more land-mobile space.

The television broadcasting services occupy three different bands in the spectrum. VHF channels 2 through 6 are assigned to the 54–72 megacycle range, VHF channels 7 through 13 are in the 174–216 megacycle area and the UHF channels 14 through 83 are in the portion from 470–890 megacycles. The JTAC argues that a single, more compact set of frequencies for all television stations would make for improved service and savings in the construction of equipment. The committee would like to have the existing band widths of television channels narrowed. It maintains that the present six megacycle band is not necessary because the average television receiver accepts only 3.5 to 4.5 megacycles of the band. It is noted by those who desire additional space that there have been hardly any changes in the utilization of spectrum space for over fifteen years.

The JTAC has also recommended consideration of the possibility of moving all local AM radio stations to FM frequencies, and permission for regional and clear channel stations to increase their power so they might be able to cover greater areas.

It is the contention of the committee, in its published study, that:

> Work on the evaluation of the need and toward improving utilization efficiency should go on even though at the outset it would appear that existing investments in stations and receivers might dictate perpetual maintenance of the status quo.

The FCC has appointed a Land Mobile Advisory Committee to study the problem as well as the recommendations of the JTAC.

POWER INCREASES

At sundown each evening, more than 25,000,000 people in the United States are uncertain whether they can get a radio signal that is listenable. This is the number of people who live in so-called "white areas," which have no primary nighttime service.

The FCC's solution for the problem is to duplicate thirteen of the remaining twenty-five clear channels and consider further the question of permitting Class 1-A stations to broadcast with power greater than the existing 50-kw limitation. The United States Court of Appeals has upheld the right of the Commission to revise the clear channels in this manner.

Opponents of higher power maintain that the Class 1-A stations would gain an unfair advantage in other metropolitan markets. The listener, however, does not respond to radio as he does to the high-budgeted television station, which "leap frogs" into his area. Radio is a habit and local medium and whenever local broadcasts are available, they are preferred by the local residents.

WGN, for example, would be dominant in Milwaukee if power and the ability to deliver a signal were the only criteria, for it can be heard better in more parts of that city than most of the local stations. Those local stations, however, are consistently the favorites of the local citizenry. An increase in power from 50 to 750 kilowatts, as has been requested, would increase WGN's signal strength not 15 times on a linear basis but rather approximately a little less than four times. (The field strength increase is the square root of how many times the power is increased). If the present signal is consistently better than most, if not all, of the stations in Milwaukee, yet does not attract those listeners, then an increase of four times or forty times the power is not going to interest them either. Milwaukee, of course, is used as an example of the reaction in other metropolitan areas.

The situation in the "white areas" is an entirely different proposition. In the upper peninsula of Michigan, for example, there are two local stations in a town of 10,000 and another in a town only twelve miles away. These stations can be heard very well in the daytime but, at night, there isn't as much as a whisper only two or three miles away from the transmitters. The only nighttime radio service these people can get is the sporadic signal from some clear channel station in Minneapolis, Chicago, Detroit and, on a few rare occasions, Des Moines. It should be time to think about a sizeable American public that is underprivileged in the matter of radio reception.

In the late 1920s and early 1930s, stations were permitted increases in power from 100 and 250 watts to 1000 watts and, later, from 1000 to 5000. There was much hue and cry then about "super" power and, in those days, there were only a few hundred stations on the air. Since there have been 50,000-watt properties operating, the number of radio stations has increased to well over 4000. It would appear that the 50,000-watt stations did not stifle competition or manifest a monopoly.

Rather, they helped greatly in the development of the broadcasting industry by their high professional standards and by helping to make the public and advertisers conscious of the merits of this medium of communications. Higher amounts of power, even on a handful of stations, could benefit every station in the land, regardless of size or location. It could furnish proof to national advertisers that not only is radio alive but its operators are willing to continue to invest money in it and to experiment in the public interest. Many national advertisers could be returned to radio through such a sound development and sizeable amounts of new business could be attracted.

We would go further and argue that all classes of radio stations should be allowed to increase their power in order to combat the vast increases in electrical interferences and in man-made noise levels.

PERMANENT DEFENSE SYSTEM

The new Emergency Broadcast System (EBS), designed specifically for use in case of a war emergency, went into effect in January, 1964. It replaced the former Conelrad system, which had been in use since 1951.

EBS uses AM stations basically, with FM and TV aural channels assigned to relay and network assistance when necessary. Under the alert system, a federal government message would be issued to the Associated Press and to United Press International. They would flash the alert to stations via their teletype services. Immediately, on receipt of the alert, all regular programming must cease and pre-arranged announcements must be read. Stations not holding National Defense Emergency Authorizations (NDEA's) must advise listeners to tune to an authorized station. Then, these unauthorized stations must leave the air. Any station may apply for NDEA authorization. Stations have a right of appeal to the FCC in the event they are refused authorizations.

Priorities in the use of the Emergency Broadcast System are: (1) communications of the President and other officials of the federal government to the public before, during and after an attack; (2) local messages; (3) state programs and (4) national programs and news.

Stations authorized to remain on the air may not broadcast any commercials. They may program music, when there is no information to be carried, and they also may broadcast information to specific individuals.

In the event of an emergency necessitating the use of EBS, daytime only AM stations could operate beyond their normally licensed hours if no other service is available in the area. Unlimited-time AM stations could maintain their daytime facilities at night.

The United States Weather Bureau makes use of EBS for hurricane, tornado and other physical-catastrophe warnings.

7

National Sales

He toiled and strove
But no one knew it:
He had a horn:
He never blew it.

He died and this is not
Surprising
In secret without
Advertising!

—ANON.

IN PRECEDING CHAPTERS, we have identified the roles of the programming and the engineering departments in radio and television stations and have cited management's most important concerns in those areas. Neither of those departments could operate in a commercial station were it not for the contributions of the sales department. This branch of the broadcasting entity produces the revenue which pays for all of the station's activities and, through good management, makes a profit for the owners of the station.

The sales department is the station's principal contact with people in the world of business. Given a strong radio or television station in a community, the sales force can provide a needed service for merchants and institutional advertisers. Those businessmen depend upon mass communications media to reach people in order to inform as many as possible concerning products and services available. Few business enterprises question the values of advertising. Their corporate concerns are which media to use and which specific representatives of each of the media chosen will most effectively reach present and potential customers.

All of the station's initial efforts, then, must be in the direction of building technical and programming assets to the point of promising excellent returns for the business community. It follows that it is vital that the sales representatives of the station be selected with care. A good station can become even better by reason of good salesmen. Good salesmen can become even better by working under good sales managers.

QUALIFICATIONS AND FUNCTIONS OF THE SALES MANAGER

The ideal sales manager is one who has had experience not only as a salesman but in other phases of broadcasting as well. Since it is his function to market the station's product, the more he knows about the total station operation the better he is able to design the various commercial campaigns to achieve maximal results.

He should be fully aware of the strengths and weaknesses of all media of communication. This knowledge enables him to study the competitive offerings of other media as well as those of other radio or television stations and be able to determine how his station can achieve leadership over that competition by providing better service. He needs to be knowledgeable concerning newspapers, magazines, supplements, direct mail, billboards and all other advertising vehicles.

The ability to analyze media includes a sensitivity for the values of research. A good sales manager should be able to raise significant questions for station research personnel to answer. His examination of data obtained from audience and marketing studies should suggest many sales approaches he can recommend to his staff.

The sales manager needs to be experienced in marketing and retailing. With an understanding of each advertiser's particular problems and objectives, he should be able to make constructive suggestions toward building their business volume. Sometimes, those recommendations may be unrelated to an advertising campaign. Confidence in his business acumen will cause merchandisers to place sizeable amounts of their advertising budgets on his station.

As manager of the prime income producing unit of the station, he needs to be aware of station expenses. A good sales manager is as proficient in the control of cost items as he is in the production of income. He knows how to keep expense accounts and general costs in line without diminishing the quantity and quality of sales.

The sales manager must be willing to join his salesmen on the street and to work with them in the conception and the making of presentations to clients and their agencies. The man must have the poise, together with the aggressiveness, to gain true respect from men who are successful salesmen themselves.

As an administrator, the sales manager needs to be a good organizer. He must have the ability and the inclination to delegate most of the routine paper work to capable assistants. The time he saves may then be devoted to the four main functions of his position. These are: (1) the coordination of network and/or agency accounts carried on the station, (2) the maintenance of contacts with the station's national and/or regional representative, (3) the direction of the station's local sales and service and (4) sales development. We will discuss the first two of these functions, covering national sales, in this chapter. Local sales will be discussed in the next chapter.

ADVERTISING AGENCIES AND BROADCASTING

When the annual corporate budget for advertising is determined, the company's advertising agency considers the relative values of each of the advertising media. Then, selection of specific properties within each medium must be made. For some advertisers, a recommendation is made that most of the budget be allocated to the print media. Others are advised to place the largest share in broadcasting. Sometimes, the overall budget is fairly evenly distributed between media. The advertiser, of course, may influence the decision by expressing media preferences.

When the amount to be spent in broadcasting is determined, further decisions must be made. What proportion of the amount will go to purchase radio and what proportion to buy television? What kinds of vehicles (programs or participations) are desired and what kinds are available? How much of the budget should be used to purchase network services and how much should go into spot advertising on selected individual stations? Which markets should be selected and which stations employed in those markets?

Agency time buyers are ready with information concerning what is available in time, talent and facilities at the various networks and stations. They know, from "track" records, which availabilities are best suited to the needs of each of their clients. Continuing studies are made of the audience composition of the various networks and stations at the various times of the day. The "reach" of the station, its programming and its community image are known. Costs are determined. Finally, time is bought on the networks and stations offering the greatest return to the advertiser. Such selections have to be as productive as possible. A random choice that does not bring results can be an open invitation to the client to take his business to a different agency.

The buyers of space and the buyers of time used to be separated into different departments in the agencies and media decisions were made by account men. Today, the buying function is carried on wherever possible by people who are specialists in all media. Rudy P. Maffei, Gardner Advertising, describes the new agency media people as "bright, aggressive, young and college trained—many of whom were, in addition, products of our fine graduate business schools." [1] The former image of the agency buyer as one who had little imagination but who relied heavily on his "horse-trading" ability and his belief in numbers has changed. The modern successful buyer is a well trained, broad-gauged professional.

The new role of the agency buyer has made new approaches necessary by the people from the stations and the networks who call on them to influence their buying decisions. For the small market stations, this function is usually performed by the station representative organizations. Whenever direct presentations are made by the station, the station manager or sales manager usually make them. Many larger market stations follow a procedure of assigning specific men from the station's sales staff to call on a list of agencies. This procedure guarantees that calls are made on a consistent and an organized basis.

Sales Manager's Relationship with Agencies

The sales manager has the important task of either calling on agencies or assigning his salesmen to make calls. An efficient sales manager soon learns the particular abilities of each of his men and what each, in turn, can accomplish at the various agencies. In both radio and television, contacts need to be maintained with large, medium and small agencies on national, regional and local levels. Some of these agencies place a high value on quality in advertising, often favoring an institutional approach. Others, largely local in nature, have little interest in the image created by their advertising. Their desires are confined to fast returns noted on the cash register. Knowing these variances at agencies the sales manager must consider the makeup of his sales staff as well as of the leading buyers and other personnel at the agencies. He needs to match his salesmen with specific agencies on the basis of the probable effectiveness those men may produce from the assignments.

The sales manager should never remove himself from selling. In addition to directing his salesmen to specific targets and working with them for improvement, he needs to call on at least some agencies regularly. Time and his station's circumstances and market conditions permitting, it is important for him to be active with at least one or two agencies so that he will not lose touch with the field. His calls also enable him to keep abreast of the problems his men confront.

After every agency call by a salesman, the sales manager should receive a report from that salesman early the following morning. Whether this is a verbal report or a briefly written statement, it is a necessary requirement so that the executive may be kept posted on progress or problems anticipated.

Through the maintenance of a month-to-month tabulation of all accounts with the various agencies, the sales manager can determine the gains or losses and strengths or weaknesses not only of each salesman but of the station in its relationship to agencies and clients.

The sales manager should also maintain relationships with those agencies that are called upon by the men of his staff. He should plan periodic trips to the major advertising centers of New York and Chicago and, whenever possible, Detroit, Los Angeles and San Francisco. These trips should be made at least once every three months. In many cases, the station's location may be such that it has within its state, or in a nearby state, a regional advertising center that generates considerable sales traffic. A personal visit by the sales manager every thirty days to all of the agencies in that market should be an all but absolute necessity. Some stations in close proximity to a major regional advertising center cover those agencies as frequently as once a week. Where this is done, rich dividends in added sales usually result.

It is perfectly in order for a salesman to call upon a national advertiser directly, but it is a cardinal sin for him to do so under any circumstance without first advising that advertiser's agency. There are times when a call on an advertiser by a station can be of great help to the agency, particularly when the sales presentation may involve a completely different approach from that which is normally pursued by the agency. In such a case, the call may bring enlightenment in the relationship between the advertiser and his agency personnel. One of the most successful selling organizations in broadcasting is that of the Avco (formerly Crosley) Broadcasting Corporation. It has not only given much consideration to discussion of sales matters directly with advertisers; it has always instructed its sales personnel to advise agency executives of this intent. In no case has a strained relationship resulted therefrom and the happy results are known to the trade.

Importance of Station Image

The image of the station conveyed to advertising agencies has assumed increased importance in the placement of spot business. With so many stations trying to make impressions on the agencies, the identification of outstanding features of any particular properties has become difficult. Station assets not found in ratings need to be communicated. Agency men are in quite general agreement that local station images are of greater importance in radio than in television due to the numbers of radio stations that make media selection more difficult. Some agencies consider station image of such importance that they employ personnel to collect as much information as possible about the various local radio and television operations in each market. They are interested in descriptions and verifications of qualities and services usually not reported. Cooperation from most stations in the gathering of such data is disappointing.

If a station wants increased spot advertising, it needs to give the agencies proof of its prestige in the community and of those characteristics which make it different, desirable or unique in a market.

Agency Problems and Progress

Contrary to what some people think, life at the agencies is not exactly a bed of orchids. Rising costs for the advertiser, increased operating expenses, the switching of agency accounts and greater emphasis on proof of performance are but a few of the problems the agencies have had to encounter in recent years.

In spite of these and other problems, and in spite of the maintenance of a traditional fifteen per cent standard commission, advertising agencies continue to grow and their billings continue to set new records each year. In 1952, BBD&O billed $40,000,000 in radio and television in what was then the highest amount for a single agency. Today, some twenty agencies exceed that figure annually and many of these bill over $100,000,000 in broadcasting.

An improvement in the agencies' service to their clients has been effected through the use of electronic computers. Analyses, media decisions and billings that formerly took weeks or months of man-labor can now be accomplished in a matter of hours. Differences between media and relative strengths of stations can be determined accurately without human guesswork. Already, the mountains of paperwork involved in the buying of spot advertising have been reduced significantly. Once the computer can be used to turn audience data into sales predictability figures, time buying will become a science or at least an activity capable of mathematical expression.

SPOT BUSINESS AND THE STATION REPRESENTATIVE

The system of station representatives, commonly called station "reps," began in 1932. Before that time, the process of representation of individual stations to national and regional advertisers and agencies was true chaos. A brokerage system prevailed, organizations or individuals often represented competing stations in the same market and general price-cutting was standard practice.

In 1932, Edward Petry started the first of the modern day station-representative firms. Petry organized his company on sound business principles and ethical practices, thus establishing high standards for the firms which were to follow. Refusing to do business with time brokers, his company instead dealt directly with station managers. Petry insisted that the one station in any market which the company selected to represent must be concerned with quality operation and fair business practices. Nationally, this made a select list of radio stations with great appeal as advertising media. From an initial list of thirteen stations in the country, Edward Petry and Company grew to the point where separate divisions are now needed for radio and television in offices located in nine metropolitan centers.

In the three years following the beginning of the Petry company, twenty-seven additional station representative companies were organized. Since 1935, there has been a steady increase in the number of national and regional "reps" in broadcasting. Table I shows their growth by five-year intervals. The total of 153 firms in 1965 was approximately evenly divided between national and regional companies. In order to qualify for designation as a *national* representative, offices have to be maintained in New York, Chicago and at least one other major market.

TABLE I [2]

GROWTH IN NUMBER OF NATIONAL AND REGIONAL STATION "REPS"

(Five-Year Periods)

Year	Total
1935	28
1940	38
1945	40
1950	66
1955	94
1960	130
1965	153

No standard commission rate exists in the station "rep" business. Rates for both radio and television vary from company to company and from station to station. Owners of several station properties have been known to get a television rate as low as five per cent while other television stations even in small markets have had to pay up to fifteen per cent in order to be represented. Some "rep" firms maintain standard rate policies but throughout the business there is no standardization. Usually, radio stations are charged more than television stations for representation.

The Sales Manager and the "Rep"

The station sales manager should work closely with his station's representative in every market where that company has an office. The sales manager must arrange for the "rep" to receive regularly all updated sales tools essential to selling the station. These materials should include program schedules with all changes noted, station brochures and routine sales presentations, and all special campaigns that are prepared for specific clients. The sales representative can be no more effective in selling the station than the data supplied by the sales department permits him to be. Unfortunately, stations do not automatically receive spot business merely by signing with a "rep" firm.

The sales manager regularly has to agitate the representative organization, particularly in the case of those firms—and there are a number of them—that do not show much aggressiveness or industry. A wide variance in initiative exists among the "rep" organizations. Some of them work almost around the clock to obtain business for the stations on their lists. In those cases, the station sales managers contribute considerable energy to keep these sales entities supplied with data and give them maximum assistance. There are other station representative organizations that hardly extend themselves beyond an occasional "strike." Indeed, all too many are found in this category. It is difficult to have respect for those "rep" firms and their salesmen who get their business by sitting at their desks or at the closest, most comfortable bar awaiting agency calls for availabilities.

There is some cause for optimism in a recently expressed concern of many of the station representative companies for more station integrity in the use of their rate cards and for less expediency in selling. It should be noted, however, that off-the-card deals are made regularly by some "reps" who care little if anything about the image or the reputation of the stations they represent.

The sales manager should insist upon a weekly call report from each of the offices of the station's representative. A sales manager who does not have this control over the station's "rep" does not truly manage station sales and is derelict in his obligation to top management. With these weekly reports, he can remain current on all national sales activity, he is able to compare the monthly and annual performance of the "rep" for the station and he can analyze the station's overall ability to continue successful relationships with an agency and its clients.

Station representatives now provide services to television stations by recommending which syndicated films to purchase. The pairing of the right film purchases with the right advertiser can often result in added national spot business for a station. In these decisions, the "reps" can play an important role because of their knowledge of client desires and their accumulated data on the kinds of film packages available. Most of them maintain "track records" or ratings of the various off-network re-runs in several markets. This information is made available to the stations they represent.

Reliance of stations on Sales Representative Companies

With some disquiet, we note a substantial amount of reliance by station managers and sales managers on their station representatives for management advice having nothing to do with sales. In too many cases, the "reps" have, in effect, become station consultants without fees for extra services. It may seem absurd but it is today possible for a man to "manage" a radio or television station practically in name only. When problems arise, he has only to turn to his station "rep." There he may get answers to most of the problems that he is unable or unwilling to attempt to confront. *Broadcasting* magazine reported that reliance on the station representative "has already reached the point where many stations hesitate to buy a duplicating machine or paint the office without at least mentioning it to their reps." [3] Incredible "authority" and responsibility, thus given to sales representatives by some stations, results in a transfer of a great deal of policy control from the station manager to the "rep's" president, board chairman or operations head. This sort of referral has led to some poor decisions, damaging to individual stations and harmful to the total industry.

We are not criticizing the involvement of a "rep" firm in occasional discussions pertaining to broad station policy, past, present or future. Nor do we advocate that the station representative should absent itself from all sales promotion and sales development plans of the station. This would be sheer folly. But the willful or witless transfer of a manager's basic responsibilities to an absentee station "rep" is inexcusable. It is one of the reasons for so many cases of lackluster performance by certain stations and by some sales representative organizations as well.

We have discussed here the overall role of the station representative and we have been critical of some practices, but it should be made crystal-clear that the good sales representative firms, and there are some that are truly outstanding, have made profound contributions to the development of the radio and television arts. The negatives to which we have addressed ourselves originate usually not from desires of the representative organization, but from the ineptness of ill-trained, ill-prepared station management. There are too many men and women in capacities of authority in radio and television management who lack the slightest idea of proper management of a broadcast property. Thus, the "rep" becomes a "crutch."

Self-Representation

At the opposite pole from those stations, which have become over-reliant on the station "reps," are other stations that have terminated all relations with their national sales representative companies. Starting in 1959, a few stations began to represent themselves exclusively. Today, the stations securing national spot business without the use of station "reps," account for approximately $200,000,000 in national spot billings. This is almost one-third of the total for the radio and television industry. The trend toward self-representation has an interesting background.

In August, 1959, the FCC finalized an order requiring the networks to stop selling spot time for stations which they did not own. ABC had discontinued its spot representation division in 1952, but NBC and CBS were still in the business of representing stations. Under the FCC order, the networks could continue to represent their "o to o" (owned and operated) stations, but they had to drop all other stations from representation. The order affected thirteen stations.

Although self-representation has for the most part been confined to group-owned stations, there have been a few cases where other stations have joined the groups for purposes of representation rather than continue with their independent station "rep" organizations.

It is anyone's guess how far the trend toward self-representation may go. Evidently, it is here to stay. The size of the billings of the self-represented stations indicates that they have been able to get their share of agency and advertiser attention.

The regional representatives seem to be largely unaffected by the trend to self-representation. Their billings, of course, are considerably less but so are their overhead costs. Some regional representative companies bill as little as $250,000 a year. Others bill one to two million dollars annually.

Spot Sales

How does a buyer in an agency determine the differences between stations in those markets where there are fifteen to twenty facilities? Does the small market station have a chance at influencing the agency buyer?

With so many stations, it is difficult to make intelligent differentiations among them. Undoubtedly, there have been cases in which more logical purchases might have been made. In partial explanation, agency time buyers and station "reps" have consistently complained about the lack of standard data from the local stations. Much station sales data are poorly organized and reveals little of importance to aid buying decisions.

Competitive print, outdoor and direct-mail media supply useful demographic information. With computers now playing an increasingly important role in media and station selection, stations will have to supply their representatives and advertising agencies with information comparable to that submitted by the other media and on a regular basis. Otherwise, they will not only fail to gain but they may lose spot revenues as a source of income.

It has been said again and again, and correctly, that radio has been undersold and that its force in advertising has never truly been realized. Files are, or could be, filled with radio's success stories. Still the medium has never achieved its fair share of the advertising dollar. It has never really been properly sold. It will not sell itself.

Complete data on audience compositions at various hours of the day, broken down demographically, and opinions of audiences and advertisers regarding the station's service, contain basic information for those who have the power to spend the national advertiser's budget. Apparently, the gathering of such material and its preparation in meaningful form has been, and may continue to be, too much work for some stations to undertake, or else their managers do not understand the very basics of station operation.

It is time for station managers to realize that exaggerated statements about station effectiveness impress very few people who count. Such distortions really hurt the station in terms of its long-range income possibilities. There is no substitute for fact. One would think that managers of stations would realize this truism. Some of them persist in the use of half-truths and, sometimes, downright untruths. This is bad for the industry. It is deplorable that the same executives seem to believe that their claims are accepted.

Far too much internal warfare vexes the radio medium. Stations fight other stations in their markets. Although there is sufficient potential business for all stations, infighting too often results in losses of revenue for every station in the area. Radio management must somehow learn that the industry needs to improve in its ability to attract advertising money from other media, not just from other (and rival) radio stations. With the increase in the number of television stations in most market areas, similar conditions may prevail in the newer medium.

Consideration must be given to benefits to be derived from cooperative preparations of key data on a state wide basis or, in the cases of the multi-station markets, a city wide basis. Many small businessmen in broadcasting will benefit from this kind of federation. They *must* cooperate if they expect to compete in the spot market against the large corporations who are after the same dollars.

The crux of the matter is a realistic and honest appraisal of exactly what the individual station can do for specific advertisers. Once the station representatives and agencies can get this information regularly and know they can rely on it, the station will be in a good position to receive the spot accounts it deserves.

The data are a necessary supplement to, but no replacement for, effective personalized selling. Every station needs to campaign vigorously and steadily at the agencies and with the "reps" in order to achieve its goals.

Is there to be a crisis in national spot radio? Some agencies, admittedly the smaller ones so far, do not recommend spot radio to their clients. Salesmen from radio stations have not been given a very warm reception at some agencies for some time. Agency personnel have been critical of the presentations made by radio's salesmen, saying that they showed little understanding of the problems of specific advertisers, that they used valuable time to try to put other radio or television stations in a bad light, that they were so full of unproved claims that their sales arguments were meaningless.

Agencies complain about violations by some radio stations of the unwritten rule against calling on advertisers directly. Agency buyers have reported publicly that the salesmen from many radio stations are not as effective as those from television stations. Some of those agencies insist that radio salesmen appear to consider themselves in a training phase for later employment as television salesmen. The latter probably manifests itself in circumstances under which joint top management of a radio-and-television mutually owned broadcast entity fails to operate its properties independently or favors television over radio. It is incredible to see the number of major broadcast companies whose executives in top management fail to give more than passive consideration to radio. These men create their own problems.

Unfortunately, the use of a double-rate system by many radio and television stations tends to confuse, rather than to construct. The frequent usage in station presentations of negative remarks about other radio or television facilities, plus inflated claims about the salesman's own station, have caused some agency buyers to reject the stations which those salesmen so poorly represent.

Is there already a crisis in national spot radio? Very clearly, there is for some stations. But there is much "gold in them hills" in national radio spot schedules and, obviously, some stations are getting it.

A Caution

That there could be dangers of complacency due to progress and prosperity hardly needs to be mentioned. Competition on both the national and the local levels from other media does not stand still. In the national spot market and to a considerable extent in the local field, television and radio are competitive and must often sell against each other as well as against the other advertising media. There are advantages in a rising curve of business in the broadcasting industry but there are also dangers, one of which is the rising cost spiral which accompanies the increased income. In a later chapter of this book, we discuss the management of income and expenses in order to produce profit. For the moment, we should be aware that the figures on revenue show only one aspect of the financial picture. It is an important aspect, of course, for without a healthy income all else in commercial broadcasting could be written off as futile.

Still another danger is masked in a regularly ascending curve of income. Extra effort may not be expended to maintain and to increase rising revenues. Such increased effort is necessary in order to offset added costs. The condition calls for more energetic and more creative selling by the local-station salesmen, by the station representatives, by the agencies and the networks and by the industry sales promotion organizations, the Radio Advertising Bureau and the Television Bureau of Advertising. The chief foe of progress is—it must always be remembered—not competition, but complacency.

8

Local Sales

He who whispers down a well
About the goods he has to sell,
Will never reap the golden dollars
Like him who shows them round and hollers.

—ANON.

WE HAVE ALREADY noted that, in the case of radio, local sales constitute the largest source of income. We have also noted that in television the revenue from local sales runs behind both network and spot in total national figures. Yet, the average amount of local sales per television station is considerably higher than the average amount per radio station. The competition of the greater number of radio stations and the higher rates of television stations are two factors in the differential.

The number of salesmen per radio station is, on the average, less than the number employed by a television stations, but the income for a salesman of local advertising, whether in radio or television, can be attractively high. Other than starring roles for top performers, the sales department offers higher individual incomes than any of the other departments of a station. The most usual route to station management is through sales experience in broadcasting.

Certain definite advantages pertain to a choice of sales as a career: (1) In any industry, comparable grades of professional status are usually better paid in sales than in any other department; (2) The work of the salesmen brings constantly changing challenges; (3) The opportunities to learn human nature are boundless; (4) The good salesman need not worry about a job since there are always more positions open in sales than in most lines of endeavor; and, (5) The man who travels about meeting other people learns of opportunities that never come to the attention of the person who works with the same people day after day.

In spite of both immediate and long-range opportunities in sales, it is

149

more difficult to find good salesmen than it is to find most other kinds of broadcasting personnel. Usually, there is a surplus of applicants for most other station positions, but almost always a scarcity of people who want to sell. With the existent opportunities in sales, the field should have greater appeal than it has.

All of this should suggest advantages in the choice of a sales career by young persons of college grade. In radio-television, there are plenty of openings for the right people and there should be many opportunities for advancement.

We stress the "right people" because we are convinced that nothing can be worst than frustrations experienced in this field by those who are not by nature inclined toward a sales career. No one should ever go into sales work motivated exclusively by the money rewards. He must like to sell or he will be a failure before he starts.

SELECTION OF A STATION SALES STAFF

In view of the current shortage of candidates for sales work, one of the most difficult tasks of the sales manager is to find and select people for new or replacement positions on his staff. The responsibility is doubly important because wrong choices can be extremely costly. Losses to the station caused by the enraged client or by the broken contracts are too imponderable to try to estimate. The employment of good salesmen can result in higher income for the station and excellent relationships with clients.

Since promising sales candidates are in short supply, the selection process should not be conducted haphazardly. Personnel people are in agreement that the essentials in selection are: (1) a well defined job analysis in writing; (2) some valid testing procedures and (3) a good, intensive interview. The tendancy to employ on the basis of any single convincing physical, mental or personality trait should be avoided.

Before hiring any experienced salesman, his past record should be given prime consideration. If he has been successful in sales in the past, the chances are that he will be successful in the future; if he has been a consistent failure in the past, the odds against his success are usually too great for a canny gamble. A successful sales record in a field other than broadcasting may or may not be an indication of success in radio or television. If the man has been successful in the selling of intangibles, his chances of doing well in broadcasting may be better than one who has sold tangible merchandise. Any change to broadcasting from sales experience in a different field will require a considerable amount of time for indoctrination and adjustment.

The inexperienced person should not be ruled out as a possibility. This would be a foolish rejection of some people who have excellent long range potentials. These people need to be given careful training and supervision.

They should not be expected to produce significant results for some time after their initial employment. Given the patience, encouragement and understanding they should have, they can develop into some of the best salesmen the station can employ. Most of them will be highly appreciative of the time devoted to their development and this will be shown in the surprising amount of business they will later produce. It should be recalled that the most successful salesmen once had to be given that initial start by someone.

The interviewer should look for evidences of an extroverted personality, a high degree of intelligence, a gregarious nature, signs of perseverance, an ability to get along with people, a good appearance, correct manners, sincerity, a true interest in sales and, frankly, a strong desire to make money.

Two researchers, Charles F. Haner and Givens L. Thornton, were intrigued by the problem of trying to discover what behavior traits seemed to distinguish successful from unsuccessful salesmen with four medium sized companies.[1] While their findings might or might not apply in the case of radio and television salesmen, there could be a strong possibility of an important carryover. Haner and Thornton found that, of several hundred behavior traits analyzed, the most important in distinguishing between good and poor salesmen was the willingness of the salesman to study the needs of the customer on a careful and detailed basis. The next most important trait was the ability of the salesman to set goals and quotas for himself which he was willing to follow. Other factors, in order of their importance were: keeping the customers informed, persistence, analysis of the sales effort, knowledge of the competition, keeping the company informed and coverage of the territory. Those factors *least* valuable in distinguishing between the good and the poor salesman were: social activities, drinking habits, personal traits, home life and group activities. In summary, job oriented behavior traits were of highest importance; personal and social traits were of lesser importance.

The truly effective, truly successful salesman in broadcasting is the one who, after convincing his clients to use his station's facilities, follows through and makes sure that sales results happen which please the clients. Nothing is more desirable in sales than long term salesman client relationships.

THE SALES MANAGER AND THE SALES STAFF

Bases for Assigning Salesman's Accounts

Several factors need to be considered before assigning a salesman to the accounts on his list. His knowledge of certain retailer's stores, an understanding of the particular problems of a specific kind of business and the salesman's previous experience in dealing with certain types of retailers are all important considerations. Most important, though, is the salesman's probability of compatible relationships with the accounts. The sales manager needs to use his best judgment in the matching of salesman and client according to their temperaments, their interests and their probable general rapport. The compatibility of the salesman should determine the length of time he remains assigned to each account.

Choice station accounts are usually assigned either on a basis of seniority or successful sales experience. A younger, less experienced member of the station sales staff should be prepared to build his initial list into lucrative accounts by providing excellent service to his clients after they are sold. Accounts, of course, should not be transferred once a good relationship has been established, unless there is no alternative.

It takes a good salesman, with plenty of patience and a thorough training in radio or television, to get on a conversational basis with many of the people who are assigned advertising and buying positions with retail establishments. Some store buyers and advertising managers seem to favor the print media so exclusively that one suspects that they have ink in their veins. Unfortunately for the salesman of broadcasting, retail management listens to those buyers and advertising managers.

Radio-television salesmen assigned to such contacts should have backgrounds of experience or training in retailing as well as in the broadcasting media. They need to be able to talk the language of those who are engaged in every conceivable category of retail sales. Here a lack of merchandising know-how can be disastrous. It has been estimated that not one salesman in ten can qualify for selling the typical resistant retail establishment because the typical broadcast-media man cannot talk with the retailer intelligently about his particular business and suggest solutions for his more important problems. Nor do more than a few broadcasters understand any media except broadcasting.

Store managers, as well as buyers and advertising managers, feel comfortable with the printed ad. They can look at it, admire it and show it to their co-op people. It is a tangible; broadcasting is not. The salesman will not make headway with these men by attacking their use of the print media. Radio and television are so strong and have such an enviable success record in advertising for all categories of retailers that the positive sell is the one and only route to take. We must admit as broadcasters that newspapers will always be the basic buys for some retailers because of the nature of their fields. But these same retailers can gain much additional business through their intelligent supplementary use of radio and television. There is no profit in denunciation and derogation.

It is the place of the broadcast salesman to make the client feel comfortable in the presence of *his* kind of advertising and to show how profits can be made from its use. It is his job to bring them to an open mind about radio and/or television.

Staff Sales Conferences and Reports

The sales manager should hold daily sales conferences with the members of his sales staff. Early each morning he should meet with them to check their contacts of the preceding day. In these meetings, strategies may be worked out for that day in line with existent availabilities.

Each Monday morning, the sales manager should get individual reports from his salesmen that recapitulate their activities and reflect their work of the previous week. On the basis of these reports, the sales manager is able to spot troublesome cases where it may be advisable for him to assist a salesman with the client. Sometimes, in cases where talent is involved in a potential sale, the sales manager may decide that a follow-up presentation involving the participation of that talent may help a salesman to clinch a sale.

At least four times each year, half-day or day-long meetings should be held, perhaps on week-ends, to engage in long range planning. Representatives of the program department and the station "rep" should attend these sessions along with the sales staff. Outside consultants may also be included.

The sales manager should keep records in his office of each salesman's performance with his clients and with the agencies to which he is assigned. Regular reports of progress should be prepared for the station manager. These are not, it should be added, exercises in paperwork. They are supplementary to brainwork.

Sales Quotas

It is the sales manager's responsibility to set sales quotas. By making realistic evaluations of each salesman's list of clients and/or agencies, proper quotas can be established. These, however, cannot be rigid expectations. Many of the advertising budgets of the large retailers, particularly the department stores and the supermarkets, emphasize print media almost exclusively. The newspapers run page after page of advertisements every day for these stores while radio and television settle for a few spot commercials.

How can the local station increase its share of that retail advertising? What kind of work, determination, enterprise and imagination does it take?

We have already noted that it is imperative that a radio or television station story be supplied to the station's "rep" in order to increase the chances of attracting the investments of national and regional advertisers. That same story, with chapters regularly updated, should be used as a selling tool for the local advertiser.

The station master sales plan should be made up of basic information covering the strength of the station, circulationwise, its image in the community and within the industry and, finally, its success stories. It should include descriptions of the facilities and the special equipment which enable the station to perform its services efficiently. It should relate, in detail, the program and production repertory of the station, including whatever live talent is available and, in the case of television, the film library. If merchandising services are provided, these should be mentioned. Added to this general sales material, special applications should be included which are designed specifically for each individual advertiser.

In local sales, the uses of the data differ from the manner in which the materials are used on the national scene. Locally, the contacts are more direct and more personal. Very few deals are closed over the telephone.

Local selling involves men calling on men they have called on many times before. Tailor-made presentations and specially constructed commercials or programs must be designed to meet special needs of specific merchants.

The local salesman in radio or television used to rely on the power of his media to make good on his promises to the retailer. Today's salesman knows that there is no magic in a broadcast campaign unless it is targeted to a particular client's needs and objectives. The modern salesman becomes as interested in helping the advertiser to grow and prosper as he is in his commission from his sales efforts. In a way, the modern broadcast salesman works as much for his clients as he does for his station.

If he is truly an authority in retailing, he should be able to make suggestions which not only will surprise the merchant but can make the salesman's counsel so valuable that the businessman will come to depend upon him for ideas. The retail-oriented salesman—and he'd better be—will know that the advertising he can supply will be successful only if the store is modern in its services, its facilities and its customer conveniences. The salesman should be able to show the retailer how to accomplish that modernization.

So the station's local sales representatives, its salesmen, must be experts in helping the retailer to grow. The advertising on radio or television is but one service which the salesman must be privileged to provide.

The Salesman's Preparation for the Sale

Before a presentation is made to any local retailer, the salesman should make a study of that firm's past and current experiences in all forms of advertising and of its business successes in general. The field in which the retailer does business should be carefully studied by the salesman so that he will be able to converse intelligently on the prospective advertiser's interests and problems.

Such study will disclose, for example, that the problems of the owner of a shoe store are completely different from those of the owner of a jewelry store, say, in the month of April. The salesman will discover what the peak business months in the year are for such other enterprises as grocery stores, hardware stores and drugstores. Seasonal fluctuations that differ within various retail categories need to be known if the salesman is to make the right sales calls at the right times.

In order to talk to the point in his presentation, the salesman needs to know the retailing methods of any specific client. Patterns of store traffic, uses of merchandise displays, the personalities of store clerks, the conveniences and services of the store and the kinds and quality of merchandise must be studied carefully.

The basis of all effective selling to local retailers is complete information about each specific prospect or client and his business. No one, regardless of his background or experience can be fully effective without pertinent knowledge. Studies of local retail establishments should include research into other local retail firms and those in other markets in the same category. For example, in the case of men's clothing stores, the salesman needs to know the problems of a particular store but he also needs to be thoroughly familiar with the men's clothing industry. A salesman calling on a men's-wear establishment should be well acquainted with the current ads in such publications as *Gentleman's Quarterly, Esquire* and the leading sports publications. Additionally, he should study the trade publications for the men's-wear field. Such sources of information exist for every kind of retail establishment and they are available in most large libraries.

Most radio and television salesmen have not taken the time to do their homework in the various trade publications of each retail category or they haven't known how to make that preparation. The more a salesman for radio or television knows about a retailer and his particular business category, the more successful he can be in helping to move his merchandise. This, as we have said before, must be the first objective of any good radio or television salesman.

One of many reasons why radio and television stations have not garnered their fair share of department store advertising is that their salesmen have not understood the advanced planning of store buyers, merchandisers and advertising personnel. Time and time again, we have witnessed stations spending vast sums of money for beautiful presentations to department stores six or eight weeks before the Christmas shopping season. The advertising budget for that particular store probably was established in the first quarter of the year, if not early in the last quarter of the previous year. Advertising plans in most department stores and in many retail establishments are finalized six months or more in advance of their actual campaigns. This is especially true in the case of seasonal types of advertising where certain lines of merchandise have a consumer demand for a brief period of time. If the salesman from the station makes his calls after the advertising budget has been allocated for the year he simply wastes his time. Incidentally, some long term business relationships between broadcasters and retailers have been formed by salesmen who anticipated store decisions on seasonal merchandise. The success of those short term contracts has resulted in year-round advertising by those stores on radio and television stations.

Every retailer who is engaged in a bona-fide business and who practices ethically is a prospect for radio and television. The prospect potential is almost unlimited in any market, regardless of its size. In most markets, however, and especially the larger ones that include both radio and television stations, leading retailers can be persuaded to use the broadcast media only when specific campaigns are prepared especially for them. A substantial revision in this pattern is beginning to manifest itself in some major markets.

In a small upper Michigan community, which has several radio stations, one broadcasting property boasts 101 local accounts out of 116 firms in the community. The business ranges all the way from an institutional-type show for an iron mining company to time signals for a shoe repair establishment. This is no accident.

THE SALES PRESENTATION

Few sales are made in one call. It is not unusual for a salesman to average five to six calls on a retailer, large or small, before an initial sale is consummated. Much that we will have to say about *the* sales presentation really applies to a succession of visits by the salesman.

If the retailer has an agency, no matter how small and how inexperienced it may be in the use of broadcast media, that agency should be consulted before a presentation is made. There may be a resistance on the part of many of the smaller agencies to the possible use of radio and television for their clients. Whenever this happens, it is both fitting and proper for the salesman to take his case directly to the client, explaining his intent in advance, of course, to the agency. Regardless of the attitude of the agency toward broadcasting, whether cooperative or reluctant, the station should and must have a contact with the client. The person who is contacted for the client should be the same individual, who would have been consulted had there been no agency involved. He may be the advertising manager, the head buyer or the owner-manager of a retail establishment.

In calls on retail establishments, the salesman must first sell the merits of his medium to the client. He must also sell a concept that the present advertising policy of the establishment can be improved upon and that increased sales will result. After selling his medium and his concept, the radio or television salesman must then demonstrate how the station's programming, geared as it is to the community, can be helpful in reaching the retailer's present and potential customers.

The station's coverage, its circulation and its audience composition should be shown in the sales presentation. The salesman must point out the availabilities which can do the most for the client and explain why.

The retailer needs every bit of service, advice and guidance that the salesman can give him, particularly if he is a neophyte in the use of the broadcast media.

It is a good service to the retailer to furnish him with information on the tools used by similar business establishments which employ radio and television in other cities. The Radio Advertising Bureau and the Television Bureau of Advertising have large inventories of such success stories. Of course, evidences of local successes have motivated many a non-user of radio and television to enter broadcasting.

Any salesman will find that his initial presentation is made much more effective through the use of audio tapes, films or slides. These selling aids should first of all demonstrate the impact of his medium and then, with actual commercial samples produced specifically for the store, illustrate what can be done for the respective departments and for the store in general through the use of the station.

Most large stations own broadcasting industry presentations on audio tape or on film or slides. These stations then add specific information about their own radio or television operations. Such presentations are effective; in fact, it is doubtful whether many major department stores would have given serious consideration to the use of radio or television without them.

In the smaller stations where elaborate production facilities do not exist, TvB or RAB can be of major assistance in supplying films, slides and audio tapes. Any station, no matter how small, should prepare its own supplements for each prospective client. Salesmen who have had the benefit of training or experience in radio or television production can be particularly valuable in this preparation.

A tour of the station's facilities, even if it is a small operation, can be very useful in explaining the station to the client. If conducted properly, it can make a strong impression on one who is not acquainted with the workings of a broadcasting station.

If "name" talent is being considered in the retailer's campaign, there should be an opportunity for the merchant to meet that talent. Such a meeting can be arranged during one of the sales talks with the client or at a luncheon or dinner. In most cases, it is advisable to recommend air personalities to large retailers because sponsored talent can be made available for store events or sales meetings and can be an added promotion factor for the store.

It may be noted that we have said nothing about the use of ratings in the sales presentation. Unless a station is completely dominant in its market, its ratings will not be as important in making a sale as some broadcasters think they are. Most local retailers have a very modest amount of interest in a station's rating service. Their audience index is the cash register a day or two following the start of an advertising schedule.

Local Sponsorship of Programs vs. Spot Announcements

Throughout the development of radio, sponsorship in the aural medium was largely by program segments. This was extremely effective for both local and national accounts because it permitted the closest possible tie between a sponsor and a program vehicle. Whether it was Jack Benny for Jello or the late Pierre Andre on *Captain Midnight* for Ovaltine, the bridge of sponsorship made an indelible mark on the consumer. Television began with program sponsorship only to see the shift to more spot announcement concentration as costs of television mounted and as smaller or specialized advertisers (both national and local) began to use the new medium.

We have long been of the opinion that a retailer gains much more in his home community through program sponsorship on radio and/or television rather than by the use of spot announcements. We are not arguing against the merits of announcements in terms of their sales pull; we are talking in terms of getting an audience reaction that will stimulate the community to express its response to a specific program. These reactions give store management an opportunity for correspondence with those consumers who may write letters. It also gives the management of the store, along with his buyers and other key personnel, further proof of the intimacy and effectiveness of radio and television. We have not noticed many letters that come to stations commenting on spot schedules or spot announcements.

An outstanding example of successful use of programming is the experience of Oak Park Federal Savings and Loan, formerly a one office establishment in a large western suburb of Chicago, which purchased Chicago Cubs' radio play-by-play over WGN ten years ago and has renewed each successive year. Baseball sponsorship doubled the growth pattern for the firm. The total resources of the company grew from $70,000,000 to $140,-000,000 in a five-year period.

It would seem that in both radio and television, the purchase of some programming is essential, especially if the vehicle involved is one that can reflect genuine credit beyond its basic entertainment or service value to the client. This applies generally to sports, news and programs featuring good music. Listeners and viewers go out of their way to buy well sponsored products and services.

In some cases, it may be best to recommend institutional campaigns. Such is the case with the spot schedule of Carson, Pirie Scott & Co. on some Chicago stations. Other than for particular sale periods, such as end-of-month clearances, back-to-school campaigns and pre-Christmas sales, Carsons devotes a very considerable amount of money throughout the year to promote its quality of service, conveniences for its customers, news about the expansion of various departments, additional stores added to its chain, etc. Here, of course, the client is most interested in the type of audience the messages will reach. In the case of Carsons, or any major retailer, obviously the people at the store and its agency want to know the reputation of the station and its impact on the community before a purchase of advertising is made.

Spot announcements can often be more effective over a given period of time on radio than on television, assuming, of course, that the right stations are bought. This is because radio is still very much a habit medium. Listeners tune in their favorite radio station in the morning and remain tuned all day,whether at home, in the car or on the beach. Television does not yet enjoy that kind of habitual audience. The television viewer is interested in *programs* and he tunes to the station that has the particular show he or she desires at a certain hour. Thus changing audience composition is important. The station or the agency that fails to take change into account is not honest with itself or with its advertisers.

There are no hard and fast rules for commercial schedules. Spots can be very effective movers of some merchandise and services. They can be good reminder copy. On the other hand, for some big-ticket items, spots alone without program backing may prove ineffective.

Some advertisers have soundly combined spot and program buys. The astute advertising manager of the Kitchens of Sara Lee designed a dual buy of network specials *plus* spot announcements on local television. On the network, Sara Lee is thus able to focus attention on its quality line through its selection of quality programs. The company sustains this major impact with a well balanced local spot schedule. This is good advertising!

Maxwell House Coffee elected to make a similar move but chose to concentrate on local stations where prestige program vehicles were available. The series, "Great Music," was bought originally on WGN–TV. The Maxwell House agency, Ogilvy, Benson & Mather, wanted the client identified with the community through the sponsorship of a distinguished musical offering. While the audience was small in size, it was quality in every respect. As a result, the endorsement of Maxwell House Coffee by the viewers was solid. In Los Angeles, Maxwell House made similar moves to buy documentaries on a city's problems, and the sponsorship of those specials was supported with good spot buys.

FOLLOW-UP ACTIONS AFTER THE SALE

Some salesmen resent the job of servicing a sale after it is made. These men would rather close a sale, forget about it and get started on another prospect. Such an attitude runs counter to the purposes of selling. As we have said, the object of the sale in the first place is to perform a real service for the client. If the campaign is not successful, it will take more effort to get the advertiser back on the air than it did to sell him in the first place.

While it is true that the servicing of accounts does not place immediate dollars in the salesman's pockets, in the long run he stands to gain by it. The salesman interested only in his immediate financial gain is not really interested in what advertising can do for the buyer. His selling methods can offset the very sales claims that the station makes. His quick gain can be a long-time station loss.

Traffic and Continuity

Two indispensable units of any station in client service are traffic and continuity.

Traffic is the very heart of the operating organization. Its primary responsibility is the preparation of the daily log showing all program and commercial placements minute by minute throughout each day. The people in traffic check for commercial separation of similar products, usually keeping two brand names for the same kind of product at least ten minutes (the better stations allow fifteen minutes) apart in the schedule. Traffic, at most stations, also prepares the weekly shift of assignments for all announcers and, in some cases, the assignment of turntable operators and even engineers, in unusual situations. The rate of the traffic department varies, of course, depending upon the size of the operation and whether or not a network affiliation is involved.

Continuity, in addition to the writing of copy for the station, often is assigned the responsibility for the rewriting of agency or client copy for better air presentation. The checking to the station's standards is another duty of those who work in continuity.

Before a salesman makes any call on a client, he needs to check with the traffic unit at the station to learn what availabilities exist in the schedule for the immediate and long-range future. This is his only assurance that what he may sell will be placed on the station at specific times of the day. If he makes a sale, he must inform the traffic unit immediately so that the blocks of time which have been sold may be removed from the availabilities list.

As soon as a sale is made, full information on all details of the contract must be supplied to the traffic department. Then requisition orders are made out and circulated to all units of the station affected by the filling of the order.

Once a sale has been made and reported, much work needs to be done before the campaign goes on the air. Format scripts may need to be written, preliminary production plans need to be formulated, art work, slides and film arrangements need to be made.

In the case of client or agency supplied copy, adequate time must be provided for the filing of that copy in order for it to be processed prior to air time. Most stations have found that a forty-eight hour deadline before air use of all copy, either audio or video, works best. In some cases, with certain retail establishments, this time has to be shortened in order to meet the competition from other media. Some daily general circulation newspapers and some shoppers' guides have as little as an eighteen-hour deadline on copy in advance of publication. In general, however, after a retailer has used a broadcast facility for a period of time, it is not too difficult to get him to comply with a forty-eight hour deadline on all of his station copy.

Servicing the Sale

Between the closing of a sale and the beginning of its schedule on the station, the salesman needs to maintain his contact with the client. Normally, the nature of the contacts is left to the discretion of the salesman but he should be encouraged by the sales manager to use budgeted funds for this purpose. Luncheon dates or tickets to sports events or other entertainments favored by the client are two of many possible ways to let the new advertiser know that the station is appreciative of his business. Telephone calls from the salesman, the sales manager and, in the case of large accounts, from the station manager help to keep a working relationship established during this interim period. Of course, regular contacts should continue to be maintained throughout the duration of the contract.

Once the advertising campaign begins on the station, the local client may begin to look for almost immediate results. There is no single conclusive yardstick of measurement of the effectiveness of radio and television advertising. It is the duty of the salesman to use every method available to evaluate the success of the campaign. Such measurement should begin as soon as the advertising starts and should be continuous thereafter.

The client will expect to measure the results of his advertising by noting an increase in sales. Even though there are other measures of success that could be equally important to his business in the long run, the salesman must be alert to actual sales results. If they should not develop as had been planned, adjustments may be necessary. The program or spots may need to be placed in different time periods. The commercial copy may need revision. In some cases, air personnel involved in the advertising may need to be replaced.

In any case, a regular relationship needs to be maintained between the salesman and the client. The advertiser should feel that the radio and/or television operation is his working ally in helping to build his business, his consumer strength and his image in the area. Many stations and salesmen have done just that. There are cases where outstanding salesmen, dedicated to their clients' welfare, have won so much respect that they have been rewarded for their effectiveness in helping to make the enterprise successful. Some retail stores have even held bargain days in honor of a radio or a television salesman or a station sales manager or station manager. This practice, if carried too far, can discredit station personnel because of unfavorable reactions among competitors in the same field who also advertise on the station. On the other hand, it is a token of appreciation, affection and respect and it can hardly be ignored by the business community.

All billings and collections should be the duty of the accounting unit of the station. The assignment of the collection of overdue accounts to salesmen, a common practice at some stations, should be avoided. A salesman should be employed to sell and his time should be so valuable in that assignment that it should be an extreme waste for him to engage in bill collecting.

ANNOUNCER-SALESMAN COMBINATIONS

Announcer-salesman combinations can be effective in small markets. In fact, they are employed in some of the larger cities of the nation but the announcers (or other talent) do not usually bear the combination title. Even a neophyte as an announcer in a small town is somewhat of a celebrity within the coverage area of his station. He becomes a familiar name in homes throughout the trade area. Small town merchants, especially those new to the use of radio and television, are frequently motivated more rapidly by sales visits from announcers than from other members of the selling staff because they are better known in the community.

Many small stations have only a modest amount of assistance in continuity and production to offer a retailer. Once an announcer who doubles in sales gets to know a client very well, he can be entrusted with the writing and the production of that client's commercials and the servicing of the account.

Announcers who sell should visit their clients' stores often in order to become thoroughly acquainted with the merchandise. Then they can be true sales representatives of the stores when they present the commercials over the air. The announcer-salesman can be useful, too, in store promotions.

LEGITIMATE COMPLAINTS OF SALESMEN

A salesman has a legitimate complaint when availability schedules are not ready, when his client's copy is revised without his knowledge, when the rating reports are not delivered on time. Such procedures can be costly to him in sales commissions and reputation.

An efficient broadcasting organization must have complete cooperation between sales and continuity-acceptance units. The latter office should be instructed never to contact a client or an agency, local or national, without first clearing with the salesman on the account and with the sales manager. There is nothing more disturbing to a salesman than to discover that other people at the station have established relationships with one of his clients without his knowledge. Such action causes confusion, ill will and, in the final analysis, results in inept handling of the account.

Another legitimate complaint of salesmen is the implementation of new corporate sales policy without their prior knowledge. Policy changes affecting the sales department should be made only after each of the salesmen has been consulted.

Salesmen also have legitimate cause for complaint when people in other departments of the station show little if any interest in the work of the sales staff. The station manager must make sure that every employee understands how sales are made and how accounts are kept or lost.

Compensation Plans for Salesmen

Salesmen, unlike sales managers, are not usually paid on a straight salary basis. Most stations use a method of salary plus commission for their compensation. The next most widely used method is the straight commission plan. Market size does not seem to be a factor in the choice of compensation systems for station salesmen. Most commissions are paid after billings. A few are paid after a logged account is aired. Some are not paid until after collections.

Rates and Rate Increases

In any review of a considerable list of radio and television properties across the country, one will find few stations that are overpriced. Most of them are *underpriced*.

Veteran broadcasters recall the low radio rates in the late 1930s, when sponsors were "waiting in line" to buy time and programs. There were some great stations of that era with costs-per-thousand of less than ten cents. Yet the ownership and management of those stations were reluctant to increase their rates and, when they did, the increases were not very significant. This practice has persisted to the present. Industry wide today, radio stations are much under priced for the services they deliver and television stations are even more so.

While, in small markets, there is, admittedly, some justification for both a local and a national rate, the time will have to come when every station in radio and television, regardless of size and type of market, will have a single rate structure. This change will be absolutely essential if broadcasting is to reflect its true maturity as an industry.

These are unpleasant matters to discuss. Yet some expedient station operators have not only had a double rate structure but have had various departures from it to satisfy certain clients, distributors, jobbers and brokers. The double billing practice is perhaps as vicious as any development in the history of commercial broadcasting and it has harmed the industry greatly. The practice has been especially harmful to radio stations as many national accounts have thereby become prejudiced against the medium.

Another station practice which the "reps" deplore is the bartering of goods and services. Although much of the bartering is a highly secretive transaction, it has been estimated that the practice accounts for a probable $35,000,000 annually. It is not confined to the lower-income stations but is a familiar practice in most, if not all, markets.

The barter transaction involves the trading of station time for goods and services instead of money. The usual commodities are merchandise for station contests, studio and office equipment, travel and hotel or motel accommodations.

So long as the arrangements are made on a straight trade out deal between the station and the advertiser, officially called bartering, the practice does not particularly offend the station representative companies. They seem to deplore the kind of deal that is made with a third party. The "reps" insist that such a transaction is the same as the old practice of brokerage of station time.

The bartering practice has been criticized because broadcasters, in many cases, get less in merchandise and/or services than the value of their station time. The ratio of merchandise value to time value often goes as high as one-for-two, meaning one dollar's worth of merchandise for every two dollars' worth of air time.

Call it what you will, bartering or brokerage, the real evil of the system is that broadcasting sells itself short when it does not have to do so. Radio and television are legitimate business enterprises and they have tremendous power to get results for advertisers. They do not need to maintain an inequitable system of charges. Under the barter system, all advertisers are not treated equally. One advertiser pays the full card rate at the station; another gets the time in exchange for a marked up retail value of his merchandise or service. Given a few years of use of this practice, all time would have to be sold by the barter system. Who would pay the full card rate after he discovered that the alternative was available? The Station Representatives Association says this about the practice:

> Bartering and/or brokerage of radio and television time is the most destructive practice that broadcast licensees have to contend with in their relationships with legitimate advertisers and their agencies who are willing to pay published rate cards for their facilities.

It would be unrealistic, within the confines of this book, to set up guide lines for rate structures at all of the individual radio and television properties in the country. Certainly, in addition to the efforts of RAB and TvB along these lines, NAB might do more to stress the importance of proper rate levels and the need for a strict adherence to them. Far greater stature would accrue to the broadcasting industry if more integrity were shown in radio and television rate management across the country. In some markets in this nation with four or more television stations and fifteen or more radio properties, all but two or three of those broadcast entities treat the rate card as a rubber yardstick.

Rate increases, when justified, seldom pose a problem to a good property. Prior to their implementation and as far in advance as possible, the station's own salesmen and its "rep" firm should explain in detail to the station's clients the reasons for and the merits of a proposed rate increase. When an explanation is given and sufficiently in advance, problems ordinarily do not develop. Of course, it is recommended that whenever a rate increase is to take place, three to six months' protection should be given to advertisers of current record. The fundamental justification is that the rate increase is worth it.

Sales Development and Promotion

The business of broadcasting has been particularly weak in regard to sales development. True, since the early days of radio, broadcasting's share of the advertising dollar has been substantial but it has been minor compared to what it should be when the potential impacts of both radio and television are realized.

Thanks to the brilliant individual efforts of the Radio Advertising Bureau and the Television Bureau of Advertising, industry wide progress is being achieved nationally in sales development in both media but not enough of it is in evidence on the local level. Too many broadcasters spend too much of their time attempting to conquer one crisis after another without taking adequate time to plan for the future and to broaden the base of advertiser participation in the station's schedule.

Every radio and television property, regardless of its size, should have one person under the sales manager who concentrates all of his time in sales development work. He should be young, aggressive and able to chart a course of future business potential for the station. Certainly, if any property is to grow in revenue and in profit as it should, it has to extend its range of advertisers.

Some stations have inaugurated sales-promotion departments only to find that they became catch-alls for every department in the station except engineering. There have been cases where outstanding work by a station's sales force has been negated by inept handling of sales promotion either prior to the consummation of the sale or early in the implementation of the contract. A sales-promotion department, even if it consists of only one man or one woman, should involve only those persons who have had training under more experienced promotion figures in the industry.

What can a director of sales promotion and sales development be expected to accomplish? He can gather the materials for and produce fact sheets on the market and the station and its programming, write sales presentations, develop slide, film and flip card materials, take charge of all station exhibits and make trade show and convention arrangements, negotiate trade deals for contests, prepare promos, design and produce marketing aids, write articles for the trade publications, analyze and summarize ratings reports, handle public appearances by talent, prepare trade advertising, prepare client brochures, keep the station mailing lists up to date, prepare newsletters, assemble advertiser-success stories, take charge of all station and personnel publicity, build audience promotion and prepare a salesman's handbook. If this isn't enough work for one or two people, then he can also be given the responsibility of keeping the air charged with new ideas for increased sales activity.

A good sales promotion department works with the client and/or his agency through the salesman assigned to the account throughout the course of a contract. It supplies regular reports on what has been done or is being done in behalf of a program series or a spot announcement campaign.

The sales promotion activity of a station will be strengthened considerably if its director is professionally trained in the field of research. In the months and years to come, broadcasters will be called upon by clients and agencies for more and more research data. Here is a field that merits consideration by some of the young men and women eager to enter the field of broadcasting. Good research people are needed. Their work has never been more necessary for broadcasting's growth and for its future development.

Trade Press Advertising

Too few stations take advantage of the audience that can be reached through the trade press. The radio and television industry is blessed with a number of fine publications, both vertical (broadcasting only) and horizontal (those embracing all advertising or, as in the case of *Variety*, all show business). Those stations which have advertised in both types effectively, meaning properly and frequently enough, have many success stories to tell about this area of corporate activity.

Schedules of radio or television spots or programs are very rarely sold as a result of trade press advertising. On the other hand, if the trade press is used intelligently it can be extremely effective as an image builder. While it may take many months for a station to derive any tangible benefits from a trade press schedule, the long range results are well worth the time, effort and expense. Be original, be clever. If you don't have anyone on the staff who can be both original and clever, either get someone or stay out of trade press advertising.

MERCHANDISING

The most confused, the most misunderstood, the most misinterpreted and the most ill-employed term in any form of advertising, but above all in radio and television, is merchandising.

The ineptness of broadcasters in handling merchandising is crystal clear to most agencies, large and small, whether they are national, regional or local in scope. Some stations, especially in the early days of television or during the first years of the great radio depression, all but ruined themselves by vending mistaken concepts of merchandising rather than their very real facilities.

Even now some stations make brief mention in a presentation to a client of their program strength, their ratings, facilities and station personalities and then devote volumes of space or time to tell what they can do regarding merchandising, and in-store merchandising at that.

Merchandising, when well directed, can be an outstanding service of a radio or a television property for a client. There are some clients, especially in the food and drug field, who not only desire this service but demand it. There are others who have such in-depth merchandising plans of their own that they do not want the broadcast entity involved. The concept of in-store merchandising involves station-client cooperation. But cooperation for what?

In general, merchandising costs are at a proper level when considered as a supplementary service to the station's own broadcast facilities and programming. The great error in merchandising occurs when stations spend huge sums of money to put their specific merchandising services ahead of what they have to offer the public in the way of mass communication serving the community.

Other types of cooperation with advertisers might very well be termed merchandising. It might take the form of promotion cards on behalf of an advertiser, such as a distributor for a beer or a wine, with signs appearing in restaurants and other public places. It can be in the form of pump islands with banners, flags and pennants at one or more gas stations. It can take the form of special shopping bags at a department store or a specialty shop for a particular week, with the printed material on each bag calling the attention of the public to the store's sponsorship of a radio or television series.

The man running a local business counts on—and correctly so—much assistance from advertising media in publicity and promotion. This does not mean that a station should sell its side benefits and forget about its facilities and time, but there needs to be some assistance given to the merchant. Sometimes a store is willing to include the costs of such services in its advertising budget. Most stations endeavor to be helpful through their sales promotion departments in suggesting such selling aids to the store as window displays, point-of-purchase advertising and on-the-air promos, all of which call attention to the sponsorship of programs on the station. Such aids help to increase the audience for the station's programs as well as assist the retailer.

Merchandising can bring returns if done in good taste and if it represents, in the final analysis, a contributory rather than a major service of the station.

THE SALES ADVANTAGES OF COLOR

Station managers should thrill at the possibility of having on their account lists all those retailers who have seen no merits in the use of black-and-white, but who should be excellent prospects for color television. There are the ready-to-wear stores, food manufacturers, producers of candy, interior-decorating salons, the vast home furnishings field, to name but a few. Color is important in determining the purchases people make, whether they buy automobiles, carpeting or draperies, clothing, fresh tomatoes or canned goods.

Note well that the added advantage of color will have to be sold. Anyone who anticipates that advertisers will come around requesting time on stations with color is due for a sad disappointment. The case for color will have to be taken to retailers in the form of newly designed presentations.

Broadcasters will be wise if they assess the tremendous sales potential of color television and resolve that it will not be priced lower than it is worth and that its selling will not be allowed to degenerate into another numbers game or bargain battle. For once again there is an opportunity to make use of a powerful force to activate people's buying habits. This time, it is to be hoped that *impact* will be the important consideration in its management, not cost-per-thousand or decimal points in ratings.

After all, color in television adds a fourth dimension to the trio of sight, sound and motion. This is a combination which is found in no other advertising medium.

THE TASK AHEAD

In a market in the Midwest, a broadcaster asked the president of a medium sized agency when he was going to stop chiseling on rates wherever he did business. The reply was: "As long as the industry is willing to make a deal, and almost every station is, why should I ever pay the full rate?" This agency president advised the broadcaster that it would take a miracle to get any business from him for this particular account unless a deal could be arranged. The agency president then proceeded to expound on his admiration and respect for the press, where the rate card is firm.

This is a tragic indictment of an entire industry. The area of ethics in sales should be one of the most important points of attack for the National

Association of Broadcasters. No single station or group of stations can successfully oppose what the competition may practice. This is an industry wide problem and it needs the kind of leadership that only the NAB can provide. Any number of upstanding broadcasters would give such a movenent their complete support.

Neither the National Association of Broadcasters nor any other indus· ᵥ group or association can either legally or practically implement any parular formula for rate adherence. Yet, integrity of station operation should ᵤe and needs more than mere token notice from these important quarters.

9

Managing for Profit

Profits are a measure of effective, efficient operation and should be worn as a badge of accomplishment and of honor.

—PHILIP REED, General Electric Company[1]

THE NATURE OF commercial broadcasting dictates the diversity of the manager's activities. As noted, he is regularly confronted with problems emanating from the programming, engineering and sales departments. His leadership of these three key departments occupies most of his attention and consumes most of his time.

There is, however, a primary responsibility which must not only affect his courses of action but also must condition his every decision. As the representative of station ownership, his success as a manager is judged principally by the profit return he is able to produce.

Typically, the ownership of a local broadcast entity consists of businessmen who have been successful in fields unrelated to broadcasting. To these men the ownership of a radio or television station is appealing for many reasons. It offers an opportunity to become engaged in a community service. It is an entrance to the exciting and colorful world of show business. It supplies an element of prestige and potential power. Basically, though, it can earn a substantial profit on the initial investment.

To protect that investment and to provide satisfactory returns on a regular basis requires specific knowledge and skills pertaining to broadcasting which these owners do not normally possess. A manager is employed who is experienced in broadcasting and who, it is hoped, can produce the profits the owners desire. To the degree that he is able to fulfill that expectation and also realize his own professional standards, we can equate his real contributions to the broadcasting system.

Even though most of the manager's attention is focused upon the operational procedures of the three major departments of the station, his *modus vivendi,* then, must be governed by economic considerations.

In any business, the product, its distribution and sale are adjudged as equal in importance. In broadcasting, programming may be regarded as the product with engineering as its distribution system. Sales results are highly dependent upon both.

As a catalyst for the programming, engineering and sales divisions, management should supply the vision and the leadership needed for a co-ordinated effort. As improvements occur in each aspect of the operation, station services should expand and the chances for profits should increase. The manager may delegate many tasks in programming, engineering and sales but the management of the station's finances is his direct responsibility. The important decisions affecting profit or loss cannot be avoided. Management must take complete charge of the approval and administration of the operating budget and the control of income and expenses.

In these areas, additional personnel are engaged who work directly under the manager's supervision. Their work crosses over the program, engineering and sales departments, serving all three as part of the administrative function. Such are employees who perform the office duties—the secretaries, clerks, receptionists and the telephone switchboard operators. So, too, are the "right arms" of managers in the area of financial administration —the accountants. The accounting function is to furnish management with accurate data concerning income and expenses, thus helping to assure fruitful decisions in situations in which figures are either red or black and there are no gray shades.

STATION ASSETS

Assets, in the case of a radio or television station, are generally different from those of other businesses chiefly in respect to: (1) the nature of the property, plant and equipment, (2) the ownership of certain broadcasting rights and (3) the possession of a unique kind of good will.

Property. Amounts expended for land for the station structure and for its transmitter, tower and antenna system are considered station assets. The costs for voluntary improvements on that land, including sidewalks, parking lots, roads, landscaping, etc., are counted as assets, as are all assessments charged against the property and representing permanent improvements.

Plant. The cost of buildings constructed to house a station and/or its transmitting facilities is classified as an asset, as are the charges for permanent additions or alterations to those buildings. Stations renting or leasing buildings may count the costs of any improvements in either land or plant as assets.

Equipment. Radio or television equipment normally considered station assets includes the transmitter, tower and antenna systems, studio and mobile equipment, office furniture and fixtures and the vehicles used by the station.

Broadcasting Rights. All rights to broadcast program materials that have been purchased but not yet used (that is, they are unamortized) are station assets. Such rights may include public events where admission is charged, such as sports or concerts. They may also include such program staples as taped features, syndicated films and recorded libraries.

Good Will. Often when an established station is sold, the asking price exceeds the total net assets of the station. The difference between net assets and the selling price represents the good will which the station merits by reason of operations. Factors contributing to a station's good will may include an affiliation with a network, the existing number of contracts for future network, spot and local advertising and the station image in the community. Sometimes a seller will agree that he will not compete in the area of coverage for a specified length of time. Such an agreement can be advantageous to a new owner and may represent an asset. The possession of patents, copyrights or leases, likewise, may be included as a part of a station's good will.

Other Assets. Other assets consist of items similar to the ordinary assets of standard business organizations. They may include: cash on hand or on deposit; all investments; accounts and notes receivable; those expenses that are prepaid (e.g. taxes, insurance, rents and expense-account advances); and unused inventories in the possession of the station.

The amount of gross investment in tangible radio properties in the United States increased from a total of $55,000,000 in 1937 to over $500,000,000 by the end of 1964. The increase in the five-year period, 1960–1964, was almost $100,000,000.

In 1960, the Collins Radio Company sponsored a study by the Industrial Marketing Studies of the University of Illinois to investigate radio technical facilities and equipment assets throughout the United States.[2]

All the then existent radio operations in the country, including commercial and educational AM and FM stations, were studied. Of the total assets of those stations, 43.9 per cent were in technical equipment, with an average investment per station of over $90,000.

The average age of transmitters then in use was 7.7 years. Slightly over three-fourths of all the 50-kw radio stations had been on the air for twenty years or longer but over one-half of those stations were using transmitters less than ten years old. A trend had begun for the retention of used AM transmitters for stand-by auxiliaries during possible power failures. The average station experienced more than five technical problems, in addition to power troubles, in an average year, all serious enough to force the station off the air. The average length of time that radio stations were off the air due to each technical difficulty was three hours and forty-eight minutes.

The findings of the study showed that 30.2 per cent of all radio stations leased all or part of their land, 15.9 per cent leased buildings, 30.4 per cent leased office space and 8.3 per cent leased vehicles. No significant number of stations leased technical equipment.

Depreciation. The Collins study showed that the average life expectancy for studio equipment and office furniture and fixtures came to slightly under nine years. In only about one-fifth of the radio stations were there plans to replace studio equipment before its full depreciation. The average annual expenditure of AM radio stations for studio sound equipment was approximately $1690 per station. The average annual expenditure for office furniture and fixtures was $746 per station.

Depreciation write-offs have been a problem for the broadcaster due to the rapid increases in price of most broadcast equipment. Some managers prefer a fast depreciation rate that permits them to replace station equipment prior to its obsolescence. Other managers prefer to take a slower rate and retain their equipment for the full depreciation schedule or longer.

In the Summer of 1962, the Internal Revenue Service adopted a new schedule recommending a six-year depreciation period for broadcasting equipment. Other recommended depreciation schedules of interest to broadcasters were: land improvements, including tower and antenna systems, twenty years; buildings, forty-five years; office furniture, fixtures and equipment, ten years; automobiles, three years; light trucks, four years; and heavy trucks, six years.

STATION LIABILITIES

The ordinary liabilities of a station include: amounts due for prior purchases of goods and services; any collections made in advance for station services not yet delivered; unpaid balances on long-term notes, mortgages, bonds or other debts; dividends declared but not yet paid; tax monies due and all miscellaneous accrued expenses.

The category of miscellaneous accrued expenses includes various obligations of the station due at some future date. Normally, these liabilities encompass such items as: employee salaries, wages, commissions and other benefits; sales and use taxes; interest due on notes, mortgages, etc., and materials received and used in trade or barter arrangements for which airtime payments have not yet been made.

SOURCES OF INCOME

It has been noted that the predominant source of revenue for any station is the sale of time for network, national or regional spot and local advertising. Secondary sources may include the sale of talent, the sale of recorded or transcribed materials, the rental of station facilities, merchandising activities and interest and dividends from station investments.

NORMAL STATION EXPENSES

Station expenses are usually categorized and budgeted under the four headings of programming, engineering, sales and general and administrative.

Normally, the largest single operating cost of any station is for salaries and wages. This includes, in addition to the regular payroll, all overtime pay and the costs of paid vacations and holiday pay. Also included are the station contributions to various employee benefits. These include social security, unemployment insurance and workmen's compensation. Additionally, some stations provide such benefits as profit sharing plans, bonuses, group insurance, hospitalization and retirement pensions. For the convenience of employees, payroll deductions may be effected for such purposes as the purchase of U. S. Savings Bonds or for donations to organizations such as a united community fund. In such cases, the added cost of administration of the service must be regarded as a station expense.

Programming Expenses

The program department usually is the most expensive station unit in terms of salaries, wages and benefits. Other normal expenses of the program department include: the cost of rights to broadcast certain programs and events; music license fees to ASCAP, BMI and SESAC; recordings and transcriptions; news wire services; film rental or purchase; shipping costs; sets and props; the costs of remote originations, including line charges, and any other miscellaneous expense for program production. Film programming, when bought in package lots, can be amortized over the period when all the films in a package will be shown.

Engineering Expenses

In addition to the payroll for supervisory and non-supervisory employees of the engineering department, other expenses usually include such items as: cost of tubes for transmitter, studio and remote units; cost of audio and/or video tape; rental charges for transmitter lines and parts and supplies used in the station's technical equipment and in its maintenance.

Sales Expenses

Sales commissions and expense accounts are added to the usual costs of salaries, wages and benefits in this department. Other normal expenses may include: public relations, advertising and promotion that is directed to the audience; trade advertising and promotion; commissions for the station rep and the cost of rating services.

General and Administrative Expenses

The salaries and wages of the station manager and all other employees of the station not assigned to programming, sales or engineering are included on the administrative budget. Additional expenses include some items associated directly with management and others used by all departments with their budgets controlled by the central administration of the station. These expenses ordinarily include: the maintenance and repair of buildings and equipment; heat, air-conditioning, light and power; rents; telephone and telegraph; stationery and office supplies; postage; travel and entertainment; membership fees and dues; subscriptions; the costs of operation of station-owned automobiles and trucks; real and personal property taxes; state and local taxes; insurance; station contributions to charitable, educational, religious and welfare organizations, and legal, auditing and other consultant fees.

RADIO INDUSTRY PROFITS

In the first two years of the period 1956–1965, the margin of radio revenues over expenses established a peak that was not reached for another six years. In 1958, the increase in revenues failed to keep pace with increased expenses, resulting in a sharp reduction in industry profit. Then, in 1961, total radio revenues took a real setback from their 1960 total, causing the margin of profit to reach the lowest point since 1939. More radio stations showed losses in 1961 than in any previous year since the FCC started publishing financial data about stations. Almost forty per cent of all radio operations lost money. By the end of 1963, all preceding marks for profit were broken and the decade closed at its highest point.

Generally about sixty-five per cent of radio's revenue is from local advertising. Thirty per cent is received from national spot and only five per cent from the networks. This follows a pattern whereby local sources of revenue have become increasingly the main support of radio stations and network income has declined steadily.

Over the years, the costs of radio station operation divide roughly into some thirty-six per cent of total expenses for general and administrative, thirty-three per cent for programming, nineteen per cent for sales and twelve per cent for technical.

Wages and salaries are the highest expense item, slightly above fifty per cent of total costs. Other major expenses include royalties and license fees, depreciation, talent and news costs other than salaries.

To take 1965 as a typical year, the radio station showed revenues of $120,300 and expenses of $111,100. Profits for the "typical" station were $9,200 for a profit margin of 7.65 per cent before federal taxes.[3] The margin of profit in the industry in 1961 was 4.8 per cent.

While 2708 radio stations reported profits in 1965, no fewer than 1150 stations suffered losses. Nor was there any consistency among the stations enjoying profitable operations. Thirty-seven stations showed profits of over $500,000 for the year but thirty stations made profits from total revenues of less than $25,000. There were ninety-one stations with revenues over one million dollars. Of these, six did not show profit.[4]

The majority of radio stations in 1965 operated very close to the line between profit and loss. The margin of gain or loss for the year for sixty per cent of the stations was around $15,000. This was hardly a desirable rate of return in consideration of the work involved in maintaining a broadcast service for a year. The investors in a majority of the nation's radio stations could have found a greater rate of return in some other forms of business enterprise.

The key factor in the determination of broadcast profit is management. Granted that there are radio stations in markets that are oversaturated or too small to support broadcasting. However, some stations do show fine profits even in these circumstances. Yet, when one station receives over a million dollars in revenue and loses money and when another station in a small market produces only about $200 a week for all its effort, it should be good sense and good business to re-assess the entities as management and business enterprises. The average profitable radio station in 1965 earned revenues almost twice those of the unprofitable stations, but their expenses were only some eighteen per cent higher. Again, the key factor is management.

Of the total of 1215 AM and FM stations reporting losses in 1965, all but 129 reported depreciation expenses. Over half of this total reported that payments were made to station owners, partners and/or stockholders. Over half of the stations with losses took depreciation expenses and/or made payments to owners, etc., that exceeded the amount of their losses. Almost one-third of all the stations failing to show profit made payments to owners, etc. that alone exceeded their losses.

A question might logically be raised as to why so many radio stations continue in business when they operate at a loss. At least a partial answer may be ventured in the observation that station owners, partners and/or stockholders are given healthy payments before profit or loss or dividends are declared. Until 1962, this data was not requested by the FCC. Station financial reports now show that about half of all licensed stations follow this practice.

TELEVISION INDUSTRY PROFITS

The general decline in profit in the radio industry in 1958 was experienced in the television industry a year earlier. Where some six years were needed for the radio industry to return to its former profit level, television came back much faster. Within two years, it exceeded its former profit record. There was a temporary slump in 1961, as there was in radio income, but it was not of any serious magnitude. Since that year, television profits have set new records annually.

The chief source of income for the three television networks is from time sales. Program and talent sales constitute the only other major income source. Television stations receive the largest share of their income from national and regional spot sales with local sales next in volume followed by income from the networks.

Expenses of networks for programs amount to approximately fifty per cent of total costs. The next highest cost is for payments to affiliates. Other expenditures, relatively less, are for agency commissions, administrative costs, payments to owned stations, technical costs and selling costs.

Television station expenses normally consist of about a third for program costs, roughly a fourth for administrative costs, and a fifth for commissions to agencies and "reps." Technical and selling costs each account for some ten to twelve per cent.

Pretax profits of the networks in the year 1965 amounted to an eight per cent return. The profits of the network-owned stations represented a forty-three per cent return. All other television stations had an average profit return of thirty per cent.

A total of 112, or fifty-nine per cent of all VHF stations, as well as twenty per cent of all UHF stations, had profits of one million dollars or more for 1965. Profits of $25,000 or less were reported by twenty-seven VHF and twelve UHF stations. Losses were reported by 13.3 per cent of the VHF stations (sixty-one) and 34.5 per cent of the UHF stations (twenty-nine).

As was the case in radio, depreciation expenses were claimed and payments were made to some television station owners, partners and/or stockholders, but proportionately fewer television stations reported making payments.

Of the television stations reporting losses in 1965, all but one reported depreciation expenses. Half of these stations made payments to owners, etc. In fewer than a third of these cases were the depreciation expenses greater than station losses. Only one station made payments to owners, etc., which were greater than the losses of the station.

THE MANAGER AND PROFIT

With over thirteen per cent of the commercial VHF television stations, almost thirty-five per cent of the commercial UHF's, almost a third of the commercial AM and most of the commercial FM radio stations showing losses, it should be obvious that the management of finances could be improved in a good many instances. One ultimate consequence of neglect of such improvement might be a reduction in the present number of radio and television stations. Much has been said about all the problems which have originated due to an excess of radio stations and it may be true that a larger number has been authorized than can be supported profitably. Any station, however, which has been authorized and has been in operation deserves a chance to survive. The accomplishment of that survival, assuming that good programming, technical and economic practices are followed, will be dependent upon the effectiveness of the station's managment.

Some managers, faced with continued financial loss, show a tendency to panic. They often decide to accept any types of commercial accounts, to cut their rates in order to get some semblance of business, to program as cheaply as possible without regard to quality standards, to cut personnel to a minimum and then hire the cheapest people who can be found, to get by with equipment that has passed its state of maximum utility, to oppose any improvements in their station facilities, to cancel their membership in state and national professional associations and in the industry Codes, and to cut all budgetary items to a point that will permit only minimal operating standards. Such action may produce an immediate financial improvement but it can also endanger the reserve potential of the station. Then, when further budgetary cuts may be necessary there can be no effective retrenchment.

The manager needs to maintain a financial or operating reserve adequate to meet possible future emergencies. Such a reserve does not necessarily need to be in cash or securities. It may be created by prepayments of certain station obligations. It may be in the form of a manpower reserve. It may consist of certain station services that can be eliminated in a crisis. There are various other possibilities. It is pure folly to destroy all bridges because in so doing the eventuality of temporary retreats can also be destroyed. The maintenance of a financial reserve is important to any manager because increased competition can force him to draw upon it in the future.

By way of contrast, there have been managers who, when confronted with almost certain financial losses, have increased station expenses in order to become more competitive. Choosing not to make radical overall budgetary cuts, these managers have eliminated wastes and inefficiencies that have caused the stations to suffer financial losses. They have accepted the possibility of even greater losses over a short period of time in order that their stations could become effective competitors in the future. These managers have had the courage to defend their strategies to their owners or stockholders. They have been fully prepared to find other employment should the station owners disagree with their policies. In every case of this nature that has come to our attention, there has been no need for any change in employment. Instead, the vision, integrity and strength of these managers has been highly regarded by station owners. In almost every case, their stations rebounded to become solid competitors.

COST CONTROLS FOR GREATER PROFITS

A station can implement various economies without sacrificing either quality or standards. Constant and careful attention to cost controls can effectuate real savings. Many relatively minor budgetary items can turn into excessive costs due to wastes, inefficiencies or extravagances. The practice of economy in the administration of expenditures requires constant vigilance. Little is accomplished if the action is sporadic. The supervision of cost controls must be almost a daily process until such time as it receives the cooperation and the enthusiastic support of the entire staff of a station. It has been said that the true test of real executive leadership comes when cost but not quality reduction becomes a major objective of the company. An effective manager can produce real savings without losing any degree of cooperation or enthusiasm from his employees. He should, indeed, grow in both.

Working Facilities

Investments in improved working facilities often produce returns far greater than the cost of the investments. Buildings originally designed for other purposes and then transformed to serve as radio or television stations often have space inefficiencies. In many cases, a simple rearrangement of the physical layout of the station facilities may result in more productive efforts by the station staff. The location of the office staff closer to the studios can improve the traffic flow and increase the work output of the station. A physical rearrangement of filing equipment or of desks may result in greater productivity. Some studio and control room arrangements require engineers to concentrate all of their attention on one activity when they should be able to oversee several. Offices can become so overcrowded that they hamper good work. Regular assessment of space considerations is recommended.

Budgeting

The budgeting of annual expenditures is standard practice in any business. Problems of budgetary control usually can be solved by the inclusions of the department heads in the planning of the budget and by the use of administrative follow-up procedures at regular intervals during the budgeted year.

The preparation of budgets entirely by management should be avoided because they will not be realistic in terms of the needs of the departments. The manager must, of course, give final approval to all budgets and he must be expected to exercise the right to veto or to cut any of the requests he deems unnecessary, but each department should be given full opportunity to propose. Each department head should be made well aware of the corporate budgetary goals and of the importance of departmental cost controls so that those goals may be achieved.

Department heads and the station controller or accountant should meet at weekly or at least monthly intervals to review actual expenditures as well as each status of the budget balance for the department. Through such conferences, it not only should be possible to curb cases of overspending but even to effect some savings.

It is a wise policy for the station manager and the department heads to review at regular intervals the annual financial reports of the FCC as well as the various data from NAB on station revenues and expenses. Station executives can gain important insights into the financial practices of typical and/or similar stations in the various categories of power, market and competition from these reports.

Mechanized Systems

The business machine age is here and it is not restricted to the accounting function. Most good-sized broadcasting operations have used one business machine system or another for several years. There is no reason why a business machine system cannot handle all of the routine traffic of a radio or television station from the time a spot is sold, including its placement in the schedule and its eventual billing.

Mechanization, in itself, is not a panacea. In cases of weak or inadequate control, mechanization only highlights the defects in an existing system. Inefficiencies cannot be eliminated by pushing a button that starts a machine. Under a properly organized and controlled operation, there are several possible advantages of a machine system to a medium or a large market radio or television station. One advantage is the speed in which clear and neat logs and invoices can be prepared. Another is the ability to produce numerous reports and analyses from basic data. Station logs can be prepared from basic data cards and at high speeds. Commercial cards can be sorted: (1) by agency code to prepare invoices, (2) by salesman code to prepare commission reports and (3) by day and time codes to obtain daily or hourly breakdowns of revenue. Even breakdowns of revenue by products can be provided. Mechanization can be particularly valuable in the forecasting of revenues and expenses.

Staff Economies

It seems to be fairly easy for employees to abuse such privileges as the coffee break or the use of the telephone for personal conversations, but of far greater importance is the development of a climate of work whereby the true potential of every member of the staff is realized. We consider this subject of such importance that we will devote the next chapter of this book to personnel practices and to the motivation of people to accomplish those creative results of which they are capable.

10

The Management
of Personnel

It is important to realize that conformity must be taught, whereas truth and principle are ultimately learned.

—ALDEN DOW, Architect[1]

RELATIVELY, IN COMPARISON with other major industries, the number of people who are employed in American broadcasting is not high. Some 100,-000 full-time personnel serve in the networks and in radio and television stations. Even so, the increase of positions has been significant. The 1960 census showed a gain of 20,000 men and 6000 women over the 1950 totals.

Men outnumber women in broadcasting by a ratio of about four to one. Yet, women hold responsible positions in all phases of the industry. According to the 1960 census, some 3200 women were either salaried managers or owners of stations.

About three times as many persons are employed by television stations as are employed by radio stations. In 1965, over three fourths of the AM and over four fifths of the FM radio stations employed no more than fifteen people. Almost thirteen per cent of the AM and forty-three per cent of the FM stations had no more than five people on the full-time payroll. The average number of employees in television stations was fifty, and 15.2 per cent of the television stations employed over 100 people.[2]

No other element of the broadcasting enterprise is capable of delivering as great a return on investment as its human resources. Superior physical plants and technical facilities depreciate in net worth over a period of years. The values of people to a station should increase as their period of employment lengthens.

The station manager should realize that his ultimate successes are dependent upon the interests and the abilities of his station employees. He

182

needs to give top priority to the maintenance of good human relations. If he regards the management of people as one of his major responsibilities and gives adequate attention to this aspect of administration, he may discover that the efficiency of his employees increases proportionately.

Whenever those employees have excellent morale plus a high degree of station loyalty, creativity and productivity may be expected to expand. Continual vigilance, then, is necessary in employee relations. Regular managerial attention needs to be directed to matters of paramount importance to the working staff. Equitable wages and salaries, proper recognition for work achievement and opportunities for advancement in the organization are vital. Most employees want assurance that if their assignments are accomplished satisfactorily, they need not be concerned about job security.

Identified as it is as a form of show business, broadcasting attracts many creative people. If such talented folk find that their work assignments are of a routine nature, the odds are that the most creative will seek positions elsewhere. Creative people must use their talents.

It is one achievement to hire the best qualified people available. It is another to keep them. To sustain their top performance is an all-important duty of great management.

SELECTION OF PERSONNEL

Broadcasters quite generally operate on a two weeks' notice of resignation basis. The notice gives the station only the two week period to locate replacements. This is hardly adequate time to look over the field of available personnel and to make a satisfactory selection. Often, as the time period for securing a replacement nears an end without any likely prospects having applied, the first available person who contacts the station is hired. Perhaps a horseshoe over the door is management's best and only resource when this happens.

Where do stations find short notice replacement personnel? Sometimes, desperate telephone calls are made to commercial and/or educational placement bureaus. A few positions are filled by drifters who just happen by when there is a vacancy. Contacts with other broadcasters may unearth a few prospects. Many stations advertise for help.

Small stations often have to settle for unemployed people. Seldom can they make offers lucrative enough to interest employees of other stations. In some cases, they turn to people who are employed in other lines of work in the community. Larger stations usually can find people in smaller operations who have worked long enough to prove their abilities. Some stations keep people on their payrolls who are not as able as they should be rather than face the task of giving notice of termination and then searching for replacements. In other words, the drift.

What about hiring personnel from other stations? What motivates people to change positions? Walter Lowen of the Walter Lowen Placement Agency has some answers. He lists four factors: greater security in the new position; more opportunity for advancement; promise of greater happiness in the new environment; more money. While money is an important consideration, usually it does not constitute sufficient motivation to change positions unless the other three factors are also favorable. [3]

College and University Recruitment

It would seem profitable even for small stations to conduct annual interviewing sessions at the colleges and universities nearest them whether vacancies are anticipated or not. Most colleges maintain facilities for the interviewing of graduating seniors. Those facilities are usually used to capacity throughout the academic year.

Seniors interested in careers in broadcasting seldom have opportunities to talk with recruiters from broadcasting stations. Consequently, many outstanding young prospects for the radio and television industry are lost to other businesses and industries. This has been particularly true of those young people who are interested in careers in sales.

It is true that the college campus is not the only source from which broadcasters may find people. It does seem wasteful, however, to disregard this resource almost completely, as the majority of station managers have done.

It is, perhaps, an insufficient concern with the long term future of stations that as much as anything else accounts for the general apathetic attitude of broadcast management toward planned recruitment.

Yet, there is enormous waste in a system that does not provide an adequate screening of employees to select the very best. Also, it hardly seems efficient for large stations to pirate people from the smaller stations as a general policy and not develop at least a few new people on their own. Somehow, it is basically wrong to expect small stations to accept all the gambles of experimentation with inexperienced people, thereby absorbing the high costs of frequent turnover. No one doubts the advantages of a good—though an informal—farm system but an essential factor even in a farm system is a carefully conceived recruitment plan.

Usually, college graduates are available at two, three or four times each year, with most availabilities coming in the months of May or June. Other times when the talent pool is replenished to some extent by the colleges are usually August, December, January and March. Correspondence with college authorities will pave the way toward interviews and selections. A college degree in itself is no automatic guarantee of excellence. Interviews with the recommended students should be combined with a follow-up check with the faculty of the students' major areas of study.

Other Selection Considerations

Neither recruitment nor replacement is an easy task. They involve a greater amount of searching than is usually done. A station committed to a rational long range employment policy will enjoy notable advantages over the station which merely fills vacancies with the first chance applicants available.

Whatever the source of new people, someone on the staff should be designated as personnel director. In the smaller stations, this may be the responsibility of the station manager or of the program manager. At the opposite extreme, some metropolitan stations that are joint radio and television properties have found it desirable to employ a full-time personnel director, who is assigned the leadership function for all non-union employees plus, frequently, a director of industrial relations responsible for union personnel.

In addition to the authority to choose new or replacement staff people, the director of personnel should be in charge of employee development. He should also be the official representative to confer with all staff personnel in matters concerning individual and corporate welfare, complaints, benefits.

A word of caution as to audition tapes: They can be poor substitutes for live performance tests because they often are not a true indication of the applicant's abilities. Tapes can be carefully planned, edited and polished by the applicant before they are submitted. The employer has no opportunity to observe how the applicant would react under pressure or how he would perform with unfamiliar announcer or news copy. Furthermore, it is always better to have an opportunity to judge the poise, personality and appearance of the applicant in addition to his submitted sample of performing ability.

It is a wise policy to have a credit check made on any applicants who seem desirable for possible employment as cashiers, payroll clerks, mailroom personnel and those who are responsible for valuable equipment.

THE EMPLOYMENT INTERVIEW

There is no real substitute for the personal interview as a method of judging the potential of the applicant. There is no substitute, either, for a skilled and experienced interviewer. Personality, manners, appearance, sincerity, emotional stability, intelligence, the abilities to articulate and listen and the applicant's opinions and attitudes about broadcasting can be judged through the interview. The nature of the questions asked by the candidate and the directness of his response to questions asked of him should be noted. Evidence of his energy, enthusiasm and drive should be sought.

Even though there may be no openings at the moment and even though many who are interviewed cannot be hired, the fact that the station provides the opportunity for interviews can reflect nothing but favor on its public relations image. Interviewing is a time consuming task, but it can bring rich dividends to the station in terms of favorable impressions.

In case an immediate job is available, specifications should be clearly explained, including duties, hours and working conditions, the wages, the fringe benefits and any other pertinent information. The actual hiring process, in most instances should not be a part of the interview even though the interviewer may feel that he has discovered the person he is seeking. The interviewer, too, may profit by a second thought. Usually, it is the better policy to let the candidate wait a day or so before extending a formal proffer of employment.

The one area where the director of personnel should be given less than a free hand is in the selection of key executives. In these cases, the personnel director may do some preliminary screening and referral of prospects to the chief engineer, the program manager, the sales manager or the station manager for further interviewing. Much valuable administrative time can be saved and much order can be given to the general employment process if preliminary screening takes place before the department heads see the outstanding candidates. For that matter, it is better to choose top executives by invitation rather than through formal application.

JOB INDOCTRINATION

We are amazed as we learn of many instances in which a new employee reports for his first day of work to find that no one has been assigned to give him any indoctrination in station policy or operations. Station practices and routines taken for granted by the employer can be complicated and strange to a new man. New duties can be downright frightening.

It should not be too much effort for some employee to prepare a booklet containing detailed information about the station and its operating policies. This could be given to new employees after they are hired and before they report for work. The Department of Broadcast Management of the NAB has prepared an excellent sample of such a manual for new employees.

Even with the booklet as an aid, proper indoctrination of new employees also requires personal attention once they report for duty. On the first day, a tour of the facilities and introductions to all employees of the station are minimal expectations. This is the time to discuss the employee's responsibilities to other employees, the station's administrative structure, its lines of authority, its functions and philosophy.

Radio and television stations are, in general, not geared for extensive training periods. Many stations, however, could profitably devote three to six months on a part-time basis for the thorough indoctrination of a few promising recruits. Even the small station could arrange a few hours each week when new personnel could learn about those activities of the station which are not a part of their regular assignments.

Caution should be expressed to station management, present and potential, regarding a special ability which should be expected of any station's key personnel. Those individuals who occupy assignments as heads of the leading departments in the station need to have the capacity to understand, direct and guide employees for whom they have direct responsibility. The most creative minded department head in the world is of questionable value to a station unless he also has skill in the direction of people.

PROMOTION POLICIES

It is difficult to set up standard guidelines for promotions. It is painful to acknowledge that some stations and some managers neglect to reward persons who make important contributions to the company. Often promotions cannot be implemented immediately, once deserved. Still, a token cash bonus can be used in lieu of an immediate promotion. Reassignment is a possibility. Every encouragement should be given the employee in the hope that he will remain with the company and aspire to an improved position. Just in case you don't have Proverbs 13:12 at hand, it reads, "Hope deferred maketh the heart sick." Also it maketh the foot loose. Laggard promotions and grudging recognition can strip a station of its most promising people.

SEPARATION POLICIES

The task of terminating an employee's employment is never easy. Authority to take such action must be vested in the heads of departments and their decisions need to have the support of the station manager.

Separation payments should be given as settlement whenever an individual is removed because of a lack of need for his future services or for some other reason best known to the company. Such payments should not be made in the cases of individuals who are *dismissed for cause,* whether those individuals are union or non-union.

Should an employee be relieved of his duties for other than a violation of good conduct or irresponsible performance, the station is advised to make every effort to find employment for him elsewhere. Sufficient advance planning will usually make other employment possible. The good will that accrues from such gestures is of lasting benefit to the station. Usually it will not be necessary to look far afield. If displaced by automation or almost any other development, intelligent and dedicated people who have been with a sound broadcasting organization all their career lives can make a contribution—and, in some cases, a superior one—in another area of broadcast activity at the same station.

HOURS AND WORKING CONDITIONS

Certainly, the forty hour week should be regarded as standard at any broadcasting station. With the higher cost of every phase of broadcasting, it would work to the financial disadvantage of the station, and in the long run to the detriment of the employee, if these hours for staff personnel were shortened. There should be no employee discontent over a forty hour week if excellent working conditions are maintained for those employees.

It goes without saying that office facilities should be comfortably arranged, clean, well lighted, warm in the winter months and comfortably cool in the summer. A few large stations have installed their own cafeterias or food services. Service is provided throughout the periods of maximum working activity at out-of-pocket cost. This convenience can be a morale builder. Furthermore, it can save, over a period of a year, thousands of hours of time otherwise lost for coffee breaks across the street or somewhere else in the building. Stations not large enough to sustain this kind of service may make arrangements either for vending by caterers or for the installation of coin operated machines, thus making clean and wholesome food and beverages available on the premises during working hours.

In large cities, free company parking facilities are important. Many stations in large markets buy real estate adjacent to their studio buildings for this purpose. Parking lot land is, of course, available for future building expansion.

In recent years, many television stations have relocated in outlying areas. Offsetting some loss of glamour in leaving the downtown area, benefits can accrue to the employee, as well as the company, in a shift to locations permitting horizontal rather than high rise building development. Television operations need space.

UNIONS AND LABOR RELATIONS

Radio and television stations in major markets have occasion to deal with most of the labor unions active in broadcasting. The programming department, especially the announcers and other talent, comes under the jurisdiction of the American Federation of Television and Radio Artists (AFTRA) and, in the case of television, the Screen Actors Guild (SAG). The International Alliance of Theatrical Stage Employees (IATSE) and the American Federation of Musicians (AFM) are active in programming aspects of broadcasting. In the engineering and technical fields, the National Association of Broadcast Employees and Technicians (NABET) and the International Brotherhood of Electrical Workers (IBEW) are the most active unions.

Smaller market stations may be involved with only one union or with none at all. At this writing, about seventy per cent of the television stations but only some twelve per cent of the radio stations in the United States are unionized.[4] Usually, the station manager and the station attorney are directly responsible for dealings with unions. In some hard pressed properties, one poor union contract can mean the difference between profit and loss. A poorly written agreement can deny a company the necessary flexibility it needs in the development of its operation.

Companies of large size, with more than one union contract, frequently have a director of industrial relations, who devotes most, if not all, of his time to the labor relations area. This individual must know every function of every union employee in the company. He must be thoroughly knowledgeable in each of the agreement clauses under existing contracts and he must be aware of what can be accomplished in future negotiations in the interest of better relationships between the union and the company.

There have been costly strikes in the broadcasting industry because either labor or management or both did not approach negotiations in a mature manner. There has been a degree of irresponsibility on both sides. Nevertheless, it is believed or at least hoped, that there can be more intelligent handling of labor-management problems in the future.

Nothing is more essential in union and labor relations than careful explanations of the rationale of company policies. When people know the reasons for doing something in a particular manner, they can be expected to have more understanding of the task. In cases where complete explanations are given, difficulties usually can be precluded. The bargaining table is, or should be, a meeting place of reasonable men.

FRINGE BENEFITS AND INCENTIVE PLANS

No standard pattern exists throughout the broadcasting industry in regard to fringe benefits and incentive plans for employees. Most workers now share in health and welfare plans at least partially supported by their employers. It is not unusual for companies to pay up to half of the costs of life insurance, hospitalization and medical care. Paid sick leave and vacations are provided by most, if not all, stations. Some companies provide such additional benefits as moving allowances, layoff benefits, severance pay, pensions, paid holidays and company financed college scholarships for dependents of employees.

Many employees take fringe benefits for granted. Often they are not aware of the extent of those contributions. It should be in the interest of the organization to see that all people on the payroll are well informed of substantial company contributions. Some stations have found it advantageous to itemize the costs of the various benefits and give this information to their employees along with their W-2 forms. In general, vacation periods, as well as other fringe benefits, tend to be more liberal in the larger markets.

Biennial NAB surveys of employment in broadcasting do not include data for office workers. However, NAB recommends that station managers review the regular studies of office personnel conducted by (1) the telephone companies, (2) The Bureau of Labor Statistics and (3) The National Office Management Association. The report of the latter organization for 1964–65 showed that the predominant pattern for office employees was a one week paid vacation after the completion of six months of employment and two weeks of paid vacation after one year of work. The trend appears to be toward the granting of eight paid holidays each year for office workers.[5]

Stations providing sick leave to workers can qualify for tax advantages of up to $100 per week of an employee's sick benefits, but only if there is an organized plan and if it is communicated to the employees.

Employees drafted or enlisting for military service are entitled to regular pay up until the time they choose to stop work. Should an employee resign and then not be accepted for military duty, or be released after he has been accepted, he is entitled to re-employment if he applies for such reinstatement within thirty days. The personnel manager must keep abreast of governmental regulations and industrial developments. Matters of military leave, adjusted compensation for men in service, and so on, become vexatious problems only if solutions are improvised out of ignorance or neglect.

Few radio and television stations have started retirement plans for their employees. After a pioneering survey, of 64 broadcasting organizations with retirement plans the NAB prepared a general guide for broadcasters who contemplate the institution of such benefits. Forty-four of the companies surveyed had fixed benefit pension plans, seventeen had deferred profit sharing plans and three companies had both.[6]

Employee Suggestion Systems

It is well for man and management to realize that the suggestion box marks a serious advance in the pooling of skill and vision.

Some of the best program concepts and some of the greatest cost-control ideas in recent years at WGN Radio and Television have stemmed from suggestions made by station personnel. Each person who makes a contribution that is used is rewarded with a special cash gift. In an operation the size of WGN (some 500 employees), suggestions are generally confined to the areas of office procedures or engineering or production techniques. Occasionally, though, a splendid idea is submitted in general programming or public affairs. The fact that every person on the staff thinks about station improvement is ample reward in itself for management.

A weekly or a monthly house organ reporting the activities of the company and its people is immensely valuable. The house organ provides for exchanges of information between employees. It is an informal channel of communication between men and management. Employee suggestions for station improvement can be incorporated in such a publication. Any changes in working conditions or hours can be announced and adequately explained. General industry news of importance can be reviewed. The nature and style of the house organ are not as important as the facility itself. In small stations, a mimeographed paper can accomplish the function and will be appreciated.

Activities of Personnel in the Community

The station manager must set the example for employee involvement in community affairs. He must show his interest in the well-being of his city, his state and the general coverage area. He should encourage all of his employees to do likewise, whether in support of a particular program of the mayor or the city government or the governor or in church or school projects or any other areas of community public service that the employee may prefer. If the employees who are active in community affairs conduct themselves properly, they will bring much credit to the station. In a business that depends so much upon public support, this is important.

One of the benefits from the outside activities of employees is the gaining of confidence and additional self-respect. Such development can add to their prospects for promotions in radio or television.

Many station managers find it desirable to keep retired employees on retainer as consultants, thus ensuring a continuity of wisdom and experience. This is an admirable idea. It may be suggested, however, that much consultative experience is, or should be, available before retirement. Too often management falls into stereotyped thinking, neglecting to make use of veteran employees who are sometimes relegated to routine tasks in corporate backwaters. The point is that management may well find consultative resources within the organization before the retirement of men by the calendar. The practice of taking thought after a man's retirement is, sometimes, an admission that insufficient consideration was given to his potentials before retirement. This is a source of creativity too frequently overlooked.

Opportunities for Employee Growth

The station manager really doesn't develop anyone on the staff. Rather, he can provide an environment in which responsible and ambitious people can develop themselves.

To this end, we recommend a carefully planned long range program of employee education with opportunities to learn about the obligations of the licensee, program responsibilities, the provisions of the Communications Act and, in general, the basic realities confronting management in a broadcasting station.

Few station employees know very much about revenues and expenses, nor are they highly cognizant of the problems of depreciation and obsolescence of broadcast equipment. Yet, they would be interested in information of this nature if given an opportunity to learn about it. Management should explain its areas of primary concern to the company employees and, in open discussion, join with them in considerations of mutual problems of a professional concern. The resources of a college or university may be employed to organize and assist with an employee-development program.

Top executives in broadcasting have many opportunities to attend professional meetings. They sometimes lose sight of the need of their employees for a wider perspective than they usually get within the limitations of their work assignments. The employee development program should pay dividends in employee appreciation and in an expansion of professional interests.

Executive Recruitment and Development

Many of the most serious problems in the broadcasting industry today stem from the lack of trained administrative personnel to manage all the new broadcast properties as they came on the air following World War II. To attain the true potential of broadcasting, the industry needs well-trained management personnel—men who, early in life, can begin the study of the problems of station administration, mindful of their very sober responsibilities and truly dedicated to a great and growing profession.

We cannot understand the attitudes of station managers who refuse to pay attention to the need for executive recruitment and training in their organizations. Some managers, particularly in smaller markets, act as if their positions might be in jeopardy should they hire assistants with management potential. We know of actual cases of the firing of staff people suspected of executive abilities.

Fortunately, this sort of selfish and stupid practice is on its way out. The able manager surrounds himself with the ablest talent he can find and brains he can afford. The fact is, also, that people of real executive endowments and potential are in exceedingly short supply.

The age group from twenty-five to forty-five, which is the source of most executive potential, constitutes a lessening segment of the population and it will continue to show a proportional decrease for several years. General expansions in business and industry, along with diversifications and acquisitions, have created unprecedented demands for executives. One recruiting firm found that there were 12,500 executive openings in the United

States during the second quarter of 1965 alone. This was an eighty-five per cent increase over the same period in 1964.[7]

Broadcast progress depends not upon systems and gadgets but upon brilliant minds. Ultimately, radio and television properties, like major-league baseball franchises, must develop their own executives. If top management takes the time to meet with and help develop young employees on its staff, there should be little need in many cases to have to go beyond the confines of the company in order to find potential talent. Where a need for future station leadership is anticipated, an orderly and effective course of executive training can be instituted for the development of young men and women for key posts in the organization. These courses of training may be haphazard in organization and in their results unless consultation is sought in their structure and administration. Some help may be gained in the organization of these programs by studying the methods and procedures of other stations with experience in similar projects.

WTOP–TV in Washington, D.C., has conducted a successful executive training program since 1952 in the areas of programming and production. The Corinthian Broadcasting Corporation has a summer executive training program for selected college students. The Avco Broadcasting Corporation has a similar program for the development of news personnel. NBC, in conjunction with Northwestern University, has operated a summer training program for interns for twenty-five years. The Michigan Broadcasters Association sponsors a program, whereby various radio and television stations in the state take interns from the state universities and pay their expenses for three month periods so they may learn station operations and management procedures while in residence at the stations. WGN Continental Broadcasting maintains a regular, around-the-year internship program for college and university students selected on the basis of their interests in either television production, arts and facilities, news, public affairs or sales promotion. Three internees are accepted each quarter for a total of twelve each year. In addition, seventeen college students are employed during the school year on a part-time basis and twelve college students are added to the payroll each summer as vacation replacements.

In all these and other equally successful programs, station executives have the opportunity to observe people at close range and on a daily basis. Those who have exceptional promise are available for future employment. At WGN Continental Broadcasting Company sometime interns are presently on the regular payroll. It would be hard to imagine a more capable and promising group assembled without the cooperation of Northwestern University and a forward looking recruitment policy. If this sounds like an enthusiastic testimonial, it's because it is.

Broadcasters are realizing they must either participate in the growing continuing education movement or be left at the post in the race for acquisition of new knowledge. A notable beginning has been made. The NAB has conducted executive development seminars at Harvard designed to develop the skills used in the analysis and solution of broadcast management problems. Seminars in sales management and in engineering have also been sponsored by the NAB. The Chicago Council of the American Association of Advertising Agencies, in cooperation with Northwestern University, held a thirty week training school for young executives. Thirty-five ad agency employees, generally in the twenty-five to thirty-five year bracket, were given rigorous training in all aspects of the agency business. The cost of $500 per enrollee was paid by the advertising agencies.

These are but samples of the kinds of activity going on in broadcasting and in advertising to update knowledge and stimulate minds. Elsewhere, state associations, group owned stations, the wire services, music licensing organizations and individual stations have arranged with colleges and universities to conduct program, engineering, sales and management seminars and workshops for radio and television employees. Instruction has been provided jointly by authorities in broadcasting and education.

The manager eager to enlighten and advance his junior executives will find academic opportunities ideal for his purpose. His people will discover new insights readily transferable to station advancements and their personal growth should be more than suitable repayment for the costs of their enrollment in the studies.

Unfortunately at too many broadcasting stations, class, seminar and conference opportunities are denied everyone except the manager and, on occasion, the sales manager. We think this is one of the most shortsighted practices in the field of radio and television management.

The well-run radio or television operation sees to it that young executive talent is standing in the wings in each department. In those stations, the senior head of the department works with those persons to encourage development in various areas of responsibility and to prepare them for possible future prime positions in the company.

Granted, the element of luck will be a factor. Many people with fine executive abilities have never had the opportunities to use outstanding talents because chance has not brought them to the right place at the right time. Still, the station must help. The station manager must be a student of human nature and a teacher of skills.

CREATIVITY IN THE EMPLOYEE

In the early days of radio, it was exciting to work in broadcasting because it was all so new. Almost anything could be tried. It was easy to be different. Innovations in programming and in production were encouraged. In those days, there were real premiums on creativity; imitated formats were rare.

The early days of television brought a renewal of emphasis on experimental programming and production. People were challenged by the opportunity to try something new and they were generally given the freedom to do so. Outstanding advancements were made in the uses of the camera, in lighting and staging and in performance techniques.

The opportunity to innovate has always been a prime motivating force for creative people. Standardized formats and routine assignments discourage men and women capable of new discoveries and new ideas. Stations that offer little or no opportunities for experimentation tend to attract a plodder type of employee satisfied by the performance of routine assignments. Highly creative people avoid this concept of broadcasting. It would seem to be to a station's advantage to encourage the development of new program formats and new production methods, thereby attracting employees capable of producing a wealth of new ideas for their own and the station's benefit.

We may be better able to understand the process of creativity by examining three studies that have been made of creative people. Revealing personal characteristics have been discovered in these studies, all of which were supported by grants from the Carnegie Corporation.[8]

The Institute of Personality Assessment and Research of the University of California conducted a six year study of the differences between highly creative people and those less creative.

The study found that while intelligence is an important factor in creativity up to a point, it is not perhaps the crucial element. A person with average or better than average intelligence can be creative if his environment is conducive to creativity.

The Institute investigated possible special aptitudes. No leads were discovered. If intelligence and special aptitudes were not the real clues to creativity, then some other factors needed to be isolated for study. The *interests* of highly creative people were investigated. Here some valuable discoveries were made.

Persons who are highly creative are not likely to be interested in small details or in the practical or the concrete. They are more concerned with what things mean and what the implications of those meanings might imply for new discoveries.

All creative people who were studied were consistent in choosing that which was complex over that which was simple. They were not bound by what was already known; they were more frequently interested in what might *become known.*

The creative person is usually a nonconformist in the field of ideas but not usually in the fields of behavior or social patterns. The study showed that the creative person is generally an independent, able to find satisfaction in those elements of challenge that other people might not even perceive.

Several characteristics of the creative person, which should be particularly desirable in an employee of a radio or television station, have been discovered by the study. These are an easy adjustment to people and situations, an attraction to problems and their solutions, a high degree of sensitivity and a wide range of interests.

The creative person's preference for the new, the unknown and the complex over the traditional, the known and the simple should interest any station manager who wants his station to be different. The creative employee should be in demand in any station where conformity is desired in behavior and social patterns but is not wanted in the field of ideas.

A second study was undertaken by a psychologist, Morris I. Stein, and the work was carried out at the University of Chicago and at New York University. This study analyzed the environments of creative people to determine which kinds of working conditions were most conducive to creativity.

Among other findings, Stein concluded that, in contrast to less creative workers, who expect quick achievement, the creative person works more slowly at first on a problem, then moves much more quickly toward a solution. The work of the creative person, in addition to being more original, is usually more efficient. Far less time is spent by the creative individual in checking back over his work once he has completed it; the uncreative person is prone to spend considerable time in checking and re-checking.

A third study was conducted by the Institute of Social Research at the University of Michigan. This involved an investigation of the conditions that seem to lead to high scientific creativity: scientists are likely to be more creative when they are in a state of uncertainty and when they are somewhat uncomfortable about it. A feeling of basic security, however, must exist. Anxiety about oneself or about the social environment or about the work itself can stifle creativity. Thus, to be creative, the scientist must have sufficient degrees of uncertainty to stimulate his interest. He must have enough sense of security in what he is doing to offset deep anxieties.

The three studies seem to suggest that the creative employee needs an atmosphere of accomplishment in order to produce his best ideas. Any time that any organization consciously or unconsciously deprives itself of the creative climate, it stands to lose important benefits—brilliant ideas, break throughs in new and exciting programs, departures from established practices in sales and public relations and (perhaps most important) the exhilarating atmosphere of the daring and the different in almost any phase of the station's activities.

Dominance and Creativity

The dominant person can be an inhibiting force on creativity. Managers or supervisors, who show concern for the employees as people, both on and off the job, normally achieve better results than those who like to show their authority. The productive person needs a considerable amount of freedom and a minimum of supervision. He appreciates constructive criticism when sensibly made and helpfully voiced. Supervisors who are given critical authority without an ability to make constructive comments can cause obstinate problems.

Creativity must be regulated by its own process of development. If it is forced by deadlines or hectored by authority the results may be disappointing. We all know how an idea may pop into the consciousness after we have struggled for days with a problem and then put it aside. The solution may appear all at once during a drive home from work or while taking a walk or even while dozing. Once facts have been gathered and after considerable study and meditation have taken place, it is not at all unusual for an inspiration to flash into the mind when least expected. The truly great idea cannot be regulated by deadlines in the same manner as the routine assignment.

The Motivation of Creativity

We have been discussing actions that can discourage creativity. What can management do to provide a favorable climate for creative people and to motivate them properly?

The creative person needs a special kind of understanding and encouragement. Once an organization hires and encourages highly creative employees, peace and quiet can be shattered. These employees are not satisfied with the birth of new ideas. They want to see those ideas implemented.

Given a staff of highly productive people and an understanding and encouraging attitude on the part of their superiors, there should be no limits to the advancements a radio or a television station should be able to make. We must re-emphasize that the ultimate test of any station's achievement is dependent upon the productivity of its people. Radio and television stations are basically people. They give stations their particular images. Whenever a station is regarded as vibrant and alive, it will inevitably have highly enthusiastic and creative employees. The personal ambitions and aspirations of the people on the staff should gain fulfillment through the gratifications of their accomplishments for the station.

All of the delightfully original contributions in writing, directing and performance that the late Ernie Kovacs brought to television would not have developed without someone's encouragement. He is but one outstanding example of many highly creative people on the network level. There should be a surprising amount of new creation on the local station level if management adopts a favorable attitude toward it.

The really important discoveries in broadcasting may not have been made as yet. Whatever progress there may be in the future will depend upon the type of people who are chosen to work in the industry and upon how they are treated. People are the most important part of any radio or television station.

The Manager
and Regulation

Men are constantly called upon to learn over again how to live together. It is a hard task. When unprecedented disputes and difficulties confront them, they repeatedly turn for help to the government, as the recognized umpire.

—ZECHARIAH CHAFEE, JR.[1]

THROUGHOUT THIS BOOK, we have cited various aspects of station management in which greater amounts of attention could result in increased efficiency. It is possible that more time could be devoted to these needs by managers if they were not regularly preoccupied with government regulation. The continuous action or threat of such action by the FCC seems to require a disproportionate amount of the broadcaster's time and attention.

Perhaps in no other activity of American life is the licensee so constantly reminded, and even threatened, that he must make modifications in his behavior in order to maintain his license over a period of years. Some reminders and threats are real; some are imagined. But the manager or owner is kept aware of possibilities of new government encroachments by several sources. There are regular pronouncements of the members of the FCC, individually and collectively. The trade press feeds speculative reports. Whenever there are meetings with fellow managers or owners, the conversation seems to be dominated by discussions of government regulation.

Why is so much of a manager's time occupied with thoughts pertaining to only one aspect of his responsibilities? Why aren't there clearer guidelines? Why must there be differences of opinion on the same basic issues that have existed all the years of broadcasting in this country? What are the causes of the differences of opinion and why haven't they been resolved? We need to review briefly the origins of federal regulation.

BACKGROUND OF FEDERAL REGULATION

In the early days of radio, between 1921 and 1926, there was much confusion in the standard broadcast band. It was easy to obtain a license to broadcast. The mere filing of an application to the Bureau of Standards of the Department of Commerce almost automatically put the applicant into broadcasting. A result of that loose licensing practice was a mass confusion on the various frequencies. An entrepreneur in South Bend, Indiana, could, for example, be assigned to a particular spot on the dial. If someone in Rockford, Illinois, or Green Bay, Wisconsin, had an affinity for that same frequency, he could use it to broadcast. As licenses increased in number, there were many cases where two or more stations used the same frequencies even though geographical separations were not very great. Some stations' broadcasts did not get much farther than the fences around their transmitter shacks.

By 1926, a potentially great medium was on the verge of perishing in its infancy. Herbert Hoover, then Secretary of Commerce, concluded that a system of allocation of licenses was the only solution to the traffic chaos. He envisioned the creation of an executive agency to implement and enforce an orderly allocation of frequencies. Mr. Hoover called upon Congress for enabling legislation and, after extended hearings in 1926 and early 1927, the Federal Radio Act of 1927 came into being. A five-man Federal Radio Commission was created. Each of these men represented geographical areas of approximately one fifth of the land area of the United States.

The five Commissioners, together with the first general counsel, the late and great Louis Goldsborough Caldwell, and the first chief engineer of the Commission, T. A. M. Craven (who retired from a period of eminent service as a member of the Federal Communications Commission in March, 1963), set out to establish a frequency pattern for all radio service in the country. As a result of their work, there came into being for the first time a designation of frequencies by class of service. The basic designations included local channels (serving cities only), regional channels (serving cities and metropolitan areas and contiguous regions nearby), Class 1-B clear channels (duplicated both day and night but protected over a wide area at night so as to reach outlying areas) and Class 1-A channels (which did not have to share their frequencies at night with other radio stations in the United States and most of North America).

The Federal Radio Act of 1927 established clearly that (1) the radio channels were public property, (2) those who were given licenses to broadcast on those channels or frequencies would be regarded as "tenants" of that property, and (3) the licensees would be expected to serve the public interest as part of the obligations of the lease. The Act further established that licensees would have to qualify for the privilege of operating a radio station through such tests as the Commission would devise. Freedom of speech, as guaranteed by the First Amendment of the Constitution, was extended to cover radio broadcasting. It was in this Act that the phrase "public interest, convenience and necessity" came into being. This was to become the standard by which every station was expected to operate and by which the regulatory powers of the FRC would be determined. A further major provision of the Radio Act gave broadcasters the right of appeal on decisions of the Commission.

By the early 1930s, the increased strength and influence of the radio industry was largely due to the clarification of the initial allocation problem. Herbert Hoover, a strong exponent of free enterprise, was reluctant at first to support governmental regulations over broadcasting but he was persuaded by the broadcasters themselves that such technical controls were necessary. Mr. Hoover went on record expressing the opinion that he was disappointed by the commercial exploitation of the medium in the late 1920s. Years later, Mr. Hoover stated on several occasions that he felt he erred in the early opinion. He later become a vigorous advocate of commercial broadcasting in the United States.

In 1934, President Franklin Delano Roosevelt recommended to Congress that the FRC be expanded to include jurisdiction over all forms of interstate and foreign wire communication. Acting on this recommendation, Congress passed the Communications Act of 1934. The new law included the major provisions of the Radio Act of 1927 and added provisions for the jurisdiction of the Commission over all other wire communications. The name was changed to the Federal Communications Commission and two additional members were added.

The present Federal Communications Commission is composed of seven members and it is still governed by the same basic regulations that were developed for radio in 1927. Yet, intervening years have seen a phenomenal growth of AM radio stations, the introduction and subsequent growth of FM and television, all the advancements in radar, in microwave relays and in space and satellite communication. The original documents that established the FRC and later the FCC have proved to be masterpieces of projectability, covering forms of communication the framers of the legislation could hardly have dreamed would become realities of the future. Still, it is possible that the two Acts of Congress of 1927 and 1934 may now have been stretched to the maximum in their applicability to modern problems of communications. At least, there has been serious thought in some quarters concerning the need for an entirely new Communications Act and for a major reorganization of the FCC.

THE FCC WORKLOAD

The overall workload of the FCC is astonishingly heavy.

The licensing function of the FRC and the FCC has been conducted on an efficient and equitable basis. At all times, the welfare of the public has been the guide in the establishment of allocation tables, the definition of technical standards, the decisions regarding changes in power, structure, equipment and ownership and in the screening of applications for licenses and renewals. These duties alone have been highly time-consuming. Some staff assistance has been provided to accomplish some of the more routine processing details but all important final decisions have had to be the responsibility of the seven commissioners. Pitifully underpaid, the men who have accepted appointment to the Commission have, for the most part, been true public servants. They have discharged their assignments in a manner to make the broadcasting industry forever indebted to them.

The establishment and supervision of technical standards in broadcasting and the approval of licensees and their facilities to broadcast should constitute fulltime work assignments. Yet, this is only a part of the Commission's responsibilities. It is also charged with the administration of the entire broadcast spectrum. This includes the approval of all assignments and the supervision of their use by the telephone and telegraph services, all short-wave and amateur radios, remote pickup equipment, relay facilities, facsimile, international wireless activities, experimental research services, various industrial functions, marine, aeronautical, land transportation, disaster communications and citizens radio.

Some 1,500,000 licensees use the radio frequencies for one purpose or another. There are close to 6,000,000 fixed, portable and mobile transmitters operated under the regulation of the Commission. In the year 1965 alone, the FCC received more than 800,000 applications for radio authorizations.[2] Yet, in true perspective, radio and television station authorizations represent a small part of the FCC's paper work.

The mere maintenance of a balanced use of the various spectra brings pressures inconceivable to the average citizen. Requests for increased spectrum space come regularly from such agents of public safety as the nation's police or fire departments, from the military establishment, from industry and from the nation's space program.

As if such a huge workload were not a sufficient assignment, the FCC has assumed the added responsibility for regulation of some 1600 existing CATV (Community Antenna Television) systems and has been given the authority to regulate this country's participation in satellite communications.

No private group could have been any more protective of the interests of the public in the administration of all of these varied uses of the spectrum.

In the area of regulation of the nation's broadcasting stations, the decisions made are many and difficult. The scope of the work of the Commission in one calendar year may be appreciated by a mere listing of the completed projects. In an address at the annual NAB convention in March of 1966, the then Chairman of the FCC, E. William Henry, summarized the accomplishments of the Commission in the preceding year. In addition to the usual weekly actions on license applications, renewals, modifications and transfers, Chairman Henry noted several major issues that were finalized. These included the assumption of regulatory powers over CATV, a proposal of new rules for over-the-air pay television, the outlawing of loud commercials, issuance of policy on overcommercialization, approval of new application forms for radio and television, a revision of the table of UHF allocations, limitations of AM-FM program duplication, action to prohibit double-billing practices and an investigation of the factors affecting network program cancellations.

There was other vital business before the Commission at that time, including decisions, determinations, mergers, investigations.

With such a volume of work, together with all the attendant pressures, the FCC could hardly be expected to have much opportunity to engage in philosophical thinking about its future relations with broadcasters. The words of Newton Minow need to be recalled:

> . . . as we re-examine the status quo, I must confess that I have found the FCC, too, a prisoner of its own procedures. The Commission is a vast and sometime dark forest where we seven FCC hunters are often required to spend weeks of our time shooting down mosquitoes with elephant guns. In the interest of our governmental processes, and of American communications, that forest must be thinned out and wider, better marked roads have to be cut through the jungles of red tape. Though we have made substantial improvements in recent years, the administrative process is a never-never land which we call quasi-legislative and quasi-judicial. The results are often quasi-solutions.[3]

BACKGROUNDS OF COMMISSIONERS

Broadcasters have not been reluctant to criticize the backgrounds brought to their assignments by many of the commissioners. Most of the appointees to the Commission have had legal training and experience. A few have come from the field of engineering. Many broadcasters have contended that at least a few people with broadcasting experience should be appointed to the Commission.

There have been few broadcasters who have evidenced a strong interest in or inclination toward such appointments, so it may be that the issue will remain open. It could be more feasible for broadcasters to arrange for in-service "education" sessions for those new commissioners with legal or engineering backgrounds.

Surprisingly, it has been only in recent years that members of the FCC have attended and participated in the annual conventions of the National Association of Broadcasters where there could be exchanges of opinions on policy matters. In general, there has been a disposition on the part of most of the recent commissioners to learn as much as possible about broadcasting. But when the combined backgrounds of the members of the commission represent considerable experience in fields remote from broadcasting, the amount of understanding acquired in short and infrequent visits to conventions or to stations is necessarily limited.

THE FCC AS PROTECTOR OF BROADCAST INTERESTS

It would be easy to gain the impression after listening to disgruntled broadcasters that the FCC is a hindrance to the progress of broadcasting. Nothing could be further from the truth.

The FCC has regularly maintained a concern for the avoidance of practices within the industry which might constitute restraint of trade. It has regularly refused station licenses to those applicants with records of attempts to affect fair competition adversely or who have done harm to their competitors in other lines of commerce. It has conducted investigations of past antitrust actions against any applicants who might be suspect. It has refused to accept applicants who might restrain competition in any way.

The establishment and enforcement of the duopoly rule and the restrictions on the number of station licenses that any one person or corporation might hold have been consistent with the Commission's determination to foster the competitive climate within the industry. The chain broadcasting regulations and the elimination of network options, while not universally popular, were adopted in the interests of individual station ownership and management. When hearings have been conducted on competitive applications or on significant policy changes in matters such as increases of licensed power (AM) beyond the established 50 kilowatts or on de-intermixture or on CATV systems or on pay TV, the high degree of objectivity that has been in evidence and the true concern with the best interests of the public have been most commendable.

Because of the Commission's concern with the protection of the individual broadcaster against unfair competition and its refusal to compromise on qualifications for station licensees, radio and television stations of the nation have been assigned, with a relatively small number of exceptions, to people of character. Thanks to the FCC, the owners and managers of broadcast facilities in the U. S. are not hoodlums or gangsters or immoral people. This element of society has been "screened out" by efficient administration of the application and transfer processes. There have been and are cases of unethical practices in business and in programming on the part of some licensees but these cases can hardly be blamed on the FCC. The record of the Commission is both clear and consistent in its concern for the selection of people of character as licensees.

LICENSE RENEWALS

The Commission has a notable record of attempts to eliminate those grantees who have failed to show proper respect for the important public licenses which they have been given.

Since 1960, a much greater amount of time and attention has been devoted by the Commission to short-term license renewals. There has been an increasing hesitancy to renew licenses for the full three-year period in those cases where the evidence seems to show that stations have been lacking in efforts to ascertain and then meet the needs of the community.

In the two-year period 1961–1963, the licenses of fourteen stations were either revoked or not renewed; fifteen licensees were in hearings to determine whether their licenses should be revoked or renewed; twenty-one stations were fined and twenty-six short-term licenses were issued. In 1964 there were four license revocations, five denials of renewal, twenty-four fines levied and nine short-term renewals. In 1965, two stations were placed in revocation proceedings, five were denied renewals of their licenses, forty-five were fined and twenty-three were given short-term renewals.

All stations in a geographical area come up for renewal at the same time. The table of renewal dates for three-year licenses follows this pattern:

1967, 1970, 1973, 1976, etc.

February 1 ....Florida and Puerto Rico
April 1 ....Alabama, Georgia
June 1 ....Arkansas, Louisiana, Mississippi
August 1 ....Tennessee, Kentucky, Indiana
October 1 ....Ohio, Michigan
December 1 ....Illinois, Wisconsin

1968, 1971, 1974, 1977, etc.

February 1 ....Iowa and Missouri
April 1 ....Minnesota, North Dakota, South Dakota,
                     Colorado, Montana
June 1 ....Kansas, Oklahoma, Nebraska
August 1 ....Texas
October 1 ....Wyoming, Nevada, Arizona, Utah,
                     New Mexico, Idaho
December 1 ....California

1969, 1972, 1975, 1978, etc.

February 1 .... Washington, Oregon, Alaska, Hawaii
April 1 .... Connecticut, Maine, Massachusetts,
               New Hampshire, Rhode Island, Vermont
June 1 .... New Jersey, New York
August 1 .... Delaware, Pennsylvania
October 1 .... Maryland, District of Columbia,
               Virginia, West Virginia
December 1 .... North Carolina, South Carolina

There has been some indication of a possible lengthening of the license period. At some time in the future, stations may be licensed to operate for five, six or even seven years before seeking renewals.

It would be in the public interest and it would contribute much to increased stability and maturity of the broadcasting art, if licenses were granted for terms longer than the present three-year period. Those who oppose this extension harbor fears that seem groundless. Now or at any time during a license period, regardless of its length, the Commission can call a station to an accounting for failure to operate in the public interest.

Hearings in Local Communities

Section 403 of the Rules of the Commission permits the FCC to initiate hearings in a station's community at any time. One of the co-authors of this book is well acquainted with the implementation of this rule since he was directly involved with the hearings conducted in Chicago during the week of March 19, 1962. The announced intent of that investigation was described as "legislative" in nature, since the hearings were to be used to determine from public witnesses and from representatives of the licensees whether or not the five Chicago television stations, four commercial and one educational, were, indeed, attempting to ascertain the needs of the community and whether those needs were being served.

During the week of public investigation in Chicago, 99 witnesses from the general public were heard. Most of them had specialized interests in their giving of testimony. While it was gratifying to hear over sixty of these witnesses, without any solicitation whatsoever from the station this co-author represents, speak in laudatory terms of its operation as a dedicated community oriented entity in television, he stands opposed to the hearing in principal. When he appeared before the FCC inquiry, he supported the position taken by LeRoy Collins, then President of the NAB, who had viewed the proceedings as unfair and unwarranted. This writer added the term "unfortunate" because it was felt that the Commission should not have instituted hearings of this nature at a time when the three network owned-and-operated Chicago television stations were awaiting their license renewals. The licenses of WGN Television and of WTTW, the educational television station, had been renewed on November 22, 1961, for a three-year period. This writer stated in his testimony that if one or all of the Chicago television stations had erred as a licensee(s), then one or all should have been called to an accounting in Washington, under the normal quasi-judicial procedure of the Federal Communications Commission, with all rights of due process given to the stations involved. In the course of the testimony by public witnesses, many of those individuals made sweeping assertions without proper understanding of the facts involved. Yet, the licensees were not permitted, through their counsels, to cross-examine any of the public witnesses.

After the Chicago hearings, the Commission conducted another public hearing in the city of Omaha in January, 1963, with Commissioner Henry in charge. Another parade of witnesses appeared to give testimony regarding the community service of the three television stations in that city. The testimony was predominantly favorable to the stations. Even the Nebraska state legislature came to the defense of the stations and adopted a resolution charging the FCC as federal intruders into both the freedom of broadcasting and the affairs of the State of Nebraska. The NAB, which had been excluded from participation in the hearing, filed a memorandum with the FCC in which it took exception to the action of the Commission in holding the local hearing and asked the FCC to call a halt to any future hearings of a similar nature.

REQUIREMENT OF PUBLIC NOTICE

Since 1961, stations about to come up for license renewals are required to give public notice of that fact. Such notice of filing must be published twice a week for two weeks in a local newspaper of general circulation. Where no local daily newspaper is published in a community, the notice must be published once a week for three weeks in a weekly newspaper in the area. Where there is neither a local daily nor a weekly newspaper, the notice must be published twice a week for two weeks in that daily newspaper which has the highest circulation in the community, regardless of the geographic location of the publication. Notices must be published immediately after the filing of the application for renewal.

In addition to the published notices, the station is also required to broadcast the notice of filing over its facilities once each day for four of the days in the second week immediately following the tendering for filing of the renewal application. All AM and FM radio stations must broadcast the notices between the hours of 7:00 A.M. and 10:00 A.M. All television stations must broadcast the notices between the hours of 7:00 P.M. and 10:00 P.M. In cases where a radio or television station is the only one in a community, it need only broadcast the notice over its facilities; publication is not required.

Information contained in public notices of a filing for a renewal must include the date the application was tendered for filed with the FCC; the call letters and frequency or channel of the station; the names of the applicants and its partners or all of the officers, directors and other persons holding ten per cent or more of the capital stock or other ownership interests; and the purpose of the application, i.e., for the renewal of license; and a statement that a copy of the application is on file for public inspection at a stated address in the community where the station is located. In addition, the following specific wording must be included as a part of the notices:

> The application of this station for a renewal of its license to operate this station in the public interest was filed with the Federal Communications Commission on _____. Members of the public who desire to bring to the Commission's attention facts concerning the operation of the station should write to the Federal Communications Commission, Washington 25, D. C., 20554, not later than _____. Letters should set forth in detail the specific facts which the writer wishes the Commission to consider in passing on this application.[4]

The station must notify the Commission, in triplicate, promptly after the notices have been properly given. A text of the notice and the dates and times that it was published and broadcast must be submitted.

THE MANAGER AND RENEWALS

The role of the station manager in renewals begins the day he accepts his position. If he is truly in command of standards of quality for the operation, renewal should be no problem. He should insist that his program manager keep him supplied with a monthly performance report. This should provide a basis for a determination as to whether proper balance and full community service are being provided. Such an insistence was instituted by one of the authors at WLW in Cincinnati in 1952 and has been employed since then by every Crosley (Avco) station, by WGN and WGN-TV, by KDAL and KDAL-TV and by KWGN-TV. There has never been a problem on license renewal since this policy was instituted at any of these stations.

If there is one function that a manager should never delegate to another person, it is the preparation of all FCC reports including applications for renewal. True, the detail work can be done by others but the manager must exercise strict supervision over its preparation. He must also approve and bear full responsibility for everything that is finally submitted. In those cases where the top operating executive has failed to manifest his leadership in programming, renewal difficulties have almost invariably ensued.

THE PROGRAM AND ADVERTISING ISSUES

From the beginning, there has been all but continual disagreement between broadcasters and the FCC over program and advertising regulation. A basic point of contention is the phrase in the Communications Act which requires radio and television stations to be operated in the "public interest, convenience, and necessity." Since the establishment of the Act, it has been next to impossible to reach an agreement between broadcasters and regulators concerning just what those words mean. All broadcasters are not in agreement as to their meaning nor are all regulators. Because of this conflict over semantics, there have been misunderstandings on both sides.

Some members of the FCC have interpreted the phrase as a command to act as watchdogs over the content of programs and advertising. Broadcasters, who are notably over-sensitive to criticism, have considered inquiries from the Commission in these areas as threats of censorship. Over the years, the "cat-and-mouse" game has resulted in a sizeable waste of energy and time.

Ever since the issuance of the "Blue Book" in 1946, a threat of government regulation of programs and commercial practices has hung over broadcasting. The tide has ebbed and flowed. Probably, it reached its highest peak of irritability to the nation's broadcasters shortly after Newton N. Minow became Chairman of the Commission in 1961. Mr. Minow provoked the broadcasters in his first appearance at their annual NAB convention with, among other castigations, his "vast wasteland" reference. He continued to admonish them to show improvement in their programming throughout his term of office.

An already overburdened Commission, made aware of possible questionable practices in broadcasting by its new Chairman, came to believe that it did have obligations in the areas of programming and advertising.

Commercial broadcasters, quite generally, resent any intrusions of the FCC into these areas. The broadcasters are of the opinion that the particular provinces of the Commission lie in the licensing function and in the maintenance of proper technical standards of broadcast engineering. Broadcasters find nothing specific in the Communications Act giving the FCC the right to intrude into program or commercial issues.

The real center of the continuing controversy on the programming issue might be focused on two words that have been insufficiently explained to the broadcasters. Those words are "balanced programming." The FCC has insisted that there should be an overall "balance" in the program offerings of stations but the station operators have no clear indication as to what is really expected of them in this regard.

The earliest advice on the matter of "balance" in programming came from the Federal Radio Commission and it was confusing enough:

> . . . the tastes, needs, and desires of all substantial groups among the listening public should be met, in some fair proportion, by a well-rounded program, in which entertainment, consisting of music of both classical and lighter grades, religion, education and instruction, important public events, discussion of public questions, weather, market reports, and news, and matters of interest to all members of the family find a place.[5]

The categories that early stations were expected to include in their overall program offerings were later changed by the FCC. They became seven in number: entertainment, news, religion, agriculture, education, discussion and talks. These, as noted in Chapter Five, have since been changed as a part of the report forms.

For license application and renewal purposes, every station's overall schedule is checked to see how much time is allocated to each program category. Presumably, a great deal of weight of the decision on the granting of licenses and renewals is based upon the distribution of these program types.

Possibly, there would be more general assent on the part of the broadcasters on the matter of program "balance" if there could be some measure of agreement on qualitative, as opposed to quantitative, standards.

One of the evils of categorical programming requests is that stations tend to conform in order to remain in the good graces of the Commission. Emphasis is not placed on broadcaster motivation for creativity but on the threat of punishment. Consequently, there have been untold cases where the dullest kinds of programming have been offered in order to qualify for overall quantitative approval by the FCC. So-called proper percentages of each category have been broadcast but little or no attention has been given to production, or to whether some of the categories really were of interest to the public. In many cases, programs in categories other than entertainment and news have been broadcast during "light" listening or viewing periods; yet, in overall quantity of time, they have "counted" with the FCC as much as if they were in prime periods.

In order to attempt to satisfy the assumed requirements of the Commission, broadcasters have engaged in other scheduling practices not known to be good programming. Church services have been broadcast at the same time that competitive stations have provided the same kind of offering. Educational and other community institutions, without much knowledge of broadcasting techniques, have been permitted to prepare and produce their own programs, which have often turned out to be exceedingly dull and wholly unrelated to the public interest. Superficial discussions of relatively unimportant issues have been broadcast. Rhythms of sequences in pro-

gramming patterns have been illogically interrupted in order to broadcast
the various categorical types.

There seems to be little question that a few broadcasters, if relieved of
any need for concern with the programming aspect as a condition for securing and maintaining licenses, would tend to concentrate almost totally on
those program types that would draw the largest audiences and would eliminate as many of the service types of programs as possible. It would seem
unquestioned, however, that in spite of this possibility, freedom in programming *must* rest with the licensee, free of government dictates. Those
few stations that would not meet certain standards would be disciplined and
ignored by the listening and viewing public and would "fail" by the twist of
the dial. It should be better to have a few ill-run broadcast properties than to
have seven men in Washington, D. C., tell the public what it should see and
hear.

Another point of disagreement between the FCC and the broadcasters
involves a value judgment concerning commercial and sustaining programs.
Sponsorship of a public service program need not necessarily reduce its
values for the general public. There have been many examples where commercials have been added to programs that had been carried as sustaining
public service features and the size of the audience has increased significantly.

Still, if no distinctions were made between commercial and sustaining
programs, then certain qualitative definitions would have to be developed.
Should a program of commercial revival religion receive as much credit as
a program carried free from an established church in the community?
Should a paid commercial for a trade school be equated as equal to a courtesy announcement for a state university?

The right of any meritorious community group to be heard even
though it does not have the revenue to buy time should always be protected
and encouraged.

The nature of commercial broadcasting, dependent upon advertising
for its source of income, requires the attraction of the largest potential audiences. Advertisers are equally interested in the largest possible audiences.
Those program types and formats having the greatest appeal to the most
people may be expected to be offered most regularly. The FCC, as administrator of a public trust, suggests that exceptions must be made in this formula in order to accommodate minority audiences. Those audiences normally are of little or no interest to most advertisers. Hence, programs
broadcast to these special audiences are usually non-income producing for
the station. Even so, the great majority of broadcasters would include programming of this nature in their schedules whether the FCC encouraged it
or not. Licensees must win the support of the total public.

Unfortunately, there are a few broadcasters who disagree and who
would maintain a 100 per cent commercial schedule if they could. In the

interest of our system of government and our freedom as citizens to determine our own course, broadcasters must determine their own programming and advertising policies. However, no licensee should be permitted to continue in the broadcasting profession if he fails his obligation to his constituency, the people of his service area.

When a broadcaster, or any other individual for that matter, makes a statement under oath he should adhere to it. There should be no sympathy for the applicant who deliberately distorts his proposal with grandiose schemes of programs merely to get a license, then proceeds to violate those promises as a licensee. Lies or half-truths in either the application or the renewal forms are inexcusable and should be punished. There is a great difference, however, in that kind of applicant and the one who is sincere in what he proposes but who must make changes after he begins operation in order to meet a competitive situation. Throughout all the years of radio and in the relatively short life of commercial television, it has been the rule, not the exception, that program adjustments must be made throughout any broadcast season. Even the networks, in their highly competitive struggle, must make changes, sometimes drastic, after the first thirteen weeks—sometimes even before—of a new entry in a fall-winter schedule. These network changes necessitate, in some cases, an adjustment by their affiliates in order to meet local competitive situations.

While the Commission has a legal and proper right to review performance versus promise, it should understand that there is no broadcaster who can predict with accuracy at the beginning of a three-year period what all of his programming will be for the next thirty-six months. Nor is there any broadcaster so lacking in competitive strength that he will be able to adhere "to the letter" regarding all the program proposals in his application. He just cannot do so and stay in a "solid" program and sales position in his market. In the final analysis, each station must perform for America's one and only true censor, the viewer or the listener with the dial who can, and usually does, exercise his rights regularly.

As noted earlier in this book, the FCC has recently given the stations greater responsibility for the determination of program balance and program quality. Each station must now make continuing comprehensive surveys of its listening and viewing audience to determine the needs and interests of the people and then make regular changes in the program offerings, if necessary and if practical, to conform to the findings of the surveys. Even though some broadcasters have opposed this ruling because of the extra effort and expense it involves, we believe that it is a fair request and consistent with the station's obligation to the people under the terms of its license. Certainly, this is *not* censorship. After all, you program for your audience or you go out of business.

Is There a Need for a New Communications Act?

In recent years, there has been an increased amount of dedicated effort for a new Communications Act which, according to the proponents of such action, would be tailored to the changed complexion of the uses of the radio (all services) spectrum in the past thirty years.

How does the broadcaster know that a new Communications Act would eliminate his present concerns? Might it not create even more restrictive situations? How many broadcasters, if called upon as consultants in the preparation of a new Act, could advise objectively concerning the content of such legislation? We are almost ashamed to admit it but we know too many cases where station managers and owners have not yet thoroughly studied the present Act. Yet, we feel that an entirely new law dealing with electronic communications is essential. Above all, it should be based upon the precious First Amendment to the Constitution.

Actually, there has been far too great a reliance by station managers upon their legal counsels for most of the important actions that are inherent in the Act. We are not arguing that stations dismiss their attorneys. Later in this chapter, we will underscore the absolute necessity for their employment. But they should be used for purposes which management cannot perform. Managers *can* study and become "authorities" on the Communications Act. This is a part of their obligation as licensees and it should not be delegated to attorneys.

We consider any lack of knowledge on the part of station executives concerning the license for their operations as most deplorable. Each broadcaster should be obliged to know the Communications Act in detail. The owners of stations should insist that all station executives make a complete study of the document and refer to it frequently. A thorough knowledge of the Communications Act of 1934, as amended, should be required of every student who proposes to find a career in broadcasting and it should be a part of every training program within radio and television stations. Such study of, and familiarity with, the Act are first essentials for a proper understanding of the many responsibilities of each station licensee and each employee.

The early pioneers in station administration did not rely upon their Washington attorneys for explanations of the various provisions of the Acts. Those early station operators set a pattern for integrity and for a knowledge of every facet of the broadcasting industry that many of the current generation of managers could well emulate. We heartily recommend that managers of today study carefully the roles of such men as the late and truly great Harold Hough, Powell Crosley, Jimmy Shouse, Earle C. Anthony and Walter Damm and others now semi-retired or retired, such as Edwin W. Craig, Mark Ethridge and Arthur Church, to name but a few who have played key roles in the establishment of favorable working relations between broadcasters and government. They had a fundamental understanding of the mutual problems of government and broadcaster; they read and digested the Radio Act and the Communications Act; they knew their freedoms and their restrictions; they were able to serve their people better by being free of the kinds of conflicts that exist today between so many broadcasters and their governmental regulators.

Down through the years, many broadcasters have continued to maintain close relationships with members of the FCC and its staff and have found themselves in a position to aid the Commission in its problems of regulation of broadcasting. These broadcasters have known most of the commissioners who have served since the beginning of the Roosevelt administration and have found that most of them were willing to cooperate on all matters affecting broadcasting so long as the practices were honorable in intent and addressed to the principles embodied in the Communications Act. Those broadcasters who have neither a firm understanding of the Act nor have made efforts to become acquainted with the commissioners except when they have been in trouble have brought about a situation whereby barriers have been erected between members of the agency and radio and television administrators, and the many have often had to suffer for the blunders of the few. We feel that it is most unfortunate that the indiscretions of some broadcasters, combined with a few notably poor appointees to the Commission, have had the present effect of establishing a bureaucratic curtain that blocks the Commission from administering its relationship with broadcasters on a cooperative and constructive basis. The broadcasters who have done so much to bring about this impasse could do much toward the raising of that curtain if they were so inclined. Since there has been no evidence of such inclination, we need to look further at other facets of the problem and search for other solutions.

REORGANIZATION OF THE FCC

A committee of the Federal Communications Bar Association, headed by Leonard H. Marks, now Director of the U. S. Information Agency, was appointed in June, 1962, to study the various aspects of the FCC and to make recommendations, if it seemed advisable, for future changes in FCC structure and function.

In its report, the committee called attention to a study, which James M. Landis had made for President-elect Kennedy in 1960. In that study, it was found that the FCC could not keep up with all the demands for policy making under its existing organization. The committee also referred to a study of FCC structure made by the management consulting firm of Booz, Allen and Hamilton. One of the recommendations of that study was that further delegation of functions in the FCC was necessary. The Bar Association committee found that the FCC did not have sufficient time either to develop a national communications policy or to carry out effective long-range planning. The pressures for adjudicatory decisions hindered both the policy making and rule making functions of the Commission. The committee recommended that the FCC be replaced by a new regulatory structure consisting of one administrator, a court of communications and a five-man policy making commission. Such a change, it was felt, would give proper weight to the various Commission functions and would insure their greater effectiveness.

At the time of his resignation from the FCC, former Chairman Newton Minow strongly endorsed a reorganization of the FCC. He recommended that the seven-man Commission be replaced by a single administrator and a court of administration. The administrator's function would be the determination of policy and the supervision of its implementation. The administrative court would conduct competitive hearings and other judicial matters. Mr. Minow said: "The administrator would have . . . to articulate effective, logical policies or the administrative court would be at a loss in deciding the comparative case. And the court would have long ago established a coherent line of comparative decisions, rather than an unpredictable crazy-quilt pattern." Mr. Minow believed that such reorganization would minimize any problems of off-the-record contacts with commissioners. "Those who make policy and regulate must necessarily have frequent contact with the industry in order to be well informed," he said. "Under the present system, the possibility of improper influence or at least of charges of such influence is always present. The administrative court, made up of jurists having *only* judicial functions, would not be a similar breeding ground for the ex parte contact." There could always be the danger that a one-man administrator might become a czar and assume control of the broadcasting industry. Mr. Minow anticipated this possibility. He stated: "His authority is prescribed by law . . . If he attempted to do so [go beyond the law], Congress and the courts would quickly check the transgressions." Mr. Minow held the belief that such appointees would tend to remain in their positions longer than the average term of employment on the seven-man Commission.

As of January, 1968, there has been no action of any kind of reorganization of the FCC or revisions of the Communications Act.

We hold full respect for the magnitude of the issue of government regulation and for the points of view of both broadcaster and regulator. The problem, however, is not impossible of solution, as it sometimes appears. It is our contention that it would take far less effort to find a satisfactory solution than it now takes to maintain what is at best an uneasy coexistence between the broadcaster and the regulator.

Is it not, perhaps, asking far too much of an already overburdened FCC to expect it to take the leadership in the framing and enforcement of qualitative standards? And is the regulatory climate conducive for the necessary subjective kinds of evaluations that need to be made in the areas of program and production quality? Aren't these the areas of the broadcaster's particular qualifications? Isn't he in a better position to know the wants and needs of the listeners and viewers in his particular community and to provide the sort of balance in programming that is tailored to meet those wants and needs?

INDUSTRY SELF-REGULATION

Many broadcasters have maintained consistently that industry self-regulation is preferable to government regulation in all areas except technical standards and the licensing function. These men have taken a point of view that most governmental actions would not be necessary once the industry removed all causes for those actions through a self-regulatory system. Such a development, they have argued, would be far more desirable than changes in either FCC structure or in the Communications Act.

We believe that the only satisfactory answer to the problems of industry standards must be in self-regulation. It is our contention that the majority of the owners and managers of radio and television properties are both capable and desirous of self-regulation. We are convinced that the standards they would adopt and maintain would be in the interests of the listening and viewing public.

The real obstacle preventing the achievement of a self-regulatory system has always been the deviant owner and/or manager. Having no real devotion to broadcasting as a profession but rather interested only in his station as a source of income, he has shown no interest in even the most minimal standards. Although in a small minority, he and his counterparts have successfully retarded the efforts of the majority to effect changes. Given a market of several stations, one operation that undercuts the rate card, accepts questionable advertising or approves sub-standard programming can force some other stations in that market to become competitive. Before long, the general image of broadcasting in the area can be damaged.

It is true that other forms of business have their deviant operators, too, as do most of our social institutions. In most of those cases, however, the predominant weight of public opinion favors those who maintain high standards that are readily identifiable. In the case of broadcasting, relatively few people in the audience are able to recognize differences between marginal operators and those who do not really approve of loose operational procedures but feel forced to adopt them in order to stay in business. The public is, fortunately, aware of those stations that consistently maintain the highest of standards. It may be time for those stations to inform the public of the reasons for their favorable images.

The nearest approximation to any sort of official "seal of approval" in radio and television is an NAB Code membership. The display of the code symbol, indicating station membership, unfortunately means little or nothing to the people in the audience.

Station membership in the Code is fairly high, considering its voluntary nature. Some three fourths of the nation's television stations and about half of the radio stations subscribe to the Code and pay membership fees. Although much has been made of the fact that sizeable numbers of stations have shown no interest in an industry code, the fact that a majority of stations do subscribe should indicate some sort of desire for industry self-regulation. It might be assumed that most, if not all, of those stations are interested in industry self-regulation.

The NAB was originated because of a need for industry representation before Congress. Thus, its first role was almost entirely that of a lobbying organization. As broadcasting has expanded, the range of functions of the NAB has grown. The scope of its services to members is shown in its organizational structure. In addition to its Code Authority and a Department of Government Affairs, there are departments of Engineering, Legal, Public Relations, Research, Station Services, Broadcast Management and State Association Liaison.

Yet, in spite of a wide range of member services and an annual operating budget of some two and a half million dollars, it has not been an easy matter to keep harmony among the membership due to the wide divergence of interests in radio and television. Within the NAB membership are 500-watt daytime stations located in small towns, large 50,000-watt 1-A clear-channel operations, independent FM stations and jointly operated AM and FM stations, group owned television properties, satellite television stations without sufficient income to support local programming and UHF facilities in VHF markets. Issues that are vital to some kinds of operations mean little to other members.

An added complication has been a general proliferation of industry trade associations. The manager may, if he chooses, belong to the Radio Advertising Bureau, the Television Bureau of Advertising, the Television Information Office, the Radio and Television News Directors Association, the Broadcaster's Promotion Association, the Clear Channel Broadcasting Service, the Daytimer Broadcasting Association, the National Association of FM Broadcasters, the Association of Maximum Service Telecasters, network affiliates groups, CATV organizations and his state association. There have been complaints about industry overorganization as well as all the membership dues that have to be paid and the number of meetings to attend. On occasion, agitation arises for the reorganization of all, or most, of these organizations into a federation.

Willard Schroeder, Vice President of WOOD-TV, Grand Rapids, Michigan, while serving as the first full-time Chairman of the NAB during 1964–1965, recommended certain changes in organization of the Association.[6] He believed the Board of Directors was too large and met too infrequently, resulting in inadequate communication between the Board and the NAB staff. Instead of forty-five Board members meeting twice each year, he proposed ten television members and ten radio members, who would meet more frequently and have a stronger voice in the generation of policies and procedures. Schroeder was critical of what he called an oversupply of committees, which totaled twenty-four. Recognizing the value of broadcaster participation, he nevertheless cautioned that

> . . . once a committee is created, it has a terrible time dying. I think that when they are created, they should be commissioned for a specific period and then automatically dissolved unless there is good and sufficient reason for their continuing.

It was Schroeder's belief that an objective study should be made of the staff of the Association

> . . . to determine if it's properly organized to do the job. It's possible that we have some personnel in some areas that are too numerous and too highly paid. It's much more likely that in some other areas, we have too few people who aren't paid enough.

A more efficient operation would be possible only if stations were to become actively concerned. Schroeder cautioned:

> I submit you can have all this if you're interested enough to elect capable, intelligent Directors and then hold them responsible for delivering the goods. If you are indifferent and sit on your hands, you'll get just what you deserve—nothing. Expression of opinion about NAB—good or bad—is constructive, providing it's well informed.

The need to caution broadcasters about their indifferences is disturbing. Precious freedoms can be lost by a devotion to the status quo or through an unwillingness to engage in common efforts to advance the status of broadcasting. Whenever individual responsibility is not identified with leadership, chaos is pursued by collapse. This is true whether it involves the destiny of a nation, an institution, an industry or even individual endeavor. Broadcasters must recognize and combat the dangers of apathy, indifference, selfishness and complacency wherever they appear in the industry. This will be the only effective form of industry self-regulation and the only sure way to offset greater dangers which could lie ahead.

The manager must realize that the powerful media of communication that he directs can perform against the best interests of the public. This can be the result whenever any station uses such devious procedures as bad taste in programming, slanted news or excessive advertising. Such practices can lead to more restrictions placed on the industry as a whole.

There are signs that certain elements of the public are sufficiently concerned about broadcasting and other media to take actions the broadcasters themselves should be taking. The chairman of the Association of National Advertisers has asked for a comprehensive study of television comparable to a study of government made by the Hoover Commission in the 1940s.

Representatives of twenty-one national organizations met in Washington late in 1966 to plan a "national congress on the rights and responsibilities of the public in commercial broadcasting." The organizations included groups from religion, education, business, labor and government.

FCC Commissioner Nicholas Johnson, in a speech before the Federal Communications Bar Association in December, 1966, deplored the absence of guidelines or principles whereby broadcast operations and their regulation may meet the challenges of the new technology. He said that "a vastly expanded and coordinated national effort at research and analysis of our communications system appears warranted."

R. Russell Porter, Associate Director of the School of Communication Arts at the University of Denver, believes that a fundamental reason for public dissatisfaction about broadcasting stems from too much reliance by broadcasters on a pursuit of numbers. Porter says:

> Broadcasting, in this pursuit, has spread its sails to the winds of public taste and has drifted wherever those winds would seem to blow, and it is now reaping not the anger—but the unconscious distaste that inevitably arises in any person who has been over-wooed, over-fawned upon, over-complimented, over-seduced. The public, having been confronted so long and so often by its own image, is bored, annoyed, often shocked with that image—and its dissatisfaction is directed, not at itself, of course, but at its favorite mirror—radio and television. . . . In the struggle to discover public fancy, broadcasting may have kept its ear to the ground—but a man with his ear to the ground has a hard time scanning the distant horizon.[7]

Professor Porter agrees that it is time for broadcasters to conduct their own study of their media. He says:

> Broadcasting, while resisting current and continuing efforts toward regulation, must actively engage in thoughtful and scientific analysis of its structure, its processes, its capacities and its proper relationship to the social fabric and must substitute these understandings for those empirical judgments that up to now, and understandably, have been its criteria for successful operation. . . . The demands on these media and the expenditures involved in their use require that a higher degree of sophistication replace our present hunches and imitative processes.

We agree that comprehensive research and analysis of this nature are needed. Meanwhile, there is much that the individual station manager can do to put his own house in order. The more he does to make his station a truly vital part of his community, the more he can rely on the people of his area to defend the station against outside interference. He should not speak to the community but rather as a part of it.

The wisdom of Lord Beaverbrook, a giant in the field of journalism, should be helpful to the broadcaster. On the occasion of his eighty-fifth birthday, Lord Beaverbrook said:

> I am not much impressed by all the talk about standards and codes. The code of a good journalist should be written on his heart. First, he must be true to himself. The man who is not true to himself is no journalist. He must show courage, independence and initiative. He must be no respecter of persons but able to deal with the highest and the lowest on the same basis, which is regard for the public interest and a determination to get at the facts.[8]

Most managers are in broadcasting because they can derive a greater sense of satisfaction than they could receive from other pursuits. They could, with business acumen, make a living in those other lines of endeavor but they could not find any greater opportunity to serve their communities. The modern broadcaster knows that the character of his station as a community force is the greatest asset he possesses.

He knows, too, that he is in a dynamic industry, one that does not stand still for very long at a time. Movement and change, unless purposeful, are not necessarily progress, however, and regular progress is necessary in order to maintain leadership.

One of the greatest needs of American broadcast management is to get away from the operational aspects of radio and television long enough and frequently enough to develop and practice a consistent philosophy of broadcasting. It becomes more and more apparent that such a philosophy is needed for the industry as a whole and for individual stations. For, if the dangers of government control are to be minimized, there must be a well defined set of principles in broadcasting, setting forth the various freedoms that are sacred to the industry and also describing the responsibilities that accompany each of those freedoms. And, *if the industry is to call a halt to the trend toward regulation of its programming, its business practices and its operational patterns, then it becomes vitally important that each station establish its own philosophy as well. The individual station philosophy should subscribe to the general overall raison d'etre of the industry with such modifications as are needed for the particular station personality.*

We have had a tendency to refer to "large" and "small" broadcasters based on differences in station power, capital investments, gross sales, net profits or number of employees. The only "small" broadcasters, however, are those who are either disinterested in or incapable of high standards of performance and who consequently need the sort of regulation that they get.

NEED FOR LEGAL COUNSEL FOR MANAGEMENT

It often has been said in jest that broadcasters employ more legal counsel and at greater fees than any other American profession or industry. Sometimes, this may seem true to some station managers. However, there are great numbers of radio and television stations, even some of substantial size, having no legal representation in Washington and little, if any, at home.

Unless a station has a manager who is trained in the laws of communications and of business, as well as additional legal areas affecting radio and television, that station needs to have local legal counsel on a retainer who is available to assist it on the various and sundry problems arising throughout the course of any year. In addition to various needs for interpretations of FCC Rules and Regulations, legal advice is needed on such matters as labor problems, taxes, depreciation schedules, libel laws and numbers of decisions associated with station promotions and contests.

Even if legal counsel cannot be employed on a regular retainer basis, there should be some arrangement whereby a station could get the benefit of local legal advice whenever it is needed. Even though legal services are expensive, the amount involved should be far less than the cost of errors resulting in suits against the station, or the manifestation of needless difficulties and attendant problems because of lack of legal guidelines. The risks of operation without at least stand-by legal counsel are too great and the chances are not worth taking.

THE MANAGER'S RELATIONSHIPS WITH STATE AND LOCAL GOVERNMENT

In this chapter, we have commented on the regulatory functions of the FCC as they relate to the station manager. It is our contention that a proper understanding of the problems of the FCC, the nature of the decisions which the commissioners must regularly make and a projection concerning possible future relationships between broadcasters and their federal regulatory body is essential to the successful management of a property for which a license is issued in the true sense of the meaning of the phrase "public interest, convenience and necessity." Of all of the governmental units in existence, the station manager is most concerned with the actions of the FCC. It is, therefore, important that he acquire an understanding of his proper role and that of the Commission. In order for the broadcaster to insist on his rights, he first needs to have a clear understanding of just what those rights are. He also must learn to accept his responsibilities to the

Commission just as the Commission needs to equate its rights and responsibilities to the broadcaster. There is no limit on what could be accomplished in American broadcasting once the broadcaster and the regulator discover their proper perspectives in relation to each other and then proceed to work together for the general good of the people.

We would be derelict if we were to omit the mention of other governmental relationships of importance to the station manager as well as to station ownership. We refer to the need for the maintenance of regular and effective contacts with representatives of state and local governments.

The station manager should and must be a first citizen of the community as far as the impressions of his mayor, his state legislators, his state governor and his area congressmen are concerned. He should have the closest working relationship with the members of his state legislature. Here, the all-important element of urgency of exchange of information is vitally important to the broadcaster and to the legislators.

Broadcasters can and will win the respect of all government officials if time is taken from the manager's schedule from week to week and month to month to work with them. Even though the manager cannot be physically in the presence of these elected representatives of the people every day or every week they are in session, he can maintain constant communication with them through correspondence and through telephone contacts.

No one in communications in any state of the nation has a greater responsibility or any more of an impact upon the community he serves than the radio or the television broadcaster. Sometimes, broadcasters fail to realize their own powers of influence. Unless they take cognizance of these powers, they can hardly expect political figures or civic leaders or even the general public to have proper respect for them or to regard them as community leaders.

Above all, the station manager must be a man before he is a manager. And he must be a civilized, dedicated, broadly gauged man before he can properly define his duties in the "public interest, convenience and necessity."

12

The Future

What is past is prologue.

—National Archives Building, Washington, D. C.

AS A PROGRAM, it was not outstanding. There were opening remarks by Jacques Marette, French minister of posts and telecommunications. Then Yves Montand and Michele Arnaud provided the entertainment. The show in its entirety lasted just eight minutes.

Whatever was lacking in program and production quality was more than made up in technical achievement. This was the first instantaneous broadcast in history from the European continent to the viewers of the United States. It took place on July 11, 1962, and was made possible by Telstar, the first communications satellite capable of relaying intercontinental television signals.

Prior to Telstar, there had been the balloon satellite, Echo, which had been used to reflect radio signals that were beamed to it. Telstar, which had been placed in elliptical orbit deliberately, was capable of reporting such space problems as radiation and micrometeorites from different altitudes. There were only from twelve to fifteen minutes each day when it came into line-of-sight vision between ground stations in Europe and Andover, Maine. An Associated Press dispatch described the technical feat of establishing contact with the satellite as being equivalent to hitting a basketball in Miami with a rifle fired in New York.

The significance of that first successful international telecast was almost entirely in its technological achievement. It was evidence of scientific progress already accomplished and of even more exciting developments to come. The event itself was one more example of the time-lag between technical advancement and the nature of the content of the communication message. Subsequent telecasts using satellite transmissions have exhibited technical brilliance; there have been no equivalent program achievements.

Satellite Communication

A. T. & T.'s Telstar and RCA's Relay, launched later in 1962, were low altitude systems that circled constantly, thus restricting their use to some twenty minutes each day. They were forerunners of the Early Bird, which was launched in April of 1965. This satellite was placed in orbit some 22,300 miles above the earth and in synchronization with the earth's movement, giving it a stationary appearance and around-the-clock use for communication between Europe and the American continent.

Even though Early Bird, like its lower altitude predecessors, was used mainly for telephonic messages, about forty hours of television transmission were accomplished during its first year of service. These included coverage of Pope Paul's visit to the United States, the splashdowns of Gemini VI and Gemini VII, a track meet in Russia and international versions of "Meet the Press" and "Town Meeting."

Lani Bird, a similar high altitude satellite to provide communication service between the United States, Hawaii and Japan, was launched in October, 1966. Troubles that developed after launching prevented Lani Bird from achieving a true synchronous orbit. Even so, the satellite could be used some eight hours each day, although the time changed from month to month. A second Pacific satellite, Lani Bird II, and a second Atlantic satellite, Early Bird II, were successfully launched early in 1967. The latter added Africa and South America to the existent links with Europe and Japan.

Difficult questions of regulation and management have pursued the satellite communications program since its inception. In the year of launching of Telstar, Congress enacted the Communications Satellite Act and, in 1963, the corporation (COMSAT) authorized by the legislation came into being. By 1966, some forty-five nations signed as investors and joint owners of the enterprise which COMSAT manages.

As if the FCC were not already submerged in work, the Satellite Act gave the Commission the responsibility for regulating the corporation. One of the major determinations relevant to that regulation was to become an issue of far-reaching consequences. This involved the licensing of the various ground stations that receive signals from and transmit signals to the satellites. A decision had to be made favoring either the corporation or the various communications carriers. While wrestling with this problem, the FCC was presented with an even greater question involving the use of satellites for domestic, in addition to international, service.

The ABC network filed a petition asking permission to control its own satellite for national network service to its affiliates, thus eliminating the use of the conventional relays of A. T. & T. The application was returned "without prejudice to an appropriate refiling" and the Commission issued a notice of inquiry that called for comment on the legality of such authoriza tions to non-governmental entities to build and operate private systems. This notice, issued in March, 1966, opened the doors wider than had been anticipated.

The first to respond with an imaginative proposal was the Ford Foundation. It submitted a plan for operation of a domestic system to be operated by a non-profit corporation. Service would be provided for the commercial networks and the profits would be used to support educational television. The system would consist of four satellites, one for each time zone, each containing twelve television channels. It was proposed that six of the channels be used for commercial networks, three for instruction at primary and secondary levels, one for college and university instruction, one for cultural and informational programming and one reserved as a spare.

The Ford Foundation proposal was well timed because of expressed interest in the advancement of educational television on the part of President Johnson, various members of Congress, the members of the FCC and officials in the Department of Health, Education and Welfare. President of the Ford Foundation, McGeorge Bundy, and consultant to the Foundation, Fred Friendly, represented a strong combination of backgrounds in the executive branch of the Federal Government and in network news administration.

Opposition to the Ford Foundation proposal was not slow in forming. COMSAT asked that there be no authorization for such independent systems as had been proposed by ABC and the Ford Foundation. As the owner of the United States part of the international communication satellite system, COMSAT argued that it alone should be given the authority to own and operate any domestic system.

A. T. & T. and other common carriers wanted a multi-purpose system capable of handling various forms of communication in addition to television. The carriers asked for authorization to own such a system and A. T. & T. submitted its own plan for an integrated operation.

The networks favored private ownership but questioned the power of the FCC to authorize the type of system proposed by the Ford Foundation.

There seemed to be two issues. First, was it feasible, either legally or technically, to allow non-government entities to construct and operate domestic satellite systems? COMSAT said no; all others disagreed. The second issue involved a determination of the entity that should be in charge of such a system. Should it be COMSAT or one of the carriers or one or more of the networks or the Ford Foundation or some as yet unidentified applicant?

Now the Commission was squarely in the middle of what was perhaps the most difficult problem it had ever encountered. Because of the complexity of the issues, an unusual third round of comments was requested by the FCC.

It appeared, hopefully, that both commercial and educational broadcasting in the United States would stand to benefit from any of the possible decisions. For the commercial networks, the savings in transmission costs would be considerable. The long awaited opportunity for a live national network for educational stations appeared probable and quite possibly in the nature of a "free ride" on whichever system was authorized.

THE ELECTRONIC FUTURE

As revolutionary as the space satellites were, they were only the overture to the main feature. Act One of an extensive production has, at this point in time, only started.

We are only on the threshold of a communications era which not even the most farsighted prophet of fifty years ago could have anticipated.

Dr. Joseph V. Charyk, President of COMSAT, has visualized the improved communications of the conventional types as only an interim phase. This interim period of time could see more flexible television, telephone, teletype, facsimile as well as aeronautical, meteorological and educational services.

Home Television

One fairly immediate consequence of technical development, refinement and mass precision manufacture will be a change in the nature of the home television audience as families become multi-set owners. Television should soon rival radio in its ability to attract the out-of-home audience due to its increased portability. Small screen sets in color made their appearance in time for the 1965 Christmas trade. Stereophonic sound for television appeared to be enough of a possibility for the FCC to issue a Notice of Inquiry late in 1964.

Already on the market, the home video recorder should come into general use in the years ahead. Refinements of equipment and reduction of costs should result in a product of wide appeal. The viewer will be able to tape programs off the air for later replay at his convenience. He may even adjust the recorder so that the television set will be turned on and a program recorded while he is away from home. Eventually, he may rent or buy programs much in the manner that he uses audio recordings today. The major appeal of the home video recorder, however, may lie in the opportunity to produce homemade tapes. With the addition of a television camera to the recorder, certain advantages over home movies occur. There can be instantaneous playback and the tape can be erased and recorded repeatedly. There will be no need to have film developed and no need to thread a projector.

Future uses of television in the home may embrace any number of purposes. Already, in Tuscon, Arizona, a seventeen-story, 411-apartment complex includes a basement grocery store that is a part of a closed circuit television system throughout the building. Women can contact the grocer by telephone, tune their television sets to Channel 2 and do their shopping by conversing with him while they inspect and select merchandise. Groceries are then delivered. The housewife may turn to a different channel that enables her to check her children at a swimming pool. A third channel permits her to inspect callers in the lobby of the building. Still another channel supplies news and classified ads.[1]

Through possible highly developed storage and retrieval centers of the future, still or moving pictures, books, music, theatrical productions or other entertainments or means of instruction may be brought into the home by television or by printout simply by dialing coded numbers. Then, the individual in the home may truly control his choices of entertainment and his means of recreation. Should he desire a newscast or a symphony or a book, he would be able to have it when he wanted it instead of at the time of a scheduled broadcast or other availability.

Media Systems

Dr. Charyk believes that communications utilities in metropolitan centers will be inevitable developments. Such systems would

> . . . link homes, business offices, and stores in a community through wide-band high capacity transmission facilities to central switching and computing centers to provide a wide variety of services. These would include color television and stereophonic FM radio, aural and visual telephone service, high speed facsimile data and newspapers, library reference, theatre and transportation booking services, access to computer facilities, shopping and banking services of all types, centralized charging and billing. Communications destined beyond this metropolitan area would be directed to a processing and transmission center which, in turn, would be linked through a suitable terminal station in the community to a worldwide satellite system.[2]

Brigadier General David Sarnoff, who predicted both radio and television, has visualized a society in which all of the mass media will merge into one system. He has said:

> With the introduction of microwave channels and the appearance of communications satellites and high-capacity cables, there is no longer any distinction among the various forms of communications. All of them—voice or picture, telegraph or data—pass simultaneously through the same relays in the form of identical electronic pulses. Henceforth—in marked contrast with the past—developments that extend the reach of one will extend the reach of all.

> This same process of unification will inevitably occur, I believe, in all media of communications. Not only television and telephone, but

books, magazines and newspapers will be converted into identical bits of energy for transmission over any distance. At the receiving end, these electronic signals will be converted into any form we choose—either visual display or recorded sounds or printed pages.[3]

The Transistor

The discovery of the transistor caused a revolution in broadcasting. For the first time, a small piece of solid matter could be used to control electric currents. The days of the vacuum tube were numbered. Transistors are now used in portable radios and television sets as well as in various other applications, including computers and space satellites.

Today, research in semiconductor devices has progressed far beyond the transistor. Already, silicon solar cells have been used to convert sunlight to electricity, to power radio transmitters in space satellites and to detect radioactive radiation.

Microcircuitry

The advances in electronics that were possible when the transistor replaced the vacuum tube have now been eclipsed by the microcircuit. Before 1970, sales of this tiny development should exceed a billion dollars a year. *Time* magazine has described the nature of the capacity of the microcircuit:

> The transistor took the complicated network of wires in a vacuum tube and condensed it into a simple, solid piece of silicon or germanium; the microcircuit reduces an entire electronic circuit composed of dozens of transistors and other components to a tiny latticework of thin metal conductors mounted on a base of such material as glass or silicon. At Texas Instruments, which shares leadership in the microcircuitry field with Motorola and Fairchild Camera, engineers have developed a piece of silicon the size of a split pea into which they have fused the equivalent of thirty-eight transistors, five capacitors and twenty-six resistors—a complete circuit one-thousandth the size of a similar vacuum-tube circuit and one-hundredth that of a transistorized one. . . .

> No consumer products have been turned out yet, but in the labs the entire circuitry of a TV set has been reduced to the size of a soda cracker; this may eventually lead to the long-heralded TV set that hangs on the wall like a picture. Scientists have also contained the workings of a hearing aid within the bows of an ordinary pair of eyeglasses, and now talk seriously of making Dick Tracy's two-way wrist radio a common reality.[4]

The Computer

The development of transistors made the amazing world of the computers available; microcircuitry now makes them more generally useful by their greater compactness, economy and reliability. The computer has already revolutionized society and it is anyone's guess how far-reaching its consequences may be.

The phenomenal memory of the computer and its ability to perform calculations in a billionth of a second make it a formidable rival to the mind of man. If station managers exhibit some concern about the future role of computers in the broadcasting industry, such feelings should be understandable. *Time* magazine has said:

> One area made mercilessly vulnerable by the computer is that of U. S. business management. The computer has proved that many management decisions are routine and repetitive and can be handled by a machine. Result: many of the middle management jobs of today will go to computers that can do just about everything but make a pass at a secretary. As much as anything else, the computer is of great value to big business because it forces executives to take a hard, logical look at their own function and their company's way of doing business.[5]

Yet, for those who are more than managers of routine affairs, the computer should make the future even more productive. *Time* says:

> Even if no further advances were made in computer technology, some scientists maintain, the computer has provided enough work and opportunities for man for another thousand years.

The executive must learn to understand the computer's powers if he wishes to keep ahead of others in the organization. He must challenge the computer regularly with his programming. *Time* cautions:

> In a sense, the computer enhances the executive's powers by cutting through all the statistics and presenting several alternatives, which the executive can act upon. But in the growing dialogue between man and machine, the man who controls the computer has a huge amount of influence in the company.

General Sarnoff believes that by 1980, computers

> . . . will respond to handwriting, to images and to spoken commands. They will commune tirelessly with one another over any distance. They will recognize a voice, a face or a symbol among tens of thousands . . . and will have the power to learn through experience.[6]

The Laser

Theoretically, all radio and television broadcasts, as well as all telephone conversations in the United States, could be simulcast on one laser beam. The term "laser" is an acronym from the phrase "light amplification by simulated emission of radiation." An extremely intense and sharply defined beam of light, the laser can be so concentrated as to burn holes in metal.

Possible applications of the laser being studied include military, medical, biological and industrial uses, as well as for communications. The International Telecommunication Union has described an early test:

> One of the most exciting laser experiments was performed on a moonlight night in May, 1962. When the beam from the laser was flashed into space for the first time in history, it lighted a small spot on the moon and then was reflected back to earth. The beam made the round trip in two and a half seconds. On three successive nights, United States scientists carrying out this project at the Massachusetts Institute of Technology sent 83 thin light beams pulsing through space, successfully lighting the moon each time.[7]

Scientists have discovered how to harness this small and powerful light beam so that information may be carried on it. Future broadcast transmissions by light waves instead of radio waves cannot be discounted as a possibility. The International Telecommunications Union has recognized this potential:

> It is hoped that eventually one laser beam will be able to carry simultaneously one thousand million telephone conversations or one thousand television programs.

The firm of Perkin-Elmer, a Connecticut manufacturer of scientific instruments, announced in 1965 that laboratory experiments had shown that a laser television system could pick up pictures in total darkness. It was reported that the images, when they appeared on a television screen, were "exceptionally sharp and clear." It was stressed that before the system could have any use in television studios it would have to be "evaluated by industry experts."

A 1965 experiment by the U. S. Army was reported in which seven television signals from New York City were transmitted by laser beam, through the use of a low voltage modulator, across a ten-foot room to a television receiver. The picture quality was considered equivalent to the same programs as received through regular transmission on a home set. The Army electronic scientists who performed the experiment said that the programs could have been transmitted by laser "over many miles, instead of the width of the room."

Other Technological Progress

At the annual NAB convention in 1965, W. Walter Watts, an RCA group executive vice president, reported that work was under way to produce a miniaturized color television set that would be "about the size of a woman's compact." It would be "cordless and operated by the heat from the human body."

The late Dr. Allen B. DuMont, a television pioneer, predicted that scientists would be able in another twenty-five years to provide electronic vision for the blind. Electrical waves would be fed directly to the human brain so that "a blind person will actually enjoy television pictures."

By the use of ultrasound, audio pulses too high for perception by humans, progress has been achieved in diagnosis in the field of human medicine. The laser has been used in experiments to perfect the methods of holography, whereby three-dimensional pictures are produced without the need for a lens.

Through the combined use of laser beams for recording and the computer for storage and retrieval, present limitations on human knowledge can be eliminated. Francis K. McCune, Vice President of Engineering, General Electric Company, told broadcasters of a new system in 1964:

> . . . Thermoplastic Recording, or TPR for short, records on plastic film or tape using an electron beam. A later relative of TPR records by means of a light beam and is known as PPR—short for Photoplastic Recording. Both systems record pictures, words, or binary data. Both can record equally well in black and white or color. Both systems offer theoretical storage density of information which was simply unimaginable before. In one square inch of recording surface, there is the possibility of storing, for example, 100 books of 30,000 words each. Here again, theory isn't yet ready to go into practice, but some seeds of change from present disc or tape recordings are surely at hand.[8]

Already the physical barriers of outer space have been conquered. Soon the space barriers on earth will no longer exist. Someday, it will be possible to reach all of the people in the world simultaneously by television and radio.

General Sarnoff, one of the great prophets of electronic development of our time, has said:

> It should be relatively easy to design and produce low-cost, single-channel television receivers for use in primitive or underdeveloped areas of the globe. These sets could be built by assembly-line techniques, housed in simple metal or plastic cases, and equipped with transistorized circuits consuming very little energy. They could be made to run on batteries rechargeable by wind, hydraulic or even animal power.
>
> Such sets could be distributed throughout the developing regions in quantities suitable to local conditions. If they were programmed from

regional stations transmitting through a few broadcasting satellites, the tragic effects of illiteracy could be virtually abolished in 10 years.[9]

It has been variously predicted that in time it will be possible for people to receive radio, television and other communications services in their homes directly from satellites. This would obviate the need for local broadcasting stations as network relays. Should such a development occur, the only justification for radio and television stations would be as originators of local programming.

Most people are not fully aware of the impact scientific discoveries will have on their lives. Most broadcasters are more aware of the future effects of science on the communications industries than they are of the possible effects of those changes on the human society.

Largely due to technological achievements, the mass media are growing faster than the present apparent ability of their leaders to master them. The many changes are often accepted as phenomena of science rather than as challenges for equivalent achievement. Again, we quote the brilliant and dedicated David Sarnoff:

Science begets humility. Its every discovery reveals more clearly the divine design in nature, the remarkable harmony in all things, from the infinitesimal to the infinite.

But the mortar of brotherhood is not a product of the laboratory. It must come from the human heart and mind, and therein lies the crux of man's dilemma. He has not yet learned, as a social and economic creature, to keep step with his science. He is technologically mature, and a spiritual adolescent. Having conquered nature, he must now learn to conquer himself.

The devices which science has given us are neither good nor evil in themselves. Their capacity for good or evil lies in the use we make of them. Thus, not in the laboratory, but in the human heart, in the realm of the spirit, lies the challenge of the future.[10]

THE STATION MANAGER AND THE FUTURE

It is more than a little frightening to realize that the world is being changed so much by scientific advancements while most people do not understand what is happening. Too many people do not care.

Station managers are being given technical breakthroughs with an amazing degree of regularity. Many of the discoveries offer these executives opportunities for outstanding achievement or for possible disaster. Yet, the top man in many broadcasting stations must still rely upon technical people for advice and, in many cases, he may not even understand the language. It now has become imperative that the station manager understand what is happening before he can make intelligent plans for using those discoveries. Robert W. Sarnoff, when he was Chairman of the Board of the National Broadcasting Company, said:

> We are entering an era when the most progressive enterprises will possess built-in electronic systems to gather, digest, measure, correlate and analyze all information relevant to management decisions. They will link every corner of an enterprise, no matter how far-flung. And they will centralize management control by endowing the manager of the future with a vast new capacity for swift and efficient response to the most intricate and varied requirements of his own operations and to the most subtle trends of the marketplace. Thus, the new generation executive must not only have a basic understanding of these powerful aids but must also realize that they are, after all, only machines, and the answers they provide can only be as good as the questions that men ask them.
>
> More than ever before, success in business and industry will require of managers that they be both specialists and generalists. They must be knowledgeable in detail of their day-to-day operations, yet steeped sufficiently in science and technology to relate research and engineering developments to the specifics of their enterprises. And they must be equipped with knowledge of the economic, social, political and cultural forces that shape their environment.
>
> To the individual this signifies a longer period of schooling and broader preparation for his career—a trend already evident in the growing number of men and women who enter their careers with graduate degrees.[11]

While all the amazing technological progress is occurring, what sort of advancement will the broadcaster contribute to his industry in the years ahead? We believe that, while his achievements may not be as sensational as those of the scientists, they will nevertheless be substantial. We venture to prophesy some of the accomplishments that should be achieved by radio and television executives in the next decade. We predict that:

1. There will be a greater understanding of the people in the audience than there ever has been before. Broadcasters will initiate two-way communication with the people they serve which will result in increased feedback of a highly useful nature.

2. Changes may be expected in traditional program patterns in both radio and television. Broadcasting will once again provide outlets for significant experimentation in program formats and production techniques.

3. A significant increase in programming research and development may be expected. Creativity, an almost indispensable commodity in a medium which demands it, will again be in good supply. Stations and networks will finance program research and experimentation at major colleges and universities and will assign some of their most creative people to assist in such projects. Similar projects will be conducted on a joint broadcaster-educator plan to establish a long-range philosophy for broadcasting. Patterns of accomplishment in programming to match those of a technical nature will be studied as will matters of taste and ethics and responsibility.

4. The world of color should envelop television and cause consequent increases in the use of color by the newspapers and magazines. Costs to advertisers will increase but the proportionate added business volume should exceed all expectations. Color, especially via television, will be a factor in the rapid obsolescence of consumer products. This will contribute to a "boom" in the national economy.

5. With the all-channel sets of the future, there should be a sizeable increase in the number of UHF stations. Undoubtedly, many of these will follow the pattern set by FM radio and transmit a heavy schedule of programming for minority interests. Meanwhile, there will always be a place for those stations which provide programs for the majority interest. And, if the FM example of programming is any criterion, when the public has both the general interest and the specialized interest programs available, the majority audience will still tune to the general interest programs.

6. CATV systems will continue to grow in number and scope of service. We hope that CATV will be limited to its historic and traditional role as a supplemental or "fill-in" service to aid areas where there are coverage problems caused by topography.

7. Educational broadcasting, both radio and television, will for the first time enjoy the advantages of a national, interconnected network. Commercial broadcasters will come to respect the quality of educational broadcasting, will cease to regard it as a competitive service and will support it both tangibly and intangibly. Many broadcasters have long advocated and supported, in countless ways, the efforts of educational broadcasting.

8. The practice of maintaining different rate cards for different clients will be outlawed. Advertising copy will be more sophisticated and creative to provide more consistently interesting commercials with greater believability.

9. Station managers and representatives of other media will join in cooperative efforts to offset government attacks on advertising. The American Advertising Federation, created in 1966 through a merger of the Advertising Federation of America and the Advertising Association of the West, will come to be regarded as the spark which ignited the movement.

10. Broadcasters will make effective use of their own media to give the public logical and studied information about the nature of radio and television and the role of the media in society.

11. Some trend may be expected toward the grouping of commercials in order to minimize the number of interruptions of program content, especially in the case of special cultural and dramatic programs.

12. The economics of broadcasting will be in a stage of expansion. Advertising expenditures in general should increase and additional clients should be attracted to broadcasting as color television saturation spreads upward. The relatively untapped local sales potential in expanding markets in both radio and television cannot help but produce increased revenues.

13. Management attention to more effective budgetary planning and cost controls will result in increased profit margins in a wider segment of stations.

14. Manpower will be better utilized and motivated. Greater attention will be given to the selection of employees and to their supervision. Station personnel will be involved to a greater extent in policy decisions. Broadcasters will support the education of future employees and the re-education of present employees by established colleges and universities.

15. The industry will move closer to professional status by (a) the encouragement of training in broadcasting before personnel are employed, (b) a more general acceptance of its codes of good practices and (c) a new emphasis on service to the people. Long before the industry is recognized as a profession, increased numbers of individual broadcasters will so qualify.

16. Network competition should increase in the years ahead. New ideas and new capital are all but certain to enter the field. There should be no weak networks in the future.

17. The station manager of the future will be able to conduct his operation under a longer license period, thus reducing his overall paper work and expenses considerably.

18. Further diversification of ownership by broadcasters may be expected. By the mid-1960s, there were many evidences of this trend. No recognizable pattern had yet been established regarding directions of diversification. Networks had bought publishing firms, a major league baseball team, engineering companies, toy manufacturing entities, research and development organizations and had invested in Broadway productions. Station owners had been disposed to increase their radio and television holdings up to the maximum number of stations allowable. Then they seemed to prefer to invest in related kinds of businesses. CATV systems appeared to be attractive to many broadcasters except for the probable regulation factor by government. Entertainment properties offered the opportunity for growth through advertising carried on the radio or television station. While compatibility with present operations seemed to be the general rule in assessing other fields of investment, one notable exception occurred when the Storer Broadcasting Company purchased Northeast Airlines. So long as broadcasting continues as a high profit industry, owners of stations will have the financial resources to invest in outside companies. The alternative is the payment of heavy taxes.

19. Competing applications for frequency and channel assignments may be expected to intensify in the future. As markets grow in population and additional allocations for those areas become increasingly more difficult to find, applications for some existing licenses at renewal time may be expected. These competitive attempts may be directed, to a great extent, against the owners of dual properties (AM-TV, AM-FM) in the same market. One such set of competitive television applications already was before the Commission in Spring of 1967.

20. By the end of another decade, there should be no need for concern over FCC interference in the areas of programming and commercials. The industry will achieve its greatest maturity by true self-regulation of these important aspects of broadcasting.

21. Resources will be provided for the preservation of broadcasting's traditions in a manner whereby they may be studied and enjoyed by future generations. Audio and video tapes, publications, equipment and other mementoes will be catalogued and preserved.

22. More and more, station images will be less dependent on ratings and clearly dependent upon community service. Station revenues will not be based on ratings as much as they will come from the gathering of data on the characteristics of any specific market and then by building the station's programming to match those characteristics. The demographic profile will be the key research factor of the future.

23. If home entertainment and instructional centers are to be possible in the next decade, broadcasters will be ready with programming which will be competitively attractive. They will *have* to be ready because the eventual survival of the media as now constituted will be at stake.

24. There would seem to be little doubt that instantaneous worldwide communication can become feasible technically in the next decade. There may be serious questions, however, about the nature of its implementation. Apathies of an economic or a political nature may delay progress for a time but they cannot stall it for long. Then, when the facility to communicate with all of the people who will listen is possible, what will we have to say? Rather than permit such an important medium to be used for routine messages, broadcasters might recall the concern of Thoreau many years ago when he said: "We are in great haste to construct a magnetic telegraph from Maine to Texas; but Maine and Texas, it may be, have nothing to communicate." We must realize that people in other countries and cultures do not necessarily visualize the world as we do nor will they necessarily interpret what they see on television or hear on radio the same as we do. One of the great challenges of the future may be to perfect the facility to convey maximum clarity and simplicity of expression when communicating to other cultures of the world.

In all of the fascinating developments of the era—the grander automobiles, the more convenient shelters, the extraordinary growth in communications and transportation—in this time when highways are wider, jet planes are superstreamlined, pictures flash through the air and astronauts drift above us—one entity remains constant. That is man himself. No new model has been announced for this year.

With his busy mind and his busy hands, man is creating miracles daily, but none that matches the miracle of himself. But man cannot sustain his present state, nor indeed soar to new heights, without the broad canopy of freedom that gives him movement and opportunity and inspiration. Given the freedom to dream and dare, man is the measure of television.

Notes

Chapter 1

1. Reuther, Walter P. "First Things First." Speech delivered at the Center for the Study of Democratic Institutions, The Fund for the Republic, March, 1964.
2. Wells, Byron G. "How to Start Your Own FM Station." *Hi Fi/Stereo Review,* September, 1965.
3. Taishoff, Sol. "Penalty of Success." *Broadcasting,* June 6, 1966, p. 102.
4. Accas, Gene. "An Open Letter to the NAB's Future President." *Broadcasting,* December 21, 1964, p. 18.

Chapter 2

1. "People in Broadcasting." National Association of Broadcasters, Washington, D. C., 1962.
2. Winick, Charles E. "The Television Station Manager." *Advanced Management Journal,* v. 31, no. 1, January, 1966, pp. 53–60.

Chapter 3

1. Radio Advertising Bureau. "The Listening Habits of Better-Educated Adults." (Booklet) August, 1963, p. 4.
2. Porter, Sylvia. "How Do You Rate on Family Income?" (Syndicated Column) Lansing *State Journal,* May 14, 1963.
3. The *Saturday Evening Post.* (Editorial) December 21, 1963.
4. *Broadcasting,* March 21, 1966, p. 64.
5. Glick, Ira O. and Levy, Sidney J. *Living with Television.* Chicago: Aldine Publishing Company, 1962.
6. Steiner, Gary A. *The People Look at Television.* New York: Alfred A. Knopf, 1963.
7. *Broadcasting,* September 30, 1963, p. 62.

8. Roper, Elmo W. Text of speech delivered in New York City, December 7, 1965. Distributed by Television Information Office.

Chapter 4

1. In 1924, Station WDAP became Station WGN.
2. Lee, Robert E. From text of speech delivered to the National Press Club, Washington, D. C., July 27, 1954.
3. National Association of Broadcasters. Bulletin no. 15, February, 1964.
4. *Broadcasting,* September 23, 1963, p. 72.
5. Federal Communications Commission. "The Mayflower Broadcasting Corporation." 8 FCC 333, 1940.
6. Federal Communications Commission. "In the Matter of Editorializing by Broadcast Licensees." 13 FCC 1246, Docket n. 8516, 1949.
7. *Broadcasting,* July 13, 1964, p. 90.
8. *Broadcasting,* June 14, 1965, p. 50.
9. Brucker, Herbert. "A Crack in Canon 35." *Saturday Review,* July 10, 1965, pp. 48–49.
10. National Association of Broadcasters. *Highlights,* June 14, 1965, p. 2.
11. *Ibid.,* p. 1.
12. Anon., "Open Meeting Statutes: The Press Fights for the Right to Know." 75 *Harvard Law Review,* 1220, 1962.
13. Joint Media Committee on News Coverage Problems. "Orderly Procedures for Mass Coverage of News Events." July 1, 1965. (Booklet)

Chapter 5

1. National Association of Broadcasters. *The Television Code.* Washington, 1965, p. 1.
2. *Time,* May 7, 1965, p. 61.
3. *Broadcasting,* June 20, 1966, p. 63.
4. *TV Guide,* February 26, 1966, p. 2.
5. Hickey, Neil. "The Day the Movies Run Out." *TV Guide,* October 23, 1965, pp. 6–9.
6. *Television,* September, 1961, p. 39.
7. Nortensen, Robert. Quoted in *Television,* August, 1961, p. 110.
8. *Broadcasting,* January 3, 1966, p. 29.
9. *Newsweek,* June 28, 1965, p. 70.
10. *Sponsor,* February 7, 1966, p. 3.
11. Press release of Zenith Radio Corporation, March 10, 1965.

Chapter 6

1. National Association of Broadcasters. Circular material (mimeographed), May, 1966.

2. National Association of Broadcasters. "The FCC Decision on Automatic Logging." (Undated Booklet).

Chapter 7

1. Maffei, Rudy P. "Timebuyers: What They Were and Will Be." *Sponsor.* February 17, 1964, pp. 30–31.
2. *Sponsor,* May 4, 1964, pp. 36–39.
3. *Broadcasting,* February 26, 1962, p. 64.

Chapter 8

1. Haner, Charles F. and Thornton, Givens L. "How Successful Salesmen Behave: A Counseling Guide." *Personnel,* May-June, 1959, pp. 22–30.

Chapter 9

1. *Time,* February 8, 1963, p. 75.
2. *Broadcasting,* June 13, 1960, pp. 98–99.
3. NAB *Highlights,* July 18, 1966, p. 3.
4. *Broadcasting,* October 24, 1966, p. 70.

Chapter 10

1. Dow, Alden. In *Creativity and Its Cultivation.* Harold H. Anderson, ed. New York: Harper and Brothers, 1959.
2. *Broadcasting Yearbook,* 1966, p. 23.
3. *Sponsor,* May 25, 1957, p. 37.
4. NAB *Highlights,* May 27, 1963, p. 4.
5. NAB, "Memo to Management," August, 1964.
6. NAB, "Retirement Plans in the Broadcasting Industry, 1963." (Booklet)
7. *Time,* August 6, 1965, p. 78.
8. Carnegie Corporation. *Quarterly Report,* July, 1961, pp. 2–5.

Chapter 11

1. Chafe, Zechariah, Jr. *Government and Mass Communications,* v. 1. Chicago: University of Chicago Press, 1947.
2. Zeidenberg, Leonard. "Is the FCC Obsolete?" *Television,* October, 1966. p. 31.
3. Minow, Newton. From text of speech delivered at annual convention of the NAB, Chicago, April, 1963.
4. Federal Communications Commission. "Rules and Regulations," Sec. 1.359

5. Federal Radio Commission. "Third Annual Report." Washington: U. S. Government Printing Office, 1929.
6. Schroeder, Willard. From text of speech delivered at annual meeting of the Michigan Association of Broadcasters, September, 1964.
7. Porter, R. Russell. From text of speech delivered to University of Denver Alumni Seminars in Los Angeles and San Francisco, January 27–28, 1962.
8. *Time,* June 5, 1964, p. 58.

Chapter 12

1. *Time,* March 20, 1964, p. 63.
2. Charyk, Joseph V. From text of speech delivered at the Broadcast Engineering Conference of the NAB, Chicago, March 30, 1966.
3. *Broadcasting,* December 20, 1965, p. 53.
4. *Time,* February 7, 1964, p. 89.
5. *Time,* April 2, 1965, p. 87.
6. *Broadcasting,* July 20, 1964, p. 65.
7. "From Semaphore to Satellite." International Telecommunications Union, Geneva, 1965, p. 333.
8. McCune, Francis K. From text of speech delivered at the Broadcast Engineering Conference of the NAB, Chicago, April 7, 1964.
9. *Broadcasting,* December 20, 1965, p. 52.
10. Martin, Harold H. "David Sarnoff's Vision." *Saturday Evening Post,* February 16, 1963, pp. 56–59.
11. Sarnoff, Robert W. From text of speech delivered at Bryant College in Providence, R. I., July 25, 1964.

INDEX

Index

A

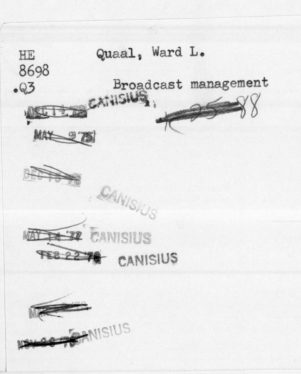